TAKE ME TO
TRUTH

UNDOING
THE
EGO

D0104487

First published by O Books, 2007
O Books is an imprint of John Hunt Publishing Ltd., The Bothy, Deershot Lodge, Park Lane, Ropley,
Hants, SO24 0BE, UK
office1@o-books.net
www.o-books.net

Distribution in:

UK and Europe
Orca Book Services
orders@orcabookservices.co.uk
Tel: 01202 665432 Fax: 01202 666219
Int. code (44)

USA and Canada
NBN
custserv@nbnbooks.com
Tel: 1 800 462 6420 Fax: 1 800 338 4550

Australia and New Zealand
Brumby Books
sales@brumbybooks.com.au
Tel: 61 3 9761 5535 Fax: 61 3 9761 7095

Far East (offices in Singapore, Thailand,
Hong Kong, Taiwan)
Pansing Distribution Pte Ltd
kemal@pansing.com
Tel: 65 6319 9939 Fax: 65 6462 5761

South Africa
Alternative Books
altbook@peterhyde.co.za
Tel: 021 555 4027 Fax: 021 447 1430

Text copyright Nouk Sanchez & Tomas Vieira 2007

Design: Stuart Davies

ISBN: 978 1 84694 050 7

A CIP catalogue record for this book is available
from the British Library.

Printed by Digital Book Print

O Books operates a distinctive and ethical publishing philosophy in
all areas of its business, from its global network of authors to
production and worldwide distribution.
This book is produced on FSC certified stock, within ISO14001
standards. The printer plants sufficient trees each year through
the Woodland Trust to absorb the level of emitted carbon in
its production.

TAKE ME TO
TRUTH

UNDOING
THE
EGO

Nouk Sanchez

and

Tomas Vieira

BOOKS

Winchester, UK
Washington, USA

ENDORSEMENTS

Take Me to Truth: Undoing the Ego

"*Take Me To Truth* is not just a book—it's a revelation. Nouk Sanchez is a gifted spiritual teacher who knows what she is talking about and has a good idea of how to communicate her knowledge. The writing of Nouk and Tomas is uncompromising, exciting and strikingly consistent." **From the Foreword by Gary R. Renard, author of:** *The Disappearance of the Universe: Straight Talk about Illusions, Past Lives, Religion, Sex, Politics, and the Miracles of Forgiveness; Your Immortal Reality, How to Break the Cycle of Birth and Death;* **and** *Love Has Forgotten No One: The Answer to Life* **(to be published by Hay House in 2009).**

"It's rare to find a book that really honors the depth of *A Course in Miracles* and provides true help on the path of Awakening...*Take Me to Truth* is both profound and practical. Illuminating, inspiring and thought provoking." **Michael Dawson, author of** *Healing the Cause: A Path of Forgiveness,* **The Findhorn Book of Forgiveness. Founding Director of the Australian Centre for Inner Peace.**

"This is a seminal book filled with wisdom on how ego integration must precede ego transcendence. Mrs. Sanchez and Mr. Vieira take us to the source of our ego-self, help us understand and accept its rightful purpose, and thereby carve a true pathway to our liberation into Love." **Jacquelyn Small, author of** *Awakening in Time; The Sacred Purpose of Being Human: A Healing Journey Through the 12 Principles of Wholeness.* **Founding Director of Eupsychia Institute.**

"A good map will show you how to reach your destination, warning of dead-ends and other dangers while highlighting wonderful views and vistas along the way. The authors have drawn such a map; a precise path through the pitfalls of Ego to the holy land of Unified Self. This is a wonderful guidebook, from someone who has field-tested every page." **Robert Rabbin, author of** *The Sacred Hub: Living in Your Real Self;* **and** *Echoes of Silence: Awakening the Meditative Spirit.* **Speaker, writer, founder of Real Time Speaking.**

"*Take Me to Truth: Undoing the Ego,* presents as a western Advaita Vedanta; more western and relevant than the traditional versions. This is non-dualism delivered in a no non-sense, simple and practical way." **John Hunt, author of** *Bringing God Back to Earth.*

"This insightful and provocative blend of *A Course in Miracles,* the Enneagram, and non-dual wisdom clearly reflects the author's deep personal investigation into the nature of Truth." **Stephan Bodian, author of** *Meditation for Dummies, Buddhism for Dummies,* **and** *Living Yoga.*

"The biggest block to wisdom is knowledge…It is about getting over our knowledge about ourselves as our identity in order to discover the Identity we already had…This book is about how to get over being smart, rediscovering yourself as a dummy, and then becoming a smart dummy!" **Dr. Brad Blanton, author of** *Radical Honesty: How to Transform Your Life by Telling the Truth.*

CONTENTS

Endorsements   iv
Foreword   1
Preface   4
Acknowledgments   9
List of Terms and Definitions   11
List of Illustrations   16

Chapter 1: An Infinite Initiative   17
Why Now?   21
The Evolution of Spirituality: How Did We Begin?   23

Chapter 2: The Ego-self: Made though Projection   28
What is the Ego-self?   29
Thought and Projection   31
Free Will   37
Fear and Now   42
Judgment   44
A Mistaken Sense of Self: Losing Our Identity
    to "I," "Me," "Myself," or "Mine"   47
The Bracelet Theory   50

Chapter 3: The Unified Self   53
Intellect versus Intuition   54
The Illusion of Attack   57
Unconscious Giving   60
I Do Not Know My Own Best Interests   62
The Power of Humility   62
Certainty   64
The Infinite State: Heaven   68
The "Tiny Mad Idea" Expands   69
The Truth is True and Nothing Else is True   71
Accepting Ego-Reality, or Loving What Is   73

The Great Escape: Commitment to Liberation   74
The Guilt Meter   76
Powerful Tool for Self-Discovery: The Enneagram   77

Chapter 4: Love Relationships   84
Specialness: Pseudo-worthiness   86
Conscious Love   89
The Unseen Child   91
The Quest for Love   93
What is a Special Relationship?   94
Special Bargains   96
Falling in Love   97
Real Love is Never Lost   101
The Unified Relationship: A Unified Goal   104
Window to Love   106
Decision to Transform Our Relationship   107
Intimacy   108
Conflict Resolution   110
Commit in Advance to Truth   112
Confusing the Body with Truth   113
Quantum Forgiveness   114
Helpful Visualization   117
The Unified Relationship: Our Relationship Goal   118
Undoing the Ego in Isolation   120
The Greatest Gift Imaginable   120

Chapter 5: The Development of Trust: Undoing the Ego   124
The Development of Trust: The Process   125
The PIQ Formula for Undoing the Ego   127
The Six Stages in Developing Trust: An Overview   129
Undoing the Ego   136
Possible Side Effects of Undoing Ego   138
Social Isolation: Cause and Effect   143
Job, Career, and Interests   144

The Body   145
Who Are Our Greatest Teachers?   146
Ego-self Esteem: The Illusion   150
Cultivating Ego-self Doubt   151

Chapter 6: The Six Stages of Undoing Ego   153
Stage 1: Undoing   154
  The First Step   154
  The Poison of Projection   163
  Absence of Guilt   165
  Giving *Is* Receiving: Undoing the "Getting" Concept   169
  Relationship Reform   174
  Ego-release: Needs and Wants   177
Stage 2: Sorting Out   180
  May the Conditions That Cause My Fear Be Removed   183
  Time, Thought, and Emotion   185
    (a) Time   186
    (b) Thought   187
    (c) Emotion   188
  An Impersonal View   189
  Temptation to Deny and Avoid   191
  Moving Out of Stage 2: "You Will See It When You
    Believe It"   192
  Contemplation and Meditation   193
Stage 3: A Period of Relinquishment   195
  The Tree of Judgment   196
  Relinquish Judgment   199
  Quantum Forgiveness and Responsibility   200
  The Unified Self   201
  Making Headway   201
  What We Truly Want   203
  The Decision   205
Stage 4: Settling Down   208
  Gathering Mighty Companions   210

Spiritual Seeking and Truth   210

Stage 5: Absolute Certainty via a Period of Unsettling   213

    From Preference to Total Trust   218

    Vigilance   221

    Possible Changes   222

Stage 6: A Period of Achievement   224

Chapter 7: Guidance on the Path   230

    We Each Have a Specific Purpose   230

    The Unified Will   231

    What Do We Fear in Ego-Release?   234

    Prayer   237

    When Prayers Seem to Go Unanswered   238

    The Now Moment   239

    Freedom is Learning to Suspend Thought   242

    Love, Joy, and Peace   244

    Powerful Keys to Freedom   247

    Problems and Now   249

    Our Unified Will   250

    The Futility of Planning   252

Chapter 8: Truth   257

    A Guide to Decision Making   260

    The Beginning   261

Appendix I: "The Work" Worksheet, by Byron Katie   263

Appendix II: Recommended Reading Resources and
    Their Websites   267

Bibliography   271

Keeping in Touch   276

About the Authors   277

Endnotes   279

FOREWORD

Gary Renard

Take Me to Truth is not just a book—it is a revelation. When I was first asked to write a Foreword for this book, I was interested because it had become clear to me through correspondence with one of the authors, Nouk Sanchez, that she is a gifted spiritual teacher who knows what she is talking about and has an ability to communicate her knowledge with refreshing simplicity and clarity. I am always interested in excellent spiritual teachers. Yet it was only through reading this book that I became enthusiastic. The writing of Nouk Sanchez and Tomas Vieira is uncompromising, exciting, and strikingly consistent.

If you think that consistency is not important, then you should ask yourself, how consistent is the world? The answer is that it is clearly not very consistent. That also applies to most of the spiritual teachings that are given to us in the world. A careful reading of many of the spiritual teachings of today will reveal that they are not consistent. That is because they lack a genuinely clear channel to a thought system that can come only from a higher Source.

How does one recognize that? Only through observation, intuition, and, most importantly, spiritual experience. The authors brilliantly discuss in their book the teachings of the Holy Spirit as found in *A Course in Miracles*, a spiritual masterpiece that reveals the fact that, despite the thousands of decisions we think we have to make in our lives, there is really only *one* decision that we need make at any given moment, and there are really only *two* available choices, and only one of them is real. That may sound simple, and it is. Yet to actually choose the one that is real is not easy. In fact, it is hard, and it is only through practice and discipline that the one meaningful choice can be

1

made consistently. The more you read and understand the observations of great teachers like Nouk and Tomas, the easier it will become to make the choice for truth.

Discussed in this book are issues that may appear at first sight to diverge from my recent writings, but I do not believe that this is so. The Holy Spirit leads all of us along our paths by speaking to us in ways we can accept and understand. Thus, fascinating bits of information that may not represent the absolute truth will appear along the way but are nonetheless there to help us realize that there is more to life than meets the eye. That is what Shakespeare meant in his words from Hamlet: "There are more things in Heaven and Earth than are dreamt of in your philosophy."

A good example of that kind of helpful information discussed in *Take Me To Truth* is the Enneagram. The Enneagram is an interesting and fun instrument of self-evaluation, and Nouk and Tomas write eloquently about it, as you will see. There is no doubt about it: there are times when the findings of such a tool will be very helpful to people. As the line from Shakespeare suggests, such captivating subjects may be the stuff dreams are made of rather than absolute truth, but they are nonetheless valuable resources that clearly help us along the way.

And there is even more than that in this wonderful book. The wisdom of great spiritual truths is presented in these pages in a passionate way by two people devoted to helping others, in a step-by-step process, uncover the Truth that is in us all. If you think about it, what more could anyone ask for from a book?

My experience of life is better for having read this book. My prayer is that everyone will get to have that same experience.

With love and joining,
Gary Renard

Gary Renard is the author of the best-selling books, *The Disappearance of the Universe: Straight Talk about Illusions, Past Lives, Religion, Sex, Politics, and the Miracles of Forgiveness* (Carlsbad, Calif: Hay House, 2004) and *Your Immortal Reality: How to Break the Cycle of Birth and Death* (Carlsbad, Calif: Hay House, 2006). His third book, *Love Has Forgotten No One: The Answer to Life*, will be published by Hay House in 2009.

PREFACE

The state of enlightenment does not necessitate total annihilation of the ego. While we still believe we are in a body, we need a small remnant of ego in order to operate in this "reality" we call life. What is dramatically different about this remaining thread, however, is that it has been totally surrendered to the Universal Inspiration. No part of a person's will is ever in conflict with the reality of any given moment; there is Absolute Trust that, no matter what, Wisdom exists at all times.

The ego is basically an intricate mess of ancient emotional attachments. If we think seriously about it, we would have to conclude that all suffering or sense of loss is derived from some form of emotional attachment to, or investment in, such things as, for example, relationships, careers, values, opinions, and objects, to name but a few. When these attachments are threatened, the result is always some form of emotional pain, ranging all the way from mild upset to complete devastation. Our desires, too, are born from this dysfunctional foundation. That is, what we want or think we need emerges from an illusion. The ego is really an emotional core that we mistakenly believe to be the "I" that we call "myself." Let us for a moment ask ourselves what or who we would be if we were to relinquish all our emotional attachments. What if we were to willingly give up all our beliefs and launch into a free-fall of trust in the process of what we term "The Undoing"? What would be the result?

We are not aware of the extent to which we form emotional attachments. An example of one such attachment is the belief that we know what our own best interests are. This idea is so absurd when we look at it from a higher perspective. It makes no sense at all because, if the "I" we accept as our identity is made up purely of emotional attachments, then everything it desires or avoids will be absolutely dominated by these attachments. Then

4

there is no room left in this identity called "I" for the Universal Inspiration to work Its miracles, no trust to invite conscious love to manifest, and certainly no grace by which to receive Its gifts. The collection of emotional attachments called "I" always does what it does best: obsessively protect its status at any cost, even if that means physical death. Despite its obvious need for love, the "I" is kept alive by one fundamental secret seed: the desire for, and belief in, separation from our source, a state in which love is impossible!

The ego must maintain its belief in a separated state in order to stay alive. If you catch on to the ego's antics, recognizing (gratefully) it is *not* who you are in Reality, you will discover the miraculous state that rests at your core.

How does our mistaken identity work? The mass of emotional attachments we call "me" believes that it is on its own; that is why it has so many *needs* and so many *fears*. At its secret core, it knows very well that it is *other* than God, that its very existence depends on how well it can stay hidden under the Divine radar while fooling us that we are on the right track.

When we ask the ego the question, "How could such a loving God have created such an unloving world?," its standard response is: "It's a chaotic, random, merciless, and unfair world, but God created it, so all we can do is try our best to protect ourselves and our loved ones, maintain control over our lives, seek pleasure and happiness while trying to avoid pain, try to stave off illness and death for as long as possible, and hope for the best."

Once we start clearing away the debris during the process of undoing ego, we come to recognize a monumental incongruity. If the ego, called "me," is a mass of emotional attachments, how can it successfully navigate this world of seemingly random chaos? If we spend our lives struggling for protection and control, seeking happiness while trying to avoid pain and postpone death, then what is left for God to do? What is the purpose of having a God if we are playing that role continuously?

Have you ever thought about our individual and collective purpose here on earth? Our purpose is *not* to run around, lifetime after lifetime, acting out the dramas of our mistaken identities. And what happens when the body dies? Are we let off the hook, returning to a temporary state of bliss, only to reenter yet another life of seemingly random drama?

While we remain under the spell of ego, clinging to our unquestioned beliefs, the meaning of what we call "life" will remain a mystery. There is no God — or whatever we may call this Universal Presence — outside us! We are part of It, and It never, ever leaves us. Of course, at times we feel as though It is not there, but that is only because "we," who have *chosen* to "separate" from It, remain unaware of Its presence *in* us. Being an ego with a bundle of uninvestigated fears and attachments, we are all too busy juggling our daily control issues to question the meaning of life, let alone to question our very identity.

We might also ask ourselves: If God is supposed to be all-loving, why is it that we are capable of being so *un*loving? The answer is that God did not create this "reality" we call the world; *we* did — and it is all made up! We came from the original state of an all-inclusive and unconditional Love, which means no pain, no loss, no fear, and no separation. We were *one*, and we still are, beyond the illusory individual lives we choose to live. In Reality, we had no need for time or space or matter; these are manifestations of separation. We were blissfully content as *one* that is, until we decided to seek something else beyond the totality of Oneness. The choice we made for separation resulted in our current experience of "duality" (meaning two-ness, or otherness), a state in which we perceive a world of opposites: good versus bad, up versus down, and so forth. The "I" perceives itself as separate from everyone and everything. In this ego-state, we truly believe that we have needs that may not be met and that we are vulnerable to loss.

These beliefs are responsible for some rather absurd ideas, including the popular misconception that love can turn to hate. If we have ever been aware of this dynamic in our relationships at any time in our lives, we must ask ourselves: "Who" had the experience? Who was the "you" who perceived that love disintegrated and became hate? And, if we have had that experience, then we can be absolutely sure that the "love" that turned to hate wasn't love at all and we are thus perfect candidates for the process of "ego-release." Only the ego believes that love can diminish or transform into hate. The Love that we are in Reality is unknowable through the ego. Love isn't a feeling resulting from something that seems to happen to us, nor can it be found in something or someone "out there," outside ourselves. Trying to get to know love while still believing we are who we *think* we are is akin to jumping off a sixty-story building, convinced that we will fly. Until we are prepared to take the journey into undoing the ego's perception, we will never know who we *really* are or what our true purpose in this life is.

Take Me to Truth isn't a religious book, nor does it point to any one religion as being the means to liberation. Its teachings have no affiliation with any one particular belief system. We encourage you to make up your own mind as to the truth contained in the following pages. The truth will resonate within you. It doesn't always present itself as peace. Sometimes it shows up as resistance (which, for example, could take the form of offense, defensiveness, denial, outrage, or anger). Often it seems challenging or even unattainable (as the ego would have us believe) but, deep down, feels right. All of us know Truth. Deep within ourselves, we all recognize It because at our core we *are* Truth, Love, Peace, and Joy.

Truth transcends all language and belief systems. It exists in Eternity, beyond the confines of time, space, and matter. It radiates a charge that literally bypasses the intellect and gently removes the ancient blocks that have so long prevented us from recognizing and living in Love's presence.

Take Me to Truth is a simple book that calls to *who* we are behind our limited ego self-image. It seeks to release us from fear and limitation and to restore our memory of our rightful inheritance as Co-creators. This book asks you to go beyond interpreting at the intellectual level, because that is easy—indeed automatic—and requires no real change in your perception. After all, we have been thoroughly taught and conditioned in the complicated ways of the ego. It asks you, instead, to translate its principles into an experiential way of consciously and diligently applying them in your daily life.

Take Me to Truth was written with a compassionate and loving intent to assist all who have abandoned the ego's search for love and are now ready to find *real* and abiding Love, Peace, and Joy.

As you read these pages, you will find that many of the principles discussed in this book are derived from *A Course in Miracles*,[1] with references contained in the "Endnotes" section at the end of the book. The ideas represented herein are the personal interpretation and understanding of the authors and are not necessarily endorsed by the copyright holder of *A Course in Miracles*.

ACKNOWLEDGMENTS

This book is a collaborative project brought about by the commitment of a group of people who, within their intertwined Unified Relationships, embarked upon a study and practice of the development of Trust as found in *A Course in Miracles, Manual for Teachers*, "Development of Trust" section.[2] The original family who commenced their journey in 1990—over sixteen years ago at the time of the original writing of the book— consisted of Nouk Sanchez, Tomas Vieira, and Rikki Vieira. They were later joined by Janine McFarlane, Lana Scott, Nick Sanchez, Jennifer Sanchez, Sparo Arika Vigil, and Nouk Sanchez's mother, Evelyne Tayler, whose spirit-presence was essential in completing the book. Nouk Sanchez and Tomas Vieira gratefully acknowledge the assistance of these individuals who have been and continue to be their greatest teachers; without them, this book could not have been written. Thank you.

We wish to also thank the following present-day Wisdom teachers for their generous out-pouring of Love and Truth: Adyashanti, Dr. Brad Blanton, Stephan Bodian, Andrew Cohen, Michael Dawson, Dr. Wayne Dyer, Frank Fools Crow (Lakota Holy Man — deceased), Lynn Grabhorn, Russ Hudson, Byron Katie, Jed McKenna, Robert Rabbin, Gary R. Renard, Don Riso, Jacqueline Small, Eckhart Tolle, Neale Donald Walsch, and Kenneth Wapnick.

Thank you also to the following people:
- Sparo Arika Vigil, who oftentimes stayed up late at night typing the manuscript and for many of the earlier illustrations. .
- Debbie and Jack Funfer and Terry Favour, for proof-reading the earliest draft, consulting on the Enneagram, and helping us figure out our Enneagram types.

- Ben Malley, for being open to Spirit and generously offering valuable insights.
- Hal Kahn, for assistance with early grammatical editing.
- Benita Romero, for introducing us to Byron Katie and her "The Work."
- Jan Cook, for help with promotion.
- Gloria Webb,[1] editor, for assistance with first publication edit.
- Damian Codotto,[2] for illustrations and website.
- Russ Edwards,[3] for front and back cover art work.
- Rikki Vieira, for front and back cover photographs.
- Lenore Dittmar, for her kind gift of this latest polished edit of our book. We are honored.
- Rogier F. van Vlissingen, author of *Closing the Circle: Pursah's Gospel of Thomas and A Course in Miracles*, for his ongoing advice, support, and friendship.

[1] www.word-fix.com.au/
[2] www.mindwire.com.au
[3] www.worxbyruss.net.au

LIST OF TERMS AND DEFINITIONS

Take Me To Truth Terms	General Meanings and/or Synonyms
ACIM	*A Course In Miracles*; referred to by some as "the Course" (see Bibliography)
Co-creator Unified Co-creator	the Unified Self, Whose function it is to eternally extend Love together with Its Creator, **The Source**
concepts	abstract notions that we hold in our mind, all of which are part of the ego-self's made-up world, non-existent in Reality (see **time-thought-emotion** concept)
defense and judgment	forms of attack
ego-error	the original desire for separation; *A Course in Miracles'* "tiny, mad idea"
ego-reality	illusory world of separation from **The Source** in which ego-self finds itself, believing it to be real; state of wrong-mindedness, duality, sin, guilt, fear, chaos, and suffering
ego-self	false-self, little self, dreamer of the dream, whose voice speaks to us most of the time (opposite of **Unified Self**)
ego-self belief system	thought system resulting out of mass guilt over the seeming separation from **The Source**, charac-terized by a belief in sin, guilt, and fear (opposite of the thought system of the **Universal Inspiration**)

ego-self will	false-self will, subjective intent in motion, through guilt-driven projection
Extension Principle	the fundamental truth that states that: all giving, extending, and sharing is receiving; we keep what we give; and others are a reflection of ourselves
Forgiveness Principle	the fundamental truth that states that by forgiving others we forgive ourselves
Infinite Light	energy of **The Source**; **Infinite Wisdom**
Infinite State	Heaven, Nirvana, Wholeness, Oneness, **Infinite Light**, Ultimate Consciousness; our only and true, eternal Home
Infinite Wisdom	Truth beyond what can be comprehended or understood in the ego-self in the state of separation; attribute of **The Source** and Its **Co-creators**; Infinite Knowledge; True Knowledge
judgment and defense	forms of attack
now moment **present moment**	a suspension of time, in which we choose to access the Universal Inspiration's guidance instead of our ego's preoccupation with past and future; *A Course in Miracles'* "holy instant"
Optimal Reality	state of mind of the **Unified Self**, in which we live with the knowledge that we are and have an endless supply of Love, Peace, Joy, and abundance of spirit; pure non-

	duality; state of Wholeness, Oneness, Unity, **now-moment** awareness, right-mindedness; Heaven; Truth
Peace Principle	the fundamental truth that states that: having Peace is giving Peace and what we give we receive; offering forgiveness brings Peace; and absence of judgment, attack, or defense brings Peace
"PIQ" Formula	a helpful tool for Undoing the Ego; P = Presence, I = Inquiry, Q = Quantum Forgiveness
Principle	see **Extension, Forgiveness, and Peace** principles
Quantum Forgiveness	the interpretation of attack in any of its forms as a call for help rather than sin; Love in action
the separation	illusory state of being separate from **The Source**, state of confusion and chaos, operating on guilt, characterized by fear, anger, depression, anxiety, judgment (condemnation) of others; denial of Oneness, denial of **The Source** (opposite of Heaven, Oneness, Wholeness)
The Source	God, our Creator; Universal Presence; Infinite Love; Unified Love
time-thought-emotion concept	the idea that the ego gains control of purposive function through time, thought, and emotion
Trust	Absolute Certainty in (a) the **Universal Order** and (b) the unfailing inner presence and

guidance of the **Universal Inspiration**, characterized by a total and joyous willingness to relinquish the ego-self belief system and surrender to the **Universal Inspiration**'s process of awakening to the state of Oneness

undoing
The Undoing the process of unlearning the beliefs and values of the ego-self; "letting go," relinquishment, or dissolution of the ego-self; ego annihilation, ego-death, ego-release; Infinite Initiative

Unified Identity identity of whole, healed Infinite Beings, Who have integrated into their earthly lives the awareness that in truth they are dreaming (this life), the truth of Who we are in Reality, but without denying the body in the process, that is, beings Who live "in the world but are not of it"

Unified Relationship our healed and restored special relationship with **The Source** as One with It, the prototype from which all our special relationships in the world will naturally heal; cf. *A Course in Miracles'* "holy relationship" (opposite of special relationship)

Unified Self Whole and healed Self, Infinite Self, Authentic Self, Sacred Self, **Co-creator**, powerhouse of Truth and Higher Wisdom, Whose sole function is to extend Love eternally (opposite of false-self)

Unified Will
Unified-Self Will   the Unified Self's objective intent in motion and expression of eternal giving of Itself through extension of Love, its eternal essence and sole purpose as **Co-creator**; Authentic Will, Infinite Will, True Will; Love, Peace, Joy, sharing, and creative inspiration

Universal Inspiration   Holy Spirit; energy/light of the **Unified Self**, whose Voice speaks to us when our ego-voice is silenced; our shared communication link between **The Source** and our **Unified Self**; Universal Presence

Universal Intelligence   Wisdom of the **Unified Self**

Universal Order   state of harmony of Heaven, Oneness, Truth (opposite of the chaos of the world)

"The Work"   Byron Katie's "Four Questions and the Turnaround" in her books *Loving What Is* and *I Need Your Love: Is That True?* (see Appendix I: "The Work" Worksheet)

world   entire universe, our dream experience of reality

LIST OF ILLUSTRATIONS

FIGURE NUMBER   PAGE

1.1   The Separation Sequence

2.1   Alternate Perception

2.2   How We Create Our Reality: Projection

2.3   Mistaken Identity

4.1   The Unseen Child

4.2   Falling in Love

4.3   Undoing the Ego

5.1   Six Stages of Ego-release

6.1   Needs and Wants

6.2   The Ego Cycle

6.3   Temptation to Cycle and Bypass

CHAPTER 1

AN INFINITE INITIATIVE

What is that elusive *something* that we are always seeking but somehow never find? Is it happiness? Well, no, not really. If we think about it, much of what has brought us happiness in the past has also caused us pain through its loss or change. And whatever is making us happy is continually under threat of possible loss or change. So, what do you think will make you happy? Forever?

What do you imagine could bring us permanent happiness that would not also be susceptible to loss, destruction, or change and then cause us pain and suffering? Money? Possessions? Relationship and romance? Children? Family? Friends? A home? Career? Status? A cause? Our opinions? Our values? Our beliefs? Recognition? Approval? Praise? Fame? Honor? Glory?

All of these can cause us pain and suffering; yet we blindly and frantically pursue them in our quest for lasting happiness. The truth is that whatever brings us happiness sooner or later causes us pain. This is a universal fact of life.

Once happiness is acknowledged as coming from the same source as that of pain and is recognized as the fickle and fragile state that it is, then we may ask ourselves: Why do we exist? What is this elusive *something* that we desperately seek, yet never find? What is that emptiness that can still be felt even after achieving a goal? What is that haunting feeling of incompleteness trying to tell us?

A gnawing discontent is in all of us, all the time; however, we keep ourselves so distracted, so occupied with the demands of life that we hardly ever dare tune in to our deep unhappiness and listen intently to its call. It usually presents itself at different times in our life, beckoning us to question ourselves, our values, and the meaning of our lives. Unfortunately, we usually don't confront these questions unless or until we are faced with extreme pain or suffering. Life crises tend to provide the stimulus for us to us stop long enough to question life and its meaning.

The question is: "What do we yearn for so deeply?" And the answer, which doesn't come in the form we may expect, is: "We yearn deeply for an infinite, absolute communion with Love itself." The experience that we seek and that will ultimately satiate all our physical, emotional, mental, and spiritual hunger is, and always will be, to know ourselves as whole, integrated Infinite Beings. We want freedom from chaos, fear, insecurity, and confusion. We want liberation from scarcity, limitation, and mediocrity. The fact remains that we cannot ever know real safety, real peace, real security, real love, or real joy until we acknowledge and willingly initiate this journey to wholeness. We will never be free from chaos and be able to fully commune with Love itself until we identify the one and only cause—separation from our source—of all our pain and suffering.

The seat of all chaos lies within our false and separated self, which is the cause of *all* individual and collective suffering in the world we perceive. There are no exceptions. In our natural Infinite State, we are Whole and connected to our Creator, God, or, as we will be referring to It in this book, "The Source." This is the nature of our Unified Self which, although often hidden from our awareness, is the Self who is in eternal communication with The Source.

We have reached a point in our evolutionary development where we are called to awaken to the truth within. This means we need to courageously question who we think we really are. It requires us to unflinchingly examine our ego-self, which includes its conditioning, beliefs, and values. As Jacqueline Small states in her *The Sacred Purpose of Being Human*:

Research indicates that there are some 50 million people in the United States today forming a new subculture interested in experiential personal growth and transformation, and in creative problem solving for the making of a better world. These are not "new agers" or dropouts from society. They are scientists, architects, university professors, novelists, artists, homemakers, physicians, and other opinion-makers….[Researchers] speculate that these "cultural creatives" may be reshaping our larger culture as well. You are the folks, I believe, who are stepping out of old, fragmented ways of being and coming into your true selves.

We've gone as far as we can in our separatist ways of living ego-centered lives. As you can see, we're unconsciously destroying our planet as well as our quality of life. The Self, our true nature, is calling us now to wake up and take responsibility for becoming healthy and whole human beings. We are evolving into our next and greater identity.[3]

We need to learn the identity and nature of the only oppressor in the universe: our ego-self. In its recognition and undoing, we will begin to experience a unified sense of self, to which we earlier referred as our Unified Self, that brings us the immense and unlimited Love, Peace, and Joy that we so deeply yearn to experience.

This Undoing is an Infinite Initiative whose time has come. We have evolved to a point where we cannot afford to languish in ignorance any longer. Our ego-self simply can no longer sustain us and our planet.

Undoing is the process of literally removing our existing "blocks to the awareness of Love's presence."[4] Undoing simply means unlearning. It is the unlearning of any conditioning, beliefs, or values that have, until now, distorted our perception and obstructed Love's presence in our mind. It is the greatest and noblest of all journeys, leading us deeper through the stages in the development of Trust, which we will explain in detail in chapters five and six.

Our purpose now is to integrate life on earth with our Unified Identity, which is the meaning of the words "be in the world but not of it," a goal of many ancient wisdom traditions. In undoing the ego, we lose nothing and gain everything. When we recognize Unified Will and voluntarily surrender our resistance to it, we will find that It only wants for us what we have always searched for but could never find—until now.

We are living in an exceptionally opportune time. A dramatic and significant shift in awareness, which has ushered in a higher order of consciousness, has recently occurred. Many people consider the return of this higher order of Christ Consciousness[5] as the "second coming." At one time, it was believed that Infinite Wisdom was confined to One Being; We have now become aware that It is available to all, and all who resonate with its calling will hear it. No one is special! We will detail this development under the section "Why Now?," which follows.

This new consciousness is about the discovery of Truth. The Truth reveals that we are all infinite fragments of the same cosmic mirror that exploded eons ago. In that one tiny error, we forgot who we are and the very reason for our being. Our mission now is to recall, both individually and collectively, our original pristine essence as infinite shards of the one sacred mirror.

Undoing our ego-self calls for us to join in dismantling all the illusions that have been responsible for trapping us in a world of chaos, suffering, devastation, uncertainty, unreliability, limitation, and mediocrity, with no apparent way out. Embracing Trust is the essence that liberates us from the stranglehold of our ego-self. We learn of the immeasurable security gained by accepting the unknown. The level of freedom and joy you experience depends on how ready and willing you are to trust the mysterious and powerful process of Undoing.

Why Now?

The concept of enlightenment today, compared to that during the time of the incarnations of both Jesus Christ and the Buddha, is perceived quite differently. Our consciousness has evolved at a progressively accelerated pace over the last 2,500 years.

As we mentioned earlier, in the past, enlightenment was widely considered to be for only the spiritual masters of the day. It was generally believed that only mystics could achieve enlightenment, the transcendence of the world of matter. In the East, the objective of enlightenment was to end the cycle of reincarnation, with the ultimate aim of overcoming the need to live a human life on earth. The objective of Christianity was to earn, in one lifetime, a permanent entry into Heaven. Both belief systems seemed to be mutually exclusive in the sense that human existence in the world of matter and time could only be used as a means to an end, the end being perceived as some sort of other-worldly Nirvana, or Heaven. We now live in a time where heightened consciousness has shifted our perception to include a far broader view of enlightenment than that embraced by our forefathers.

A new awakening is occurring. Right here, right now, the healing of duality—the dissolution of the perception of separation and the recognition, and acceptance of our Oneness—is quickly gathering momentum. More and more people are recognizing separation, or the split within, as destructive and are willingly and desperately seeking to restore love and harmony in their lives. They are responding to a deeper call to Truth. Again from Jacqueline Small's *The Sacred Purpose of Being Human*:

> We humans are a hybrid species made of both spirit and matter. Mystics throughout the ages have always known this. And today, scientists are catching up. Realizing that you are both human and divine is the act of Self-remembrance that lays the founding principle for everything you aspire to do

and be. This new evolutionary impulse is awakening in our psyches now, demanding to be known. No longer do we see ourselves as mere egos needing to be fixed; we are uncovering a deeper truth of our being, realizing (making real) that we are both human and divine....Both sides of our nature are to be made legitimate now, or we will never feel whole.

We ultimately learn from traveling the path of awakening that being "only human" doesn't satisfy our soul. It's very tempting to try and be "just spiritual" and rise above our human problems, but this doesn't work, either. We can never transcend anything we've not healed and integrated in our personal life.[6]

The Source, or the concept of the Creator, is not a Being "out there" somewhere. It is extremely important that any idea representing The Source as a separate entity Who judges us in any way be totally rejected. In order for Love's presence to be realized by any one of us, we must first be willing to surrender now and forevermore all notions of a separate, judgmental, vindictive, and punitive God. To believe The Source is outside and above us renders us helpless and vulnerable, totally at the mercy of a whimsical entity of some sort. The concept of a separate Source disempowers us and denies us our rightful inheritance as a Co-creator.

To be truly liberated and to initiate peace both personally and globally, we need to become conscious of our unconsciousness. Only then can existing fears and limitations be undone. Any feeling of gnawing discomfort, any vague sense of urgency, or any unquenched thirst for fulfillment are all signs of a deeper calling from within. The pain born of ignorance, of not knowing that we have long been unconscious, is becoming too much for us to bear. The end of suffering and chaos will become our reality when we relinquish our limited and outdated perception of who we are, what The Source is, and the purpose we were created to fulfill.

The Evolution of Spirituality: How Did We Begin?

How did we begin? Where did we come from? Where are we headed? Originally we existed in a state of perfect Oneness, meaning that nothing existed outside or apart from us. We *were* everything and *had* everything. We were everywhere because everywhere existed within us. There were no individuals, nor was there anything to perceive, as we belonged to the Infinite State, the loving inclusiveness of The Source. Then, an idea occurred from within the Oneness, an idea of separation. And although this tiny idea occurred in less than a split second (a "tiny tick of time,"[7] as *A Course in Miracles* states it), it nonetheless exploded into a manifestation of duality. Suddenly, what seems to us to be billions of years ago, time, space, and matter appeared to emerge, and our desire to experience something other than Oneness, Wholeness, was initiated.

The concept of the separation—the idea that we could separate from The Source and be on our own—is called a "tiny, mad idea" in *A Course in Miracles*,[8] and thankfully it is a mere illusion, although it seems real. We decided collectively to experience something other than Infinite Oneness. However, The Source cannot produce or acknowledge illusion. *We* made it up. And we did so by entering a *dream* of the separated state, making time, space, matter, and separate entities an apparent reality.

Our Higher Mind is eternally at one with The Source. However, the ego-self depends entirely on projecting the notions that this world is real and that we are all separate human bodies who are at the mercy of random chaos. Yet, while we appear to be here, having this dream experience we call "life," our Unified Self is perfectly unaffected and is joyfully extending Infinite Love in a Reality of which we are unaware while in the dream state.

We all have dreams while asleep. We experience those dreams as real. However, when we awaken, we realize very quickly that what we *experienced* as real isn't real at all; it was just a dream. And oh what a relief it is when we awaken from a nightmare! Our ego experience here in this world is analogous to our sleeping dreams; when we finally "awaken" from the ego's dream of separation, we will be absolutely overjoyed, not just temporarily, but eternally. We read in *A Course in Miracles*:

> Yet the Bible says that a deep sleep fell upon Adam, and nowhere is there reference to his waking up. The world has not yet experienced any comprehensive reawakening or rebirth.[9]

When viewed metaphorically, this statement supports the notion that Adam, who symbolizes our collective descent into the separated state, became unconscious. From that point onwards, humanity's dream continued to unfold, and to this day there has not yet been any significant global awakening from the ego-dream. It seems that we, like Adam, undertook a mammoth journey into unconsciousness. However, just as we wake up from our sleeping dreams, so too will we eventually awaken from the dream of our illusory world to reclaim our divinity along with all the endless blessings that come with it.

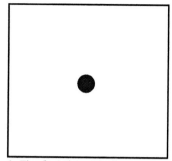

1. The first thought of separation.
Duality is initiated and time,
space and matter are made manifest.

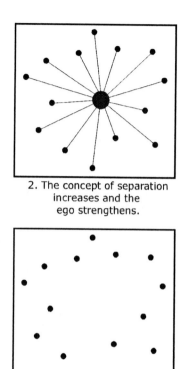

2. The concept of separation
increases and the
ego strengthens.

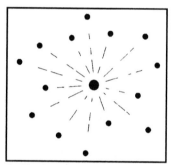

3. The burden of guilt causes us
to further fragment.

4. Separation complete.
Our deep guilt is hidden and
projected through the ego.

Figure 1.1: The Separation Sequence

As the human ego evolved and reinforced its belief in the separated state, so did it increase its capacity for acquiring relative knowledge. In other words, our brains developed through the constant seeking of external information. Compulsive thought was born, and intellectual capital became the ego's most envied prize—one that is still highly valued and rewarded in the world today.

We forgot that the Light resides within us and is the only Source we require to live a life of spiritual value and fulfillment. Wisdom was forgotten in favor of intellectual prowess and material accumulation. Thinking and doing became glorified attributes, while the quiet, reflective states of being and realization were cast aside and drowned out by the ego's "raucous shrieks," as *A Course in Miracles* puts it.[10]

As the ego gained more of its seeming independence from The Source, its fear of The Source increased. The notion of "fear of God" could be translated to mean: a sense of shame, guilt, helplessness, and vulnerability. Perhaps its most common manifestations are the haunting feeling that "something is wrong" and the experience of fear in any form (paranoia perhaps being paramount), as well as the chronic and impressively prompt impulse to blame when experiencing anger or upset in any of its wide-range of forms. Fear of The Source in every possible disguise is purely lack of trust in Love's presence.

In evolutionary terms, it is "turnaround" time. We have wandered far and long from our original intent, and now it is time to heed the call home to our true nature.

We are beginning to recognize that we alone create our own reality in the here and now. And it has taken us until now to evolve sufficiently in order to grasp the concept of an eternal all-inclusive life of higher consciousness within the world of time and matter. Some of us have awakened to at least the prospect that, since we cannot fix the world, we don't need to wait until we do so, nor do we need to experience death of the body or devastating crises to motivate us to seek to reclaim our rightful place as a Unified Co-creator. We can fulfill all our deepest yearnings with our willing commitment to heal our own split mind. Now, more than ever, it is possible—and indeed inevitable!—that human consciousness will eventually wake up, thus creating an experience of Heaven on earth. Before we awaken completely from the dream of separation, we will all experience what *A Course in Miracles* calls "the happy dream,"[11] which is experienced when ego has been undone and the illusory idea of separation and suffering disappears into the "nothingness from which it came."[12]

Undoing is a sacred remembering, through the unlearning of that which prevents us from realizing and experiencing the essence of who we are in Reality. It is a reinstatement or recalling of the Absolute Trust and certainty we had before our mind became split. The process itself is directed by the Universal Inspiration, or Holy Spirit (or God, if you prefer), and success depends entirely on your honesty, courage, intent, willingness, and commitment.

CHAPTER 2

THE EGO-SELF:
MADE THROUGH PROJECTION

Let us begin by asking ourselves the questions, "Who am I?" and "How do I define myself?" How do we define who we are? Is it by our primary role, such as parent, CEO, spiritual teacher, artist, or student? Or do we define ourselves by our values, accomplishments, beliefs, personality, past experiences, childhood, body, (age, gender, size and shape, color, state of health), nationality, or perhaps our hopes, dreams, mistakes, regrets, grievances, and fears?

Most of us mistakenly confuse our meaning and identity with one or many of the above categories. We are obsessed with two ideas: *getting* what we want or think we need but don't have (for example, material possessions, relationships, people, money, or happiness); and *becoming* what we want to be but have not yet become (for example, happy, peaceful, loving, healthy, wealthy, famous, successful with a good career or status, or a good parent). The truth is that none of these things define *who* we are now, and none of them could possibly be used to define *who* we will become at any moment in the future.

Before we dare think that we could ever be truly happy in this lifetime, we need to discover who we are *not*. Once we realize that we've always been mistaken in how we looked at ourselves, we are released to awaken to *who* we really are and receive the limitless gifts that come with this knowing.

We have been led to believe that we are separate, independent human beings. Yet, to accept as true any of the labels that, we claim, have defined our identity results in our being co-dependent and severely limited. All that these definitions do for us is reinforce our limitations. The very fact that we depend so heavily on them for our sense of self reveals just how unaware we are of our own dependency on external conditions to make or break who we think we are.

This means we do not know *who* we really are; we do not know our true purpose, and we do not know what will truly make us happy. So, how could we possibly be free from suffering and experience joy in our lives?

It is a dangerous misperception to accept as true the widely held beliefs that (1) happiness depends on external conditions and (2) we are not totally responsible for ourselves and the life we create. Both of these ideas lead to the belief that we are helpless victims, that is, at the mercy of others as well as random chaos. And both of these beliefs are to be reevaluated and transformed before we can know *who* we truly are and begin a new life filled with purpose and meaning. Recognizing just where we have misplaced our identity and meaning shows us also where we have invested our trust. Whatever we value mentally and emotionally is where we place our trust in life. For most of us, that trust has been placed anywhere and everywhere except where it belongs: with our one "Unified Self," the self we were created to be.

To get to know the Unified Self, we must first identify the source of the distorted and misguided thought system responsible for all the pain and suffering, disillusionment and disappointment in the world. Next we must step back and objectively give it a thorough examination of its purpose and *modus operandi*.

What is the Ego-self?
As mentioned earlier, the ego-self was made at the point of separation that we chose eons ago. In the beginning, there was only one Will, and that was The Source's expression of eternal giving of Itself, or Infinite Love. The formation of the ego-self came from the splitting of our minds, and we forgot our unified nature in favor of a false image that we made up, based on the

belief in our separation from The Source, resulting ultimately in the state of fear and chaos in which we find ourselves now.

Let us look at what makes up the entity of ego-self and what drives its belief system in order to unlearn it, or undo it, and become whole through regaining Trust. *The ego-self is a belief system resulting from the mass of guilt acquired through the seeming separation from The Source.*

The ego-self is unconsciously in direct opposition to our Unified Self. It "knows" it separated from The Source (although in Reality, of course, separation from The Source is impossible) and, having suppressed that idea out of sheer terror, spends its existence in vehement denial of its perceived betrayal of The Source. That was the birth of duality, the state in which we (1) perceive opposites, with "good versus evil" perhaps being the ego-self's predominant purposive focus, and (2) constantly seek pleasure while trying to avoid pain. The ego-self makes itself most known to us through its preoccupation with judgment and desire; most, if not all, our suffering is caused by these two distractions and experienced through painful emotion. However, we are not conscious of this dysfunctional process, that it alone is what drives our existence, that is, every aspect of our thinking and behavior. The entire world runs on the ego-self belief system.

At the seat of all our emotional needs, beyond the search for love or joy, lie a deep sense of abandonment, a sense of persistent threat, and a feeling of inadequacy. Unfortunately, this is the legacy of the ego-self, and it is always trying to eradicate these ancient feelings through distraction.

The saddest, most pathetic and insane aspect of the ego-self's past-time is that it drives all our thoughts, desires, feelings, and consequent actions, knowing very well that it can never fulfill us. Indeed, as *A Course in Miracles* says, its rule is: "Seek and do not find."[13] The more we deny the pain or struggle to resist, fight, or remove it, the more it will intensify! The ego-self will *never* find the source of all our disappointment and suffering. Why?

Because *it alone is the problem*. To expose this truth once and for all would render it obsolete forever. Is it any wonder that it fears your discovery and undoing of its false perceptions?

We asked earlier, "Who am I?" If we are not to confuse our identity with externals such as our roles, relationships, careers, accomplishments, or the past, then could we define ourselves by our thoughts, or maybe our feelings or emotions? Or could we define ourselves by our conditioning, our beliefs, or our values?

The answer here is that you very well may define yourself using any of the previous examples; however, you are only describing your ego-self's image. The question of "Who am I?" can never be answered with a fictitious response.

Thought and Projection

Thought is an independent energy that is used by the will of the ego-self. Negative and positive thought exists in our perception only. Outside us, without a brain to perceive, thought would not have any effect. Thought has no meaning of its own. We actually give thought all the meaning it has for us every instant of our lives. There are no neutral thoughts. Why? *A Course in Miracles* puts it this way: "Neutral thoughts are impossible because all thoughts have power."[14] In other words, every thought has a consequence. And every thought is the cause of an effect. Nothing happens without there first being a thought to cause it. Therefore, we must always be aware of the content of our thinking. Meaningful thought is crucial for creating the deep and abiding happiness for which our soul yearns.

Thoughts create beliefs, which are then projected outward, and the outside manifestation of that belief is mirrored back to the mind that projected it, thereby reinforcing the original belief. Belief is thus created through projection and therefore can never be trusted as reality. After all, our beliefs are only projections that we accept as real, because they are mirrored back to us that way. What we think becomes what we perceive, and what we perceive becomes what we believe. As we are taught throughout *A Course in Miracles*, "projection makes perception."[15]

Who, then, is responsible for what happens to us in our lives? If thought creates reality, then we ourselves must take total personal responsibility for the reality we alone unconsciously create. Speaking about reality, most of our thoughts, beliefs, and values are hidden from our conscious self; yet they are responsible for the experiences we have. Can you imagine the enormity of the so-called "reality" for which we must take responsibility? All the people, places, events, and circumstances that affect our lives are in some way created either by us individually (usually unconsciously) or by the joined mass conscious or unconscious beliefs of the world's population. Again, we give our thoughts all the meaning they have for us. It is our thoughts alone that cause us pain. Nothing external to our mind can hurt us. There is no other cause of oppression than that of our erroneous thoughts. Nothing but our own perceptions affect us.

The world we see does nothing of its own accord, and it has no effects at all because it merely represents our thoughts and mirrors them back to the mind. Everything we perceive with our eyes and ears is a symbol of our thoughts. We can change our perception, or interpretation, of the world we see by changing our thoughts about it. If thoughts are the cause and the effect is our past, we can change the past by interpreting it differently. This is the meaning of "letting go." A very threatening habit of the ego-self is to convince us that attack of any kind is real. We tend to immediately take offense at any unkind word directed at us. *A Course in Miracles* tells us, "'What you project you believe,'" and that means, "...you will learn what you are from what you have projected onto others, and therefore believe they are."[16]

The truth here is that, if we tend to experience a hostile world, it is because, whether we are conscious of it or not, we harbor that very hostility within us. And if we have grown accustomed to seeing ugliness in others, it is because we secretly hold on to ugliness within ourselves. Whatever we perceive in others, we strengthen in ourselves. So, wisdom tells us to become more aware of what we are so convinced of seeing in others in order to undo whatever our own ego-self is hiding from us. On the positive side, if we tend to see inner beauty in the people we encounter, we can be sure we are seeing a reflection of ourselves. Whatever we acknowledge in others we acknowledge in ourselves, and whatever we share we strengthen. So, realizing this truth, we may be more vigilant about just how we perceive each and every person we encounter from now on. This truth can be summed up by the following text from *A Course in Miracles*:

As you see him you will see yourself.[17]

We create our own reality and increase that reality by sharing it. A mass conscious belief gains strength and momentum because it is a shared projection among minds. That is why we need to become more aware of our unquestioned beliefs and openly challenge them.

Quantum physics has discovered the phenomenon of what it calls the "observer effect." The "observer effect" supports the theory that we do indeed create our own reality. The theory of the observer effect states that there is no reality unless or until an observer observes it. Furthermore, everything we observe is literally affected by our perception of it. As Wayne Dyer likes to say, if you change the way you look at things, the things you look at change. This means that we can change our lives for the better by paying attention to our thoughts and feelings.

In the quantum-mechanics world in which we live, we, as observers, ultimately and fundamentally affect the universe whenever we observe it or anything in it....Thus the world is really not as it seems. It certainly seems to be "out there" independent of us, independent of the choices we might make. Yet quantum physics destroys that idea. What is "out there" depends on what we choose to look for.[18]

For example, take a look at the following picture (Figure 2.1). What do you see?...Look again. Now what do you see? We may see either a white goblet or two profiles in silhouette facing each other. Mentally, we acknowledge that both interpretations exist at the same time. However, we are incapable of perceiving them both at the same time. When we are seeing two profiles, we are *making* it two profiles, because that is how we choose to perceive it in that moment. In the next second, we *choose* to see it differently, this time as a goblet, and hence it becomes a goblet in our perception.

Figure 2.1: Alternate Perception

The picture is merely an assortment of black and white shapes, dependent on our own perceptions to make it any reality we want. Likewise, our entire world, too, is nothing more than a mass of oscillating energy that we call matter, time, and space. Everything in our reality is affected by how we perceive it, that is, by what we choose to see and focus upon at any given moment.

We, along with the rest of the world, have until now chosen "objectivism," which means a belief that all reality emerges externally from and independently of the mind. The truth is, however, that we always have created and continue to materialize our reality individually and collectively through our thoughts and beliefs. Again, no reality exists externally from, or independently of, the mind. In other words: we do reality; reality does not do us.

Our world can and will be miraculously transformed through the healing of our belief system. This shift of thought actually changes our perception, and our life becomes a magnificent reflection of the beauty, Joy and, Love that we recognize as ourselves, our own true nature.

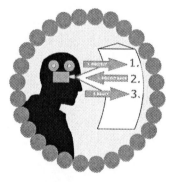

Ego perception is founded upon projection. In this diagram we see how it works.
Our seeming reality begins with our personal and collective beliefs being unconsciously projected outward. The world is the screen that reflects our projections back to us and we will react depending on what we imagine we see out there.

1. We project our reality
2. It reflects back as "real"
3. We then react to it

Figure 2.2: How We Create Our Reality: Projection

Every thought, belief, action, and attitude we project outward is reflected back to us, although what we see with our eyes and hear with our ears is usually disguised as being external to, and independent of, us (Figure 2.2). When we are not aware of the psychological dynamic of projection, we will react to any seemingly external people, places, events, or circumstances as if they are random and separate from us. We become victims of life. When we become knowledgeable about projection and how it works, we take responsibility for our own perceptions, and we are thereby empowered to create a vastly more meaningful life.

In other words, whether we realize it or not, we are largely under the spell of the ego-self's thought system. But the advantage of acknowledging and accepting this fact is that we are then able to choose and, again, embrace a radically more empowering way of perceiving and thereby gain confidence in the truth that we indeed create our lives.

If we choose our thoughts, then what about our emotions, like sadness, anger, depression, frustration, hatred, or rage? Again, if we didn't have a brain to interpret thought, we would not experience emotion, because thought is the original cause of emotion. All emotion is e-motion, "energy in motion," coming from some root in thought, though it is usually frustratingly hidden from our awareness. This is why, when serious depression, anxiety, or phobias set in, we usually turn to the school of psychology and its method of psychotherapy, or psychoanalysis, in the hopes of exhuming and dispelling the erroneous beliefs that caused the symptoms to manifest in our psyche.

We do not consciously choose an emotion, however. All the emotions we feel come from deep-seated experiences, thought patterns, and beliefs that have conditioned us to respond emotionally. Emotion is the psyche's way of getting our attention, whether it is negative or positive. Emotion is there for good reasons, but if not properly understood and directed, it will often turn against us. How does it do this? When we *express* our emotion in negative ways, we attack others physically (violence) or psychologically (verbal or emotional abuse). If, on the other hand, we *repress* negative emotion, as we so often do, the result is *self* attack, expressed in various ways throughout the body (including illness, "accidents," and death) and through self-destructive behavior (self-sabotage, for example). When negative emotion surfaces in our awareness, it is a red flag, and we would do well to be alert and pay attention to what it is trying to tell us. What we do with that emotion and where we direct it will determine whether it is destructive or empowering to us.

Like our thoughts, emotion in any form, whether negative or positive, is neither good nor bad in and of itself. We have established so far that we are neither our thoughts nor our emotions. They are not *who* we are. The same can be said for all our responses to any given situation, that is, how we respond does not determine who we are.

What about our bodies? Can we confuse our identity with the body? If we do, then we can be certain that when the body changes due to accidents, sickness, aging, or dying, our identity will be tragically crushed or at least altered to some degree. Likewise, we can become elated with a body makeover, weight loss, new hairdo, new clothes, or cure of disease, but of course that new identity doesn't last and will therefore never bring us happiness. It is important to remember that *we are not our body*.

Free Will

The Source created the Infinite State (Heaven, or Nirvana), which is eternal and totally untouched by our temporary separated state in time and space. *When we separated, we fell asleep and began to dream.* Our Unified Self was, is, and always will be part of the Infinite State, even though our earthly evolution is but a *dream experience.* The world we see seems to exist outside and independently of our minds. Every form of fear, including anger, attack, lack, and anxiety, are all projected fragments of our dream and therefore can be healed through *awakening*. However, as long as we believe this dream is real, our ego-self (dreamer) is the producer and director of all our make-believe plays on the world's stage, and all the traits of the characters components of the dreamer's psyche.

At the time of the separation, when our minds split, we formed a will, or intent, that ran counter to the infinite expression of Love's presence. This is the will of our little self, or ego-self.

To begin to grasp why the ego-self's will is so antithetical to that of The Source, we need to look carefully at its core belief. The ego-self believes it made itself; yet somewhere, in the back of its psyche, it "knows" (or, rather, *fears*) that there exists outside itself a gigantic Source that created everything else. It is terrified of this Power and flees and tries to hide from It with all its might because it "knows" it abandoned It and continues to turn away from It. A bottomless pit of guilt drives its need to maintain control. It has a terror of ever being found out and sought in revenge, and with its fearful thoughts it projects a notion of The Source as being separate, judgmental, vindictive, and punitive. This is absolute fiction. Even so, the ego-self is so fearful of its manufactured notion of The Source's punishment that it delivers its *own* judgments and punishments. It desperately hopes that, by judging and punishing its owner through illness, accidents, loss, devastation, victimhood, or guilt, it will escape the full wrath of The Source. In other words, punishing itself in any of these ways is the ego-self's way of avoiding an even more severe, though imagined, response from The Source.

At the core of the ego-self's free will is the belief in separation, "sin" (our imagined betrayal and abandonment of The Source), judgment, and retribution. This is what our personal ego-self believes and, frighteningly, this is the same value system from which most of our world operates, *no questions asked*. From politics and law to corporations and our education system, institutions unconsciously teach and learn fear, because that is the core and foundation of the ego-self's nature, both individually and globally. Fear, not Love, is the hidden motivator of all the agendas and designs of free will that operate in our entire world.

All pain and suffering, all accidents and disasters, are not caused by a wrathful and punitive Creator. The Source, who created us, allowed us to become extensions of Itself and to freely choose to enter the dream dimension of time and space. Our minds split, and we formed the illusion of separate bodies along with the idea of free will. Temporary amnesia of our natural inclusive state of Love and Joy overtook us, allowing the ego-self and its fear-based perception to take the reins of our human will.

When we realize this truth, we can then begin to appreciate that there *is* a Universal right order in our world. It is not governed by chaos or influenced by some outside evil force. There are two *wills* (intents) in this world, one is not real, the other truth. Let us examine both. First we will look at our own personal will, the one we hold dear, defend, and value so highly.

(1) *Ego-self will* is **subjective intent in motion** through *projection*. It is expressed as guilt, fear, judgment, attachment, control, thought, emotion, having, and becoming. The ego-self will was conceived through separation, and at its core is the belief in sin and guilt, which leads to fear, the need to control, chaos, scarcity, and struggle. Operating in the ego-reality of time and space, it is subjective rather than objective. It is compelled by its natural function, which is to contract (in direct contrast to Love's function, which is to expand, or extend), separate, and project.

The ego-self will is intensely personal, conditional, judgmental, exclusive, restrictive, and biased. It is experienced through thought, time, and emotion. Because it must maintain total control of its purpose and function in order to survive, it skillfully uses its attributes to ensure that we stay stuck in the disempowering cycle of seeking pleasure while trying to avoid pain, all for the sake of maintaining our cherished individuality! The basis of this thought system depends on the ideas that attack and defense are real, and that giving is sacrifice or loss. Our personal will (ego) cannot conceive that anything of value such as Love, Peace, or Joy could ever only increase when shared. It gives conditionally, that is, it gives only so that it may receive something in return. When giving, it perceives there is a finite amount to give, and it is angered when its giving is not reciprocated. It is convinced that giving can only mean sacrifice or loss. It staunchly resists reality if reality differs from its expectations. Our ego-self will is *always* going to lead to suffering. Fortunately, it is not real. It does not exist in Reality.

(2) *Unified-Self Will* is **objective intent in motion** through *extension*, namely, Love, Peace, Joy, sharing, and creative inspiration. The Unified Will understands that all attack or judgment is a disguised call for Love, and that "giving *is* receiving" [italics ours].[19] It perceives *all* behavior as either a call for Love or an expression of it. Its response is the same to both: Love. Recognizing only Oneness, It is incapable of distinguishing between the two. The Unified-Self Will is inspired by Infinite Love and Joy. It is compelled to extend itself endlessly. It is objective rather than subjective, and, knowing Itself to be integral and inclusive, It exists independently of the mind, that is, outside time and space. It is mostly experienced on the level of the world through the means of forgiveness, or present-moment awareness, as well as at times of intuitive guidance and creative inspiration. Loving *what is*, It accepts reality without resistance. Being, allowing, accepting, undivided, inclusive, unconditional, impersonal, unbiased, unlimited, unchanging, timeless, and eternal are attributes of the Unified-Self Will. We'll be speaking more about "loving what is" in Chapter 3.

"...to will contrary to God is wishful thinking and not real willing."[20] The conflict we experience, then, is between the ego-self's idle wishes and the Will of The Source, which we share. The last thing the ego-self wants is for us to discover that we are afraid of it. And we would be, indeed, if we realized that it causes all the fear we experience, which literally drives us, resulting in our conflicts, both inner and outer. It is the cause of all seeming disappointments, suffering, and pain. It is ingenious at making sure we don't discover the pit of fear that propels our perception and therefore keeps us in bondage. Beneath the cover of the self-praise and positive attitude we strive for, the ego-self regards us as superficial, distrustful, cynical, pessimistic, distant, unfeeling, and callous. Every response to anger or threat, and every thought or feeling of fear, frustration, loneliness, or depression, are all manifestations of ego-self's foundation of separation: guilt. It skillfully disguises all the people, places, events, and circumstances (to which we respond and justify our grievances) as coming from outside us and wants us to believe we are victims of random chaos, thus further encouraging our dependence on and allegiance to it. In other words, when we *respond* to anything that appears to happen, we are giving power to the ego-self's will.

Our liberation depends on relinquishing the ego-self will's stranglehold and learning to *let go* of it in order to awaken to our natural inheritance, the Unified Will. Perhaps the most impressive trait of ego-self is its *absolute undivided devotion to one goal*, which is to maintain separation and total autonomy apart from The Source, and it does so with remarkable efficiency. The more seemingly random the chaos, the more it gains its strength. What an advantage it seems to have! We, on the other hand, do not have a single focused vision and goal comparable to that of ego-self. Instead, we vacillate incessantly, not at all certain of our goal or what we want, and that is why we experience confusion, inconsistency, doubt, and conflict. We are confused, because ego-self would not have us know we have another choice besides separation. Having now become aware that we do indeed *have* a choice, we can now learn from ego-self and use it to our advantage by examining its strategy and, *this* time, develop a corresponding single unflinchingly consistent focus and goal towards regaining the state of our Unified Self. Paradoxically, it seems, our utter *dependence* on The Source is where our power lies.

It is not Unified Will that creates suffering, pain, and death, or chaos in any form. How could Infinite Love be, or cause, anything other than the Peace and Joy that it is and extends? *Our purpose is to remember and reclaim our own True Will, the Will of the Universal Inspiration.* We align with this goal as we unlearn our misperceptions.

There is no seeming chaos that the Unified Will cannot reinterpret for us and heal. Every mistake we ever made can and will be transformed at our own heartfelt acknowledgment of our unhappiness and request for help. Once we remove the lens of fear, we can see clearly that everything that happens in our life is meaningful and not random. This is explained in the following quote from *A Course in Miracles*: "What could you not accept, if you but knew that everything that happens, all events, past, present and to come, are gently planned by One Whose only purpose is your good?"[21]

Fear and Now

A Course in Miracles explains that there are only two states, or emotions: love and fear.[22] The first is our natural and original state, that of our one Unified Self. The second, fear, is something our mind manufactures.

Love can flourish only in the absence of fear because fear distorts our perception and blinds us with a cloud of confusion. Love, being opposite to fear, is an endless energy that knows only how to extend (or share) itself, and, by so doing, it increases both for the giver and the receiver. Most of us have been conditioned to know fear more than Love, because that is what our world's culture invests in.

Fear tricks us into states of confusion, anxiety, and dread. In this book, we hope to expose and demystify fear's illusory game and provide an empowering alternative to its deluded intent.

Almost all the fear we experience is unnecessary and debilitating. The only real fear we may need to listen to in this world is immediate physical threat, the type that is instinctual and gives us no time to think. We go into a "fight or flight" response, just as our ancestors did when suddenly faced with a hungry wild animal. This type of "emergency" fear is a built-in response to ensure survival. These days, the threat could more often be mechanical rather than natural; for example, we barely escape a car racing towards us, or we flee the scene of a terrorist attack. Yet, having arrived at this point in our evolutionary development, the type of fear we are more likely to suffer from is psychological in nature. That is, we have awakened to the truth that *all* fear, in all its forms, stems from our thoughts about the past and/or the future. This type of fear would include any of our *resistance* to *what is*, which is cleverly hidden from our awareness by the ego. And it can only survive if we ponder the past or the future. However, if we remain focused in present-moment awareness, all fear disappears.

Much of our fear on this level, the world, is unconsciously rooted in our childhood or past. All the fear-based conditioning we absorbed developed into beliefs that lie largely unquestioned. This wall of fear is what limits us in all our relationships; it also limits our ability to attract abundance and to be healthy. Fear will not allow us to be fulfilled.

Our childhood conditioning was most probably saturated with beliefs stemming from words such as: impossible, difficult, have to, should, can't, do/don't, no/never, bad, and doubt. Millions of seeds of limitation and doubt were planted in our young and impressionable minds.

Our minds now can be likened to a collection of movies that

we call upon in our memory and act out accordingly. We actually live every moment through a clouded lens of past limitation. Thus, we are not relating with reality. Reality is the present moment, entirely free of the mind's past conditioning. However, we are so conditioned to perceive each moment either (1) through the smeared lens of the past or (2) by fantasizing about a future moment. As a result, we almost always exist outside the now moment, which means we are not really present, here and now. And because of this, we do not see or hear anything truthfully. All we really see or experience is distorted old-movie film footage that obliterates the now moment from our lives.

The now moment is the only "time," which of course is a time*less* experience, that exists in Reality. It is what *A Course in Miracles* calls the "holy instant."[23] All we have ever experienced are zillions of now moments, but the problem is that we were not there for them. We have been distracted from living in Reality because we have been dwelling in a useless past or the imagined future. It is a kind of secondhand way of living, not really here, yet not really anywhere real. Evading the now moment is the ego-self's way of keeping us trapped mentally, spiritually, emotionally, and physically. Later in the book, we will look at how to access the now moment and examine its importance on the path to Liberation.

Judgment

Judgment is a subject that most of us misunderstand. It is a valued quality of the ego-self, although its entire foundation is based on illusion. All judgment the ego-self makes comes from a distorted self-image that is constantly seeking pleasure while trying to avoid pain. It believes it created itself and is separate from The Source, and all its judgments are geared to keep this separation intact. How can the ego-self possibly judge rightly? It would have to have infinite knowledge and awareness encompassing all of time—past, present, and future. It would be required to know in advance all the effects of its judgment on everyone and everything in every possible way. It would need to be fully aware of everyone's most inner intent at all times and in all circumstances.

The ego-self would judge as "bad" or tragic a disaster that kills thousands of people. But because it is based on a belief in sin and guilt, separation, and chaos, it has no ability to correct its perception and do what the "miracle" does as it is defined in *A Course in Miracles*: "It [a miracle] merely looks on devastation, and reminds the mind that what it sees is false."[24] Nor can the ego-self even *begin* to fathom the truth that we do indeed create our own reality, including tragic disasters, through the psychological mechanism of projection (again, projection makes perception). The ego-self will never claim responsibility for creating reality and will always project blame and guilt outside itself, that is, onto other people, places, circumstances, events, or even The Source Itself.

One person's judgment of something as "good" is another person's judgment of the same thing as "bad." And what may have been "good" (accurate) judgment at one time may be perceived as "bad" (faulty) judgment at a different time. The ego-self's judgment is fickle and completely unreliable, and therefore dangerous.

Let us clarify the difference between the right- and wrong-minded use of judgment in our lives. We *must* use judgment, or *discernment, evaluation, comparison,* or *choice,* every day in order to make ordinary decisions. For example, we weigh the pros and cons of the duties and benefits of two job offers. But the *ego-self's* judgment is *condemnation,* which is always the result of its illusory projections of guilt onto another whom it perceives to be outside and separate from itself—and the target of its projection becomes the bad guy. As we become more and more aware of this dynamic, we would do well to be more careful when jumping to conclusions about others, because, as we said earlier, what we see in another is merely a reflection of what we see in ourselves. We do not see others as whole, because we do not see ourselves as whole; we only see a fragment of a person, and our ego-self perceives that fragment as faulty and mistakenly overlooks Reality, which is that we are one. Our ego projects qualities that may or may not be real onto people we encounter, thereby distorting reality. We are raised from early childhood to be fault-finders, thinking we help people with so-called "constructive criticism," which is an oxymoron if ever there was one. All this does is keep us stuck in a limited state that blocks out the awareness of Love's presence.

The challenge for us is to practice *allowing* and *accepting*. What we give to others, we give to ourselves. Again," giving is receiving." And each time we consciously withhold judgment of someone, which is to forgive him and ourselves, we come closer to knowing and accepting the Unified Self. We can actually be the observer of ego-self and monitor our thoughts, including our tendency to judge or condemn, giving us the opportunity to correct our faulty perceptions. This shift of perception will help greatly in curbing the ego-self's destructive habits.

We are not our thoughts, beliefs, and emotions because these are subject to our own erroneous projections. We are not our roles, our past, personality, accomplishments, body, hopes, or fears. These labels are all fragments of what we believe to be true now. They are subject to constant change and distortion by the ego-self and therefore are not Reality.

We are not the ego-self, nor are we its perception. Just recognizing this as truth is a courageous first step in the direction toward discovering *who* we really are, along with the majestic purpose we were created to fulfill.

Wherever our trust has been invested until now is the direction in which we were heading. Trusting the illusion of the ego-self has never given—and never will give —us that for which we so deeply yearn. If, at our core, we long for absolute communion with Love Itself, and if we want to know Unified Peace, Joy, security, and endless abundance of spirit, we must desire to know our Self, the one Unified Self within. This is the Self who responds to the Unified Will and is the instrument for Its expression.

An absolute prerequisite to unearthing our Unified Self and its unlimited perception is the dissolution, or "undoing," of the ego-self. We refer to this process as "ego-release," or "ego-death." However, the only aim of Undoing is to reverse, or undo, the ego-self's dysfunctional thought system. There is no actual death involved; rather, there is a voluntary abdication of all that is false and destructive. This process is made so much easier if we consistently remind ourselves, "I do not perceive my own best interests,"[25] and willingly surrender to the Higher Intelligence who does. Adyashanti explains this from another perspective: "When the role called 'I'm a human being' ends, we call that death. It's a lot easier if you let that role die before the body dies, and let it be put to rest now."[26]

We are beings seeking wholeness after eons of laboring through illusion and separation. This goal requires that we relinquish our dysfunctional false perception (the ego's separation belief system) and learn how to reverse it, the process of which systematically eliminates all existing blocks to the awareness of Love's presence. The cumulative results of this reversal are increased trust in the perfection of the Unified Will and an ever-deepening ability to let go of previous limitations. We learn to recognize and embrace Love, and in return we come to know that we, having been created by Love, *are* Love.

A Mistaken Sense of Self: Losing Our Identity to "I," "Me," "Myself," or "Mine"

The ego believes itself to be separate and alone and invests its entire concept of self-worth in the ideas of "I," "me," "myself," and "mine." As children, we all learned very early on to link our sense of self to people and all sorts of objects, circumstances, and conditions. When we became attached to something, such as a toy, blanket, or other special object, we automatically tagged it as *mine*. Giving the object the status of *mine* also gave it the destructive power to be a kind of extension of our ego-self. That is, making it *mine* amounted to linking it as another addition—another bead on our identity bracelet (see the section on "The Bracelet Theory," which follows)—to our extended ego-self identity, a false substitute of our Self.

The acquisition of things, as we mistakenly learned, seemed to add substance to our developing self-image. We classified and named the special objects that we desired and coveted and claimed them as ours—*mine*—as part of our identity. We soon learned to attach great personal value to these things, confusing them with who we really are. Who we are has nothing to do with *what* we identify with, because who we truly are needs no thing, object, person, or circumstance in order to be complete.

The trap that snared all of us as children was one of ignorance. Not recognizing or valuing the real self (Unified Self), we were conditioned to make one up. The ego-self gathered even more strength as we learned to personally identify our sense of self with added extras, such as attitudes, beliefs, opinions, and values. We collected myriad judgments and assimilated them as illusory parts of our image. Then when these attachments, too, were threatened, we would take offense and often retaliate.

When we take offense or feel defensive, it is usually because we are personally identified with something such as an idea, belief, or opinion that is not consistent with who we are. The truth, of course, is that "nothing real can be threatened,"[27] so what is it that the ego is defending against? Whatever it may be, it must not be real because Truth never needs defending. So, what do we defend? Eckhart Tolle answers the question thusly: "You are defending yourself, or rather the illusion of yourself, the mind-made substitute."[28]

Put very simply, we confuse our *true* identity (Unified Self) when we emotionally attach ourselves to something, most often using the concepts, "I," "me," "myself," and "mine." Whenever we consciously or unconsciously claim ownership of someone, a role, an object, outcome, belief, or opinion, we mistake them for our eternal essence, our real identity. Note that claiming ownership can also include *negative* identifications, such as illness, disabilities, a sense of victimhood, resentments, regrets, and grievances. For example, saying "I am an allergy sufferer" is literally telling yourself and others that your identity *is inter-locked with* allergies. Without being aware of it, we thus describe ourselves in terms of our suffering. The suffering then becomes confused with our identity. The truth is that your identity is whole and pure and immune from any outer influences.

Whenever we become upset, it is almost always because we have mistaken something as *ours* and have forgotten that our Unified Self is whole and without need for illusory substitutes. *My* partner, *my* job, *my* car, *my* child, *my* idea, *my* house can all too quickly become substitutes for our true sense of self. We can tell when this occurs by our emotional reactions to loss of, or change to, any one of the above items. Fear, anger, and need to control are signs of this confusion. By the same token, elation or exuberance over the gaining or improvement of such items would be a symptom of this confusion, as well.

The process of awakening will always include challenges. For example, when our attachments are threatened in any way, the ego-self steps in and promptly sets into motion its strategy to defend and protect its separation at all costs, and we need to be cognizant of that dynamic. The suffering we may feel—a sense of loss—during this process is the elimination of the "ownership factor." Once we relinquish this "ownership concept," we no longer take things seriously or personally. Nor is our happiness contingent on them. We can still enjoy the experience of some of the more pleasurable satellite identifications. However, they are no longer locked into our identity.

As we evolve, the labels "I," "me," "myself," and "mine" become less necessary in our vocabulary, and, when they are required, they are used purely for practical reasons. Overcoming the need to claim ownership of anyone or anything removes the ego's addiction to holding fixed mental viewpoints that always serve to invite chaos through their illusory need to be acquired, protected, and defended.

The Bracelet Theory

The ego, as a mistaken thought system, may be likened to a multi-beaded bracelet, a sort of "charm bracelet," with each bead representing an erroneous belief (Figure 2.3). These beads consist of both conscious and unconscious beliefs, many of which stem from ancestral heritage, race, tribe, nation, culture, and/or family. Past conditioning, education, experiences, and environment also contribute to the formation of our values and opinions. Every bead we collect —and the more we collect, the more ego-self is strengthened and reinforced—acts as an opaque barrier, blocking us off from the awareness of Love's presence in our lives, in ourselves and others.

Every one of our ego beads—each charm—has a story, and we repeat our stories every time we identify with a belief. For example, a common story may be that we were wrongly treated as children, perhaps even abused. The story feeds the belief that, "I am a victim of abuse." This belief then becomes another solidified bead in our collection of egoic identifications, which negatively affects us. Being overly identified with our accomplishments, failures, or partners means that we are mentally telling ourselves a story that feeds our dysfunctional belief system. And most, if not all, our beliefs are severely debilitating because they limit us and block us from Truth, which is Love.

Potential Mistaken Identity Beads (Ego)

- Partner/relationships
- Career or business
- Children or parents (family)
- Finances
- Accomplishments or failures
- The past or future
- Emotions
- Politics

- Nation, race, or tribe
- Body image, health, age, gender
- Beliefs, opinions, and values
- Illness or disability
- Material objects
- Friends or enemies
- Authority
- Thoughts

- Fears
- Desires
- Conditioning
- Education
- Habits
- Addictions
- Experiences
- Role or status

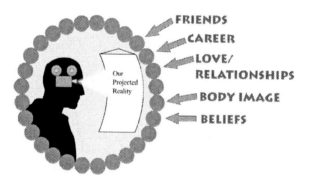

Figure 2.3: Mistaken Identity

Each of these stories tells us who we are and what we want to be. However, never will they lead us to real and abiding happiness and Truth.

Each ego bead of mistaken self-identity that we acquire reinforces yet another fixed point of mental resistance and adds one more obstruction to the awareness of Love's presence. When we identify something as "mine," we confuse the object, person, belief, opinion, emotion, or thought with the *who* that we are in Reality. Then, when any one of these items is lost, threatened, or changed, we encounter suffering. The ego, taking things personally, feels threatened when it perceives judgment or attack on any one of its *mistaken identity beads.*

CHAPTER 3

THE UNIFIED SELF

The Unified Self is a sacred shard of the one immaculate mirror that smashed eons ago when we chose the dream to separate from The Source and incarnate in this dimension of space and time. It is the pure and resplendent part of us that never left Its Source. Our Unified Self is the mystical warrior who knows everything—everywhere, at all times, all at once. Operating outside time and space, It sees us and our lives with pristine perception.

This whole and sacred Self is directed by the Universal Inspiration (Holy Spirit), and it is the part of us whose sole purpose is to express the Unified Will here on earth. The Universal Inspiration acts as a communication link between The Source and our Unified Self. When operating from this Unified Self, we are perfectly and effectively aligned with, and therefore instrumental to, the miraculous outpouring of Love, Joy, and Healing that is our purpose. *A Course in Miracles* states: "The Holy Spirit is in you in a very literal sense. His is the Voice that calls you back to where you were before and will be again. It is possible even in this world to hear only that Voice and no other. It takes effort and great willingness to learn."[29] The Universal Inspiration is "universal" because it is the shared inspiration of all mankind. It is the energy/light of the Unified Self, which induces the miraculous clarity of vision that we enjoyed before the separation.

Because the Unified Self is not governed by time, space, logic, or reasoning, it is unlimited. That is why It is often referred to as the Co-creator, whose nature is Love, Joy, and unlimited abundance of spirit. And this is what It wants for us:

- to know our enormous power as Co-creator;
- to recognize our purpose in life: to awaken from the dream;
- to realize our fullest potential;
- to experience Absolute Certainty, or Trust, in the Universal Order;
- to live in Love, Joy, and Peace, and unlimited abundance of spirit; and
- to inspire others to know and be the Love that they *are*.

The Unified Self's entire frame of reference is based upon the opposite of that of the ego-self. Unlike the ego-self, which was born in fear when it seemingly split off from The Source, the Unified Self is a pure core of Love, which cannot perceive fear. The two have nothing in common because their goals are diametrically opposed. Our minds are split, and, having forgotten who we are, we are all walking this earth in a state of psychosis.

Intellect versus Intuition

With the possible exception of the greatest of spiritual teachers, mystics, and avatars of the world, we are all challenged greatly by our split mind, which is the sole cause of *all* our inner conflict. That is because our intellect tells us one thing and our intuition another. But it seems logic and reason invariably win us over, and then later, when things don't work out, we regret that we hadn't listened to the intuitive urge.

Intellect is the voice of the ego-self. It is linear rather than abstract, that is, it operates on the level of the dualistic world of time and space. It is severely limited in its ability to perceive anything other than the mundane world of form. It is most often the louder of the two voices and the one we are proud of, respect, trust, and pay attention to first. Ego-self depends upon its intellect for all its problem solving. But because its perception is distorted, intellect is totally unreliable and not to be trusted. Because it is made up, it is actually unnatural to us and therefore requires an extraordinary amount of effort to be cultivated. While this may be hard to believe, it has only a fraction of the capability of knowing that intuition has, as it has no access to Truth.

Intuition, on the other hand, is the Voice of the Unified Self. It is abstract rather than linear, that is, it literally interconnects outside of time, space, and matter. Therefore, it can appear to be irrational to our intellect, and what it tells us seems to defy all possible explanation. It is the Unified Self's mode of communication and problem solving. Since intuition is a *knowing*, or *foreknowing*, it operates in leaps without any logical procedure or formula. It "just knows." Our intuition holds the key to absolute knowledge, or Truth. It is our natural inheritance. And It is infallible.

Our intellect is useful to be sure, but nowhere as valuable and trustworthy as intuition. Unfortunately, our culture depends on the intellect and disparages intuition. We have only to look at our education systems to see that the foundation and the goal of education are all about intellectual knowledge and the accumulation of skills. Do we see a college degree in "Intuitive Wisdom"?

The ego-self is addicted to control and uses its intellect to sustain that desire to control. It is in constant thinking and judging mode. It analyzes, evaluates, discriminates, compares, defends, and rationalizes, trying to control the past and future in each waking moment. When such thoughts occupy the mind to this extent, we leave no room for intuition. Is it any wonder we suffer from so much confusion and conflict?

True knowledge, or wisdom, is gained only when intuition becomes the driver and skillfully directs the intellect when required. Our entire world is based upon, and functions through, intellect only, and because of this we miss many miraculous opportunities. If we only knew how limited the intellect is, we would be willing to let it go and discover, cultivate, trust, and use our intuition in our daily life.

Learning to trust intuition requires regular practice. Quieting the mind and becoming the observer of thought and feeling are necessary. The Voice of our intuition never lies to us; it's just that we're not practiced enough to detect it consistently. For example, let's say you are in a situation where you wish to purchase a used car. You want to be sure it's a good buy and not a lemon, and you're challenged because you don't have a mechanical background. You like two cars, but one seems a better buy because it is newer. Logic and reason tell you that the more recent model is the obvious choice. Even your mechanic, after a quick check, logically confirms the obvious. Yet somewhere in your gut is a subtle, nagging feeling that something just doesn't seem right about the newer model. What would you do?

Typically, in this type of situation, most of us would disregard intuition in favor of all the logical facts that seem to stack up in favor of the newer car. However, if we were trained to be more in tune with our intuition, we would step back and listen to that intuitive urge that warned us *not* to purchase the newer car, regardless of the logical evidence that seems to point to its superiority. We would, through practice and experience, trust the gut feeling that the newer car is not right. A type of foreknowing reveals to us that the newer car is about to develop a major engine problem that would cost us as much as the car was worth.

That is intuition, and, if valued and nurtured, it is readily available for us every moment of our life. Trusting this wonderful gift may save us many costly mistakes in every aspect of life with people, circumstances, and material considerations.

The key to becoming aware of both our Unified Self and Its intuitive Voice is the process of what we referred to earlier as "letting go." Unless we are willing to let go of all our assumptions, judgments, conditioning, and intellectual knowledge, we cannot embrace this precious gift. The ego-self thinks it knows so much and is convinced it's always right about everything;

however, all it does is make assumptions, form conclusions, and project illusion onto others. It is in fact an obstacle to our Liberation.

Ironically, we need to befriend uncertainty in our life, because that is precisely where we will find the opportunities to learn to develop Trust. In learning to trust our Unified Self, we gradually become liberated from the ego-self's constant obsession with the intellect as being the supreme intelligence and protector of our safety and wellbeing. As our perception becomes more and more healed and whole, our Unified Self emerges in our awareness. We will acknowledge that the ego-self, with its limited frame of intelligence, can never transport us beyond its restricted abilities. Only the Unified Self, joined with The Source through Unified Will, can reveal within us the gifts we were born to enjoy as Co-creators.

The Illusion of Attack

One of our most fundamental and deceptive beliefs that requires total reversal and nothing less is the belief in attack in all its conceivable forms. For us to begin to acknowledge who we are in Truth, we must be willing to surrender the deep-seated notion that we are separate and different from each other. We, at our core, are all one and the same, having been created absolutely in Love by infinite Love Itself, The Source. Our mission at this point in our evolutionary development is to become aware of our connection with each other and to The Source, that we are one, not separate, and actually *are* Love. Our mission is achieved when we see the Sacred-Self in everyone around us, whereby we remember *who* we are. They are the key to our own healing and wholeness.

The degree to which we are able to see through others' superficial ego-self, with its beliefs, values, and behaviors, is the degree to which we will see our own authenticity. Whenever we are able to overlook ego-self error in others, we come closer to embracing the Love that we truly *are*.

The ego-self sees us all as separate and different. As a result, we perceive our values, beliefs, opinions, possessions, and bodies as being under constant threat of loss, change, or attack by others. To prevent others from attacking and stealing from us, the ego-self has set in place its preposterous strategy of defenses and counterattack, which it then ingeniously finds ways to justify.

The ego-self's insane belief that it is separate from The Source and therefore requires special protection is at the seat of our investment in the personal. By the word "personal," we mean that the ego-self always sees things from its individual vantage point, and consequently takes things personally.

The ego-self is refined in its ability to analyze and form rationales for either defense or attack. Its conclusion is always that it needs to defend or attack in order to protect itself from others. If we interpret another's behavior as a personal attack on us, we can be sure the ego-self has conjured up a false picture and projected it outward so that counterattack can be justified. It cannot under any circumstances know the reality of the situation as it is occurring in the now moment, because it is projecting an image made up by itself, based on past experiences or future fears, not Truth. It has no way of seeing truly in the now.

Embracing Unified-Self awareness requires that we suspend our usual reaction of taking personal offense when we perceive attack. This calls for discipline in retraining our minds. To experience liberation, we need to liberate others first, and in so doing, we liberate ourselves. That is, in suspending our usual judgments of others, we learn to see ourselves in a purer light. Also, our intuition is strengthened in the process, as it alerts us to any obstacles that the clouded judgment of our ego-self previously obscured, and then those situations become opportunities for Undoing on the road to Liberation.

At the very foundation of the Unified Self's existence is the Extension Principle, the fundamental truth that *all giving is receiving*. This is in direct contrast to the ego-self's basis for its very existence: it seeks to receive for the self alone, gives to get, and believes that whatever one person wants, another will have to relinquish. To the ego-self, giving means losing, gaining is another's loss. It has no idea that *all* giving truly *is* receiving.

Whatever we give we keep, whether is it Love or judgment and attack; this is a universal truth. For example, if we have the intent to give forgiveness to a loved one by choosing to overlook his mistake, we in turn receive that very gift that we offered, and we, too, are forgiven. We may not be conscious of it at the time, but each and every act of forgiveness releases us immeasurably from the grips of the ego, enriching our lives in ways we could not imagine at the time.

If, on the other hand, we attack another with blame or condemnation, we are in fact also giving. In this instance, we are giving judgment, guilt, anger, and hatred. The principle of *giving is receiving* remains exactly the same in this case; whatever we project or give to another person we invariably accumulate internally. Ugliness given away returns as ugliness. That chaotic dynamic can be seen occurring in myriad forms throughout life.

As we said earlier, every thought has an effect. There are no neutral thoughts. If every thought we have causes an effect, can you imagine what the cumulative effect of making thousands of false judgments would be? Especially now that we realize that all we give, both good and bad, returns to its source? There is no escaping this truth. However, we can decide to be pro-active about it and become aware of our thoughts, feelings, and actions. By so doing, we open the door to the Unified Will, and the quality of our life improves dramatically. Simply stopping when anger surfaces and objectively observing our thoughts and feelings is wonderfully freeing. Realizing that you are not your thoughts or feelings and that you can *elect* to detach and observe yourself is probably the fastest way to empower you and transform your life. This process will be discussed in detail in the section, "The Now Moment."

Again, with each and every encounter we have with one another, we are given the opportunity to either imprison or liberate ourselves. We can choose to overlook error and see Truth or we can enforce chaos in our lives by choosing to perceive the ego-self as real. Whatever we give we keep.

Love itself can only increase by being shared. Extending Love *ensures* its increase. Every loving thought, or every opportunity we take to think, see, feel, or act in loving ways, such as forgiving, listening, being grateful, allowing, accepting, and giving, will manifest as Love in our lives. The more Love we give, the more we receive, and it keeps extending infinitely.

Unconscious Giving

Most if not all of us, however, engage in a kind of giving that we will refer to as "unconscious giving" (wrong-minded, faulty, or dysfunctional giving). Some of us just cannot say "no," and we find our lives filled with endless acts of giving. The frequent feelings accompanying this type of "giving" are exhaustion, resentment, anger, paranoia, and a nagging sense of being used, without our realizing the source of this discomfort. The urge to blame or criticize the other promptly follows.

There are certain trademarks of unconscious giving that you may recognize as your own behaviors. These include a craving or drive to give something to someone even though the other person may not actually feel he or she needs or wants it, doesn't express a desire for it, or doesn't ask for it outright. One who engages in unconscious giving is trying to establish a connection with the receiver of his "generosity," which, if accepted, eventually becomes a co-dependent relationship (or what *A Course in Miracles* calls a "special relationship," a topic we'll be discussing later on). The giver's underlying motive is rooted in a deep-seated need to be loved or to gain someone's approval, *not* altruism, because his intent stems from an unconscious persistent sense of lack, incompleteness, or emptiness. Invariably, the giver will attract users and abusers or classic victimizer-personality types. This cycle of giving and receiving is disempowering for both people involved because neither the giver nor the receiver is coming from a truly loving, selfless intent. When during honest self-inquiry we find that our underlying motivation for giving is to get love, recognition, acknowledgement, approval, favor, or praise, or that we desire to feel needed, then the giving is conditional and, consciously or unconsciously, demands recompense.

To remedy this type of dysfunctional giving requires diligent vigilance of all our thoughts and feelings, and, as soon as this all-too-familiar urge to "give" arises, we might start by asking ourselves, "What is my deeper intent?" We must acknowledge where this impulse is coming from—our own mind and *not* outside us—and take full personal responsibility for it. Secondly, we must entrust this bad habit to the Universal Inspiration and, with complete honesty, holding back nothing, ask for help and guidance. By so doing, we become the observer of our ego-self, and the Universal Inspiration gently and patiently coaches us through our temptation. This entire process is the essence of Quantum Forgiveness (which we will discuss in the following chapter), or being in now-moment awareness, and it strengthens the Unified Self while, at the same time, loosens the grip of the ego-self.

The ego-self is a master at trying to conceal our deeper intent from us. It wants desperately to be seen, approved, needed, valued, and desired because, under all that bravado, is a yawning chasm of emptiness and sense of worthlessness. It uses either "good" or "bad" labels or behaviors—whichever tactic seems to lend it the most power at the time—to gain attention or recognition. Either way, both tactics are equally dysfunctional at the intent level, that is, they both come from the same misidenti-fication with ego-self and are therefore a mistaken belief. We must be willing to relinquish ignorance and wholeheartedly desire to know Truth and act on it.

I Do Not Know My Own Best Interests

We have said that much of what our ego-self has learned will need to be unlearned if we are to behold and embrace our true nature and purpose in this life. Probably, the first of all conscious acknowledgments to be made is the undeniable truth that we do not know our own best interests. Our ego-self has absolutely no idea what is best for us and will always lead us into confusion. In order to begin the process of Undoing, it is important to keep reminding ourselves, "I do not perceive my own best interests."[30] This helps to shift the balance of power from ego-self to Unified Self and stimulates our desire for Unified Will to flow through us in the form of intuition.

The Power of Humility

The Unified Self is an endless store of Higher Wisdom to which most of us have not yet yielded. It is a powerhouse of Truth and knowledge far beyond the ego-self's finite intellectual realm because it is the direct receptor of The Source's miraculous intention. The more we peel off the outer layers of ego-self perception, the stronger our capacity to extend and receive Love, Joy, Peace, and Wisdom. Attack in any form, including defense and judgment, is not part of the Unified Self's reality. Defense in itself is the belief that attack is real and therefore justifies counterattack as a defense. The real and true Self can never be attacked and therefore requires no defense.

The ego-self has an enormous investment in its image. These investments include its ideas, beliefs, opinions, people, careers, and possessions. It guards these idols intently and is on the watch for any perceived threat of loss or change to any one of them. It uses defense as a means to resisting *what is*.

Humility contains the power of defenselessness because the

Unified Self is invulnerable and therefore needs no defense. The ego-self, on the other hand, perceives itself as vulnerable and therefore needs to defend in order to uphold its insane thought system of separation. It rises in defense whenever its identity is threatened by our possible discovery of the preposterous illusion that it is. Only illusion needs defending because, if illusion of any kind were to completely withdraw defense, what would be left? If fear itself in all its guises withdrew all defenses, what would remain? Very simply: Love, the only essence that could possibly remain once illusion is no longer protected. The ego-release experience is purely the setting down of defenses that have, until now, protected our illusions, all of them, including our ego-self image. Surrendering defenses leads to the awareness and embracing of Truth, which is Love in action.

Ego-release would not be necessary if we could fully embrace true humility now. The ego-self is like an armed fortress, ready to battle against anyone or anything that threatens to de-stabilize its seat of power. We need to ask the questions, "What is our ego-self protecting?" and "What value lies in upholding such a gigantic illusion that blocks us from experiencing the ecstatic bliss of Love's presence?" If we were to surrender whole-heartedly to the recognition that our most valuable asset is humility, we would become enlightened in this very instant. Both the intensity and duration of the ego-release experience would be diminished if we would only embrace humility.

We need to encourage conscious, now-moment presence and total self-honesty in order to gain humility, which means eradicating the ego-self's desire to edit or justify our thoughts, feelings, and responses in its favor. As we discussed earlier, the key here, once again, is to maintain awareness while exercising discernment in our everyday decision-making but not use judgment as condemnation, which fosters guilt.

Our seeming vulnerability in defenselessness is where our strength lies, when recognized from The Source's perspective.

Not only can we afford to become more vulnerable (from the ego's standpoint), but we *must* become more "vulnerable" if we are to grow to trust the wisdom of the Unified Will working through and around us. Ego-self defenses are meaningless, because all the areas within us and in our life that we consciously or unconsciously defend are illusion! Our bodies, feelings, values, beliefs, and status are all illusion.

If we could only refrain from attacking and defending and instead hold present-moment awareness with the intent of allowing Truth to unfold in our awareness, we would gain insight and Peace. One more layer of illusion would be removed, and we would gain yet another gigantic step forward to reclaiming our Unified Self and the joyous life for which we yearn.

Certainty

There are only two realities between which we can choose in this world, one is illusion, the other Truth. There is either fear or Love. Where there is fear, there can be no Love. Where there is Love, there can be no fear. Love cannot co-exist with fear. Fear cannot co-exist with Love. They are mutually exclusive. At any given moment, we live in a state of total fear or total Love. There cannot be a fearful love or a loving fear.

Love itself is the only real essence in our world. This leaves fear to be recognized for what it is in its totality: illusion. No part of fear is real. It only seems real when our minds believe it and use it as a filter on our lens of perception through which we see and consequently believe that people, things, and circumstances are trying to attack us. We cannot exist peacefully with some love and some fear; it is not possible. Love produces certainty, fear confusion.

How do we grow to understand and embrace our Unified Self? If the Unified Self is Love, then its only perception must be Love. All perception emerging from any other place stems from guilt, in the form of fear, the need to control, resistance, anger, hatred, and judgment. If at any moment we see fear in any form, we must realize that we are not seeing Truth, but an illusion. Seeing or feeling any form of fear, then, must mean we are mistaken and must have misunderstood Love's call. At this point, we must pause, objectively observe ourselves and our thinking from now-moment awareness, and surrender the need to take action. Once having done so, *whatever* action we may take will be loving because Love will be flowing through us.

Every appearance of fear is a sign that our minds have chosen to see through the ego-self's distorted lens. This need not happen. At the moment we feel pain or resistance, we need only ask to be returned to right-mindedness, and the Universal Inspiration will carry our thoughts gently back to a state of Peace.

All fear comes from resistance to *what is*, that is, the need to control our external world. Resistance is the poison that forms fearful thought and therefore fearful beliefs. Reality seems full of disappointment, suffering, and tragedy. Yet it is only our thoughts and beliefs about these that truly give us suffering.

Nothing in and of itself can make us suffer. Our *perception* alone causes us pain, and if we act out of fear, it then causes us more pain. If we would only let go of all our thoughts and beliefs and surrender to Reality, we would find Peace this very moment!

Our deepest yearning is for Love, for Absolute Oneness. Ultimately, all of us yearn for this. Our natural state, Unified Self, is one of immaculate connection to "All That Is." It is our ultimate home, where no conflict can enter and no loss is possible.

Ironically, our greatest opportunity for liberation from ego-self lies within this very dream-reality of ours, because our daily lives present us with the most magnificent opportunities for inner transformation. Every day, no matter where we are, no matter what the circumstance, no matter which people seem to surround us, we, in any given moment, have the power to choose our experience. We either let the experience define our inner reality, or we choose the only Reality that truly exists, the Reality of Peace.

Our thinking and beliefs are the cause of any and all anxiety or conflict we may feel. We unconsciously carry fearful or threatening thoughts with us most of the time, because we haven't yet realized the tremendous power that our uninvestigated beliefs hold over us. If we're in a hurry to get to work and there's a traffic jam, our usual and immediate response is anxiety, anger, upset, impatience, frustration. Why? Because we perceive the problem to be *outside* ourselves. That is, reality—the world we see with our eyes—presents the traffic delay. There isn't a single thing we can physically do to change it, so our ego-self's thought propels us into instant anxiety. Why? There's always only one base reason: the ego-self rigidly resists reality, or *what is*. The ego-self says that *what is* is wrong. *What is* is not supposed to happen since it conflicts with our own will. *What is* should be something else. How many times a day are we faced with these mini-conflicts and disappointments? A problem at work, a flat tire in heavy traffic, our partner lets us down. This is reality as it occurs each and every day. We have no control over what this reality presents at any given moment. However, we are very much in control of our own reactions to it.

In her remarkable book *Loving What Is*,[31] author Byron Katie gives us a simple yet empowering process that involves a day-by-day, minute-to-minute strategy for easily and quickly seeing right through illusion. Her system is called "The Work" (see Appendix I). "The Work" consists of four little questions that are aimed at exposing Truth, which in the end reveals the Love that was there all along. "The Work" enables us to identify and take apart the disabling beliefs that breed anxiety, anger, paranoia, blame, criticism, and depression. Her ground-breaking discovery has helped many of us to clarify and adjust our thinking, leading us to peace within ourselves and all our relationships.

Katie identifies only "...three kinds of business in the universe: mine, yours, and God's." She continues, "(For me, the word *God* means 'reality.' Reality is God, because it rules. Anything that's out of my control, your control, and everyone else's control—I call that God's business.) Much of our stress comes from mentally living out of our own business. When I think, 'You need to get a job, I want you to be happy, you should be on time, you need to take care of yourself,' I am in your business. When I'm worried about earthquakes, floods, war, or when I will die, I am in God's business. If I am mentally in your business or in God's business, the effect is separation....If you are living your life and I am mentally living your life, who is here living mine?"[32]

In other words, when we are mentally in another person's business, we prevent ourselves from being present in our own business. If we are separate from ourselves in this manner, is it any wonder our lives aren't working?

If we don't even know what is in our *own* best interests, how could we possibly know what is in another's best interests? The only business we need concern ourselves with is our own. When we feel anxiety, fear, or conflict, we need to stop and ask ourselves, "Whose business am I in?" Mentally, this exercise allows us regular reality checks and the opportunity to see just how often we have not been truly present because we have been mentally living in other people's business most of our lives.

Furthermore, we begin to realize our own business is not what we may have believed. As we evolve, we discover that the Unified Self runs on a type of Universal Autopilot that dispels the need for the ego-self's obsession with control. This Universal Autopilot is the Unified Will being expressed through us.

The ego-self uses its thoughts to create desires and plans that are geared toward sustaining and reinforcing itself. As its "natural" state is one of scarcity, it depends on searching outside itself for things, circumstances, outcomes, food, or people to satiate its endless need to have or to become. Because its intrinsic drive is based on lack, the ego-self's will is destined to resist *what is* (reality) unless that reality is in line with its particular interests and expectations.

When our ego-self resists *what is*, it is defending itself against Reality. It does this at serious cost to our peace of mind because, in its resistance, it tells us that life is wrong, it's not the way it is *supposed* to be. And if that message is repeated often enough, we lose trust in life, in others, and in ourselves. Next time we find ourselves disappointed by someone or something, we have another opportunity to choose to be conscious of our inner resistance to *what is* (see the four questions and "The Turnaround" in "The Work" Worksheet in Appendix I). We can observe our reaction and gently remind ourselves to allow Reality to *be as it is* rather than resist it. By accepting *what is*, we learn the real meaning of Peace. Experiencing the peace that comes from doing this work will verify the truth in the following words, cited earlier, from *A Course in Miracles*: "...everything that happens...[is] gently planned by One Whose only purpose is your good."[33]

The Infinite State: Heaven

At the point of separation, we did not leave the Infinite State. We remain inside this Ultimate Consciousness, but we are asleep, or unconscious of it. As we discussed earlier, the ego-state is much like the dream-state we enter while asleep. That is, just as we experience our sleeping dreams as real, so too do we believe our dream-life in this world to be real. Just as we need to awaken from our sleeping dreams, so too do we need to awaken from this dream-life. Therefore, our liberation depends on our becoming cognizant of this deception. Our purpose, then, is to wake up from the dream and to become lucid Co-creators. The only Reality that has value in our lives is Love. And Love increases in proportion to our degree of awakening from the ego-state. The more we realize this truth, the more we see that our purpose is to awaken to our Unified Self.

The Source is Infinite Light, or Love, everywhere, always. This energy exists everywhere, always. It never changes. In our separated state, we live the illusion of separated selves, believing that giving is sacrifice and that attack and defense are real. The truth is that the Infinite State exists in its totality all around us, but all-too-often we are blind to its beauty and deaf to its harmony.

The "Tiny Mad Idea" Expands

A Course in Miracles explains that we believe that, with our "tiny, mad idea"[34] of separation, we actually shattered Heaven, and that we proceeded to make up a new world of time and space by selecting only some fragments of the Light while rejecting others. We took from Wholeness and produced a fragmented world, with no regard to right relationship between these parts, and deluded ourselves into believing our world to be real.

In order to deflect the insurmountable guilt caused by this act, we projected it outside of us and created a reality that seems to separate and attack. Such a world is governed by chaos. This way, we could believe that the world is the cause and we its effect, that is, we are victims of it and not responsible for it. "The world you see is an illusion of a world. God did not create it, for what He creates must be eternal as Himself. Yet there is nothing in the world you see that will endure forever."[35] Within this illusion, we perceive The Source as a supernatural force existing outside us with the power to create and to destroy, resulting in the illusion of birth, life, and death. Everything in this world and the universe seems governed by the law of constant change; whatever comes into form eventually passes away and dies. Even the relationships we form seem governed by change. They are sometimes loving, sometimes hateful; we stay a while, and then we leave.

If The Source is Unified Love, without change or limitation or end, then separation in any form, within the realm of The Source, is literally impossible. Realizing this truth, we may then begin to grasp the idea that we are in truth fast asleep, dreaming. In our dream-state, we unconsciously believe that we shattered Heaven with our "tiny mad idea." We believe we betrayed The Source and deserve to be punished. All of this of course is utter nonsense.

We in fact suffer from amnesia. We simply do not remember that we, and not The Source, made up this world. We do not remember who we are in truth. We enter this world in complete confusion, not remembering how we got here. The only True Reality is one of Love, and now we need to learn how to remember the Love that we *are*, so that we can awaken from this dream of limitation.

In the pre-separation state of perfect Oneness and Wholeness, we had no needs. There was no need for projection or perception, because we are all One; there is no object outside us to perceive. These concepts were born from separation and duality. In the state of perfect Oneness, we knew only the beingness of infinitely extended Love and Joy. There was nothing apart from this. How could there possibly be anything apart from perfect Oneness? Duality, the realm of opposites, introduced division in the form of observer and observed, a separation of the One. In the dream of this separated existence, we forfeited our awareness of the pure, radiant essence of our loving extension in exchange for the ego's cheap, shabby imitation of Life. We denied our place, our Oneness, with The Source, and that denial turned into projection, making this entire ego-reality. That is the story of how our universe came into "existence." We are dreaming this reality as external to us, we think we had no part in its making, and we appear to be victims of the world we see.

This world of ours is an hallucination that we ourselves assembled, using selected parts of the Infinite State. The changeable nature of the world is the external picture of our state of mind. We unconsciously believe we changed the Changeless, so we see a world of change! We may be living a dream experience here, but there is a part of us that is Divine and, in so being, has manifested loving aspects of our distant memory into this reality, which serve as sacred reminders of our absolute Oneness and Joy. The existing outward reality of humanity, animals, plants, minerals, and organic substances is the disguised form of what is actually at its essence: Infinite Perfection, which has never changed from its state of Infinite Love and the subsequent extension of that Love.

This entire universe is an illusion, made by our desire to fragment and become free from The Source. The Source did *not* make this reality; *we* did. The more quickly we awaken to this undeniable truth, the faster we will find Peace, and then no matter what may appear to happen from without, we still have Peace within, always. Nothing not made of Love exists. Nothing not eternal exists; nothing that seems to change is real. Therefore, nothing in this "reality," except for Love, is real. All else is illusion, a dream of birth and death, of beginnings and endings.

The Truth Is True and Nothing Else Is True
We belong to, and are eternally part of, The Source. We are Co-creators with our Creator. Our Unified Self and the Higher Mind within It *is* The Source. In other words, we are equal to, but not higher than, The Source. It created our Unified Self. However, we did not create It. The immaculate perfection of The Source is absolute, meaning that it is *always* consistent and coherent. There are *no* contradictions within The Source because It never vacillates, It never changes, It never ends. It is all Love, all Joy, all Peace, all knowledge, and all eternal. The power of The Source is never diluted and can have no opposites. This is Truth.

If The Source and everything It created is at one with Love, then are we not this same Love? If The Source created the Infinite

State, and our egos chose to adorn our existence with parts of that State within this world, what are the qualities of those parts? The only possible answer is Infinite Love. Everything—every thought, emotion, person, and circumstance—that is loving, forgiving, joyous, and peaceful is *real*. This means that if we perceive anything other than this Reality, we are hallucinating, which means hate, anger, and fear are *un*real. "...the truth is true and nothing else is true."[36] Only the ego-self can project the opposite to Love and believe it. We, our true Unified Self, cannot.

There is no evil, no demonic power that battles against The Source, because It and Its all-Loving Intent is the only Truth that exists everywhere, always, all at once. So, when we see or feel fear in any way, we are seeing or feeling an illusion that only *seems* real. The Source and the Universal Inspiration cannot acknowledge anything not created in Love; they see nothing where we see fear, anger, and guilt. They cannot see sin, because it does not exist. We make mistakes caused by the hypnotic sleep of the ego-self and call it "sin." In our ego-self insanity, we make sin real and demand retribution. All attack, blame, and guilt, on the level of thought or deed, whether self-inflicted or projected onto someone else, are all the same. There can be no degrees of illusion. For example, to take offense is the same illusion as to give offense; there is no difference between giver and receiver, because we are one. If we make the mistake of seeing or taking any offense as real, we then invest in the illusion of hate just as much as the perceived offender does. Any and all mistakes originate from this one and only place of ignorance: our belief in the reality of illusion. Every mistake, every offense perceived, in oneself or another, is *a call for love*, but it is disguised as attack because of the utter confusion of ignorance.

The separation instilled in us a seemingly insurmountable level of guilt. This guilt is so massive that it propels us to incarnate over and over again, thinking we can escape both our guilt and our fear of The Source. But what we do instead is project the guilt *outside* ourselves and make it real by believing it is caused by others or external circumstances. Then we blame, shame, or accuse. Not realizing that by doing so, we accumulate even more guilt each lifetime because we're not yet aware and willing to face the Truth that there is only one of us in this dream. We're all one. In Reality, separation and individuality are an impossibility, all illusion.

In any situation where judgment, fear, anger, grief, or guilt are experienced, the only remedy is to ask the Universal Inspiration to return our thoughts to right-mindedness. "Return me to right-mindedness" becomes an instant thought or prayer that takes us back to Peace.

There is extreme simplicity in Truth: Truth is Love, and all that exists is Love. To perceive complexity and anything other than Love is illusion. If Love is all there ever is, was, and ever shall be, then why do we experience everything but Love on a daily basis? Because it is what we *choose* to experience.

Once we realize the truth that Love is a choice and that reality is Love, then there is only *one* choice to lead us to Liberation: Love. Active Love is forgiveness, where forgiveness is the overlooking of an error that, while seeming very real in this ego-dream, never really occurred in Reality. Thus, forgiveness is Love in action. Before we began to catch on to the ways of the ego, we were confused, believing in a world that consisted of part love and part hate. We were lost to the whims of chaos. But not anymore!

Accepting Ego-Reality, or Loving What Is

If, in truth, there are no opposites of Love, then we must withdraw investment in anything other than Love. There are no exceptions. Yet daily we see, hear, and experience the opposite of Love. How can we overcome this conflict? Paradoxically, the only way to overcome the illusory world is to *accept* it. We reinforce error if we *resist* it. Learning to allow reality to present itself without arguing its existence, or attempting to change it, is releasing error's hold on us. Investigating our beliefs is the key to this liberation.

Quoting once again from *Loving What Is*, its author Byron Katie says, "In reality, the pain we feel about a past event is created in the present, whatever our past pain might have been. Inquiry looks at this present pain."[37] In a review of the book, the *Los Angeles Times* says the following: "The Work...when applied to a specific problem, enable[s] you to see what is troubling you in an entirely different light. As Katie says, 'It's not the problem that causes our suffering; it's our thinking about the problem.' Contrary to popular belief, trying to let go of a painful thought never works; instead, once we have done The Work, the thought lets go of us. At that point, we can truly love what is, just as it is."[38]

If all we really want is to be free from chaos in every form, and if deep and abiding Peace is our goal, the fact that there is nothing "out there" (external to us) that can be a real barrier to achieving this goal is reassuring and comforting, to be sure. There are no objective barriers to attaining peace and happiness; every barrier we encounter is subjective, existing only in our minds. This fact, coupled with the truth that all that really exists out there and in here is Love, means we can make a conscious choice now for liberation. What other choice would deliver us from suffering and limitation? Accepting reality without resistance brings us closer to experiencing Unified Reality, where Peace is restored.

The Great Escape: Commitment to Liberation

If we truly want to be free from suffering, then it is important to look willingly at the fundamental cause of suffering for our liberation. The ego deals with day-to-day problem solving from a severely limited perspective. It first perceives a problem and tags it as such from its distorted idea of reality. The ego-self becomes both disappointed and delighted by circumstances that make no sense to itself. When it perceives a problem, it quickly tries to fix it. Seen from a conscious, objective perspective, the ego's attempts at problem solving are laughable. Nothing it ever thinks it has remedied can possibly last, because its entire foundation is based on the illusion of separation, and its "outcomes" will lead eventually to pain of some sort.

Ego problem solving is like trying to eradicate a field of weeds by pulling out only their tops. In a few days, the weeds are back, stronger than ever. If we are truly committed to solving our problems in a lasting way instead of merely cleaning up the top soil to make it look pretty, we must get at their source and pull out the entire root of the weed, that is, we must look below the surface, not on the surface, to undo the ego.

Consciously embarking on the Undoing journey will *take us to Truth* because it leads us to the root of our ego-self and therefore to Liberation. This choice is really one that we all will inevitably make, but making it sooner rather than later *saves us time* and delivers us from more suffering.

To get what we wholeheartedly desire, we must first prioritize. Before we take any action, we first make an internal choice to act on the decision we have made. Committing to becoming whole and liberated necessitates that we place that goal as the conscious priority in our mind, before any personal desires. This priority becomes the absolute intent beneath every decision and action we make from now on. This is an ongoing commitment to perfect fulfillment in the now moment through renouncing a belief system based on chaos and separation. Peace, and therefore Love, become the intent for all our interactions. And when we make this decision, we acknowledge that all other desires take second place to this.

Let's look at a Love that we are soon to know, described in a quote from *A Course in Miracles*:

Perhaps you think that different kinds of love are possible. Perhaps you think there is a kind of love for this, a kind for that; a way of loving one, another way of loving still another. Love is one. It has no separate parts and no degrees; no kinds nor levels, no divergencies and no distinctions. It is like itself, unchanged throughout. It never alters with a person or a circumstance. It is the Heart of God, and also of His Son [all of us, as One Son].[39]

Any suffering in us, our lives, or the world is created through our belief in separation and its ensuing guilt, that is, in fear, chaos, attack, and defense. In every person we meet, we are meeting ourselves. Everything we give, whether love or judgment, we give to ourselves, and it is strengthened in both.

If we want Wholeness and perfect Oneness, devoid of suffering and lack of any kind, we make only one choice: the total and undivided commitment to Truth, to Love. We acknowledge the insanity of believing in the dualities of love/hate, infinite/limited, holiness/evil, peace/chaos, and joy/pain. Only Love, Truth, Peace, and Joy are real; anything else is not. We say we want to be free from suffering, but do we? Do we want this more than anything? Do we want to know who we are in Reality? Do we yearn to discover and fulfill our purpose? Are we ready to know Love in its Unified and Eternal form? And is joyous liberation what we seek?

If so, ask to see only Truth and thirst for nothing less than this, always. Only then can we stop supporting illusion and allow reality to mirror our Oneness, safety, Love, Joy, and Peace.

The Guilt Meter

The "Guilt Meter" is a tool designed to help us quickly identify any unconscious guilt that causes suffering in our lives. It shows us how, in various ways, the ego-self's unacknowledged guilt manifests in us. You can gauge any unconscious guilt to the degree that you still experience the following symptoms:

- You either judge others or perceive them judging you.
- You react negatively to a perceived offense (with anger, defense, frustration, or judgment etc.).
- You judge yourself.
- You experience seeming injustice in the form of perceived attack.
- You perceive threat or anxiety in the case of personal or worldly adversity.
- Your perceived needs appear *not* to be met (money, relation-ships, etc.).
- You experience "doubt" in the beneficence of your life. You perceive scarcity.
- You feel physical discomfort, or dis-ease.

Judgment is the fuel of the ego. Guilt is its driver. Most of this guilt is not observable to us; it is hidden. Where? In others! All *your own* unhealed guilt is hidden in everyone else. Why? Because anytime you judge another, or feel attacked, you are projecting your very own guilt. Remember, there is only *one* of us, appearing as many. The remedy is always Quantum Forgiveness, which, as mentioned, we will be discussing in more detail in Chapter 4, which follows.

Powerful Tool for Self-Discovery: The Enneagram

If we are seriously intent on removing the blocks to the awareness of Love, Peace, Joy, and abundance of spirit in our life, then the Enneagram[40] presents us with an exceptional oppor-tunity to help us become aware of the manifestation of Love in our life in all its forms.

The Enneagram (pronounced "ANY-a-gram") is a creation of modern psychology that has its roots in spiritual wisdom from many various ancient traditions. It maps out nine fundamental personality types of human nature and their complex interrelationships. This powerful system enables us to:

- Acquire more insight into ourselves and others, and see our core psychological issues and the strengths and weaknesses in our interpersonal relationships.
- Discern our personal filters through which we perceive the world and take them into proper account.
- Discover the core issues that are particularly troublesome to us individually and learn how to deal with them effectively.
- Peer into the depths of our soul without fear or self-condemnation.

Self-knowledge is the key to unlocking the door to Love and the Unified Self. The ego-self is a master of illusion and trickery and will do its utmost to divert us in our quest for Truth. The authors of *The Wisdom of the Enneagram*, Don Richard Riso and Russ Hudson, state:

> Real self-knowledge is an invaluable guardian against such self-deception. The Enneagram takes us places (and makes real progress possible) because it starts working from where we actually are. As much as it reveals the spiritual heights that we are capable of attaining, it also sheds light clearly and nonjudgmentally on the aspects of our lives that are dark and unfree. If we are going to live as spiritual beings in the material world, then these are the areas we most need to explore.[41]

They proceed to identify the following three basic elements needed for transformational work:

- presence (awareness, mindfulness) [which is supplied by *Being*];
- the practice of self-observation (gained from self-knowledge)

[which is supplied by *you*]; and

• understanding what one's experiences mean (an accurate interpretation provided by a larger context such as a community or spiritual system) [which is supplied by the *Enneagram*].

Transformation occurs rapidly when we work with these three elements altogether. The Enneagram tells us a great deal about how we view the world, the values we hold, the kinds of choices we are likely to make, how we respond to stress, what motivates us, and much more. Another one of its great benefits is that we can learn to appreciate perspectives that are different from our own. The authors tell us:

> The core of this sacred psychology is that our basic type reveals the psychological mechanisms by which we forget our true nature, our Divine Essence, the way in which we abandon ourselves. Our personalities draw upon the capacities of our inborn temperament to develop defenses and compensations for where we have been hurt in childhood. In order to survive whatever difficulties we encountered at that time, we unwittingly mastered a limited repertoire of strategies, self-images, and behaviors that allowed us to cope with and survive in our early environment. Each of us therefore has become an 'expert' at a particular form of coping which, if used excessively, also becomes the core of the dysfunctional area of our personality.
>
> As the defenses and strategies of our personality become more structured, they cause us to lose contact with our direct experiences of ourselves, our Essence. The personality becomes the source of our identity rather than contact with our Being....This loss of contact with our Essence causes deep anxiety, taking the form of one of the nine Passions. Once in place, these Passions, which are usually unconscious and

invisible to us, begin to drive the personality.[42]

One of our greatest challenges in embracing real Love, Peace, and Joy is in looking at the ego's distorted interpretations of both thought and emotion and reinterpreting them in a new way. Egoic thoughts and beliefs disable and severely limit us because they are the cause of all our conflict and other emotional turbulence. Such thoughts, beliefs, and emotions separate and isolate us, making us more likely to take things personally. The more this occurs, the more likely we are to perceive attack and value judgment as a trait we need for self-protection. This endless cycle of GUILT-projection-judgment-blame-condemnation-punishment-GUILT increases our sense of separateness and reinforces our illusory desire to take things personally.

The Enneagram is an excellent self-discovery tool that helps recontextualize our interpretations of thought, belief, and emotion. We learn to perceive ourselves, others, and circumstances of life more impersonally, empowering us in our lives. Trust, Truth, and Love will grow in proportion to our level of self-knowledge, while willingness and commitment quicken our journey.

We have reproduced here a very brief overview of each of the nine Enneagram types taken from the book *The Wisdom of the Enneagram,* by Riso and Hudson:

Work with the Enneagram starts when you identify your type and begin to understand its dominant issues. While we will recognize in ourselves behaviors of all nine types, our most defining characteristics are rooted in one of these types....Keep in mind that the characteristics listed here are merely a few highlights and do not represent the full spectrum of each personality type.

Type One: The Reformer. The principled, idealistic type. Ones are ethical and conscientious, with a strong sense of right and wrong. They are teachers and crusaders, always striving to improve things but afraid of making a mistake. Well-organized, orderly, and fastidious, they try to maintain high standards but can slip into being critical and perfectionistic. They typically have problems with repressed anger and impatience. At their best, healthy Ones are wise, discerning, realistic, and noble, as well as morally heroic.

Type Two: The Helper. The caring, interpersonal type. Twos are empathetic, sincere, and warm-hearted. They are friendly, generous, and self-sacrificing, but they can also be senti-mental, flattering, and people-pleasing. They are driven to be close to others, and they often do things for others in order to be needed. They typically have problems taking care of themselves and acknowledging their own needs. At their best, healthy Twos are unselfish and altruistic and have uncondi-tional love for themselves and others.

Type Three: The Achiever. The adaptable, success-oriented type. Threes are self-assured, attractive, and charming. Ambitious, competent, and energetic, they can also be status-conscious and highly driven for personal advancement. Threes are often concerned about their image and what others think of them. They typically have problems with worka-holism and competitiveness. At their best, healthy Threes are self-accepting, authentic, and everything they seem to be—role models who inspire others.

Type Four: The Individualist. The romantic, introspective type. Fours are self-aware, sensitive, reserved, and quiet. They are self-revealing, emotionally honest, and personal, but they can also be moody and self-conscious. Withholding themselves from others due to feeling vulnerable and defective, they can also feel disdainful and exempt from ordinary ways of living. They typically have problems with self-indulgence and self-pity. At their best, healthy Fours are inspired and highly creative, able to renew themselves and transform their experiences.

Type Five: The Investigator. The intense, cerebral type. Fives are alert, insightful, and curious. They are able to concentrate and focus on developing complex ideas and skills. Independent and innovative, they can become preoccupied with their thoughts and imaginary constructs. They become detached, yet high-strung and intense. They typically have problems with isolation, eccentricity, and nihilism. At their best, healthy Fives are visionary pioneers, often ahead of their time and able to see the world in an entirely new way.

Type Six: The Loyalist. The committed, security-oriented type. Sixes are reliable, hardworking, and responsible, but they can also be defensive, evasive, and highly anxious—running on stress while complaining about it. They are often cautious and indecisive but can also be reactive, defiant, and rebellious. They typically have problems with self-doubt and suspicion. At their best, healthy Sixes are internally stable, self-confident, and self-reliant, courageously supporting the weak and powerless.

Type Seven: The Enthusiast. The busy, productive type. Sevens are versatile, optimistic, and spontaneous. Playful, high-spirited, and practical, they can also be overextended, scattered, and undisciplined. They constantly seek new and exciting experiences, but they can become distracted and exhausted by staying on the go. They typically have problems with superficiality and impulsiveness. At their best, healthy Sevens focus their talents on worthwhile goals, becoming joyous, highly accomplished, and full of gratitude.

Type Eight: The Challenger. The powerful, dominating type. Eights are self-confident, strong, and assertive. Protective, resourceful, and decisive, they can also be proud and domineering. Eights feel that they must control their environment, often becoming confrontational and intimidating. They typically have problems with allowing themselves to be close to others. At their best, healthy Eights are self-mastering—they use their strength to improve others' lives, becoming heroic, magnanimous and sometimes historically great.

Type Nine: The Peacemaker. The easygoing, self-effacing type. Nines are accepting, trusting, and stable. They are good-natured, kind-hearted, easygoing, and supportive but can also be too willing to go along with others to keep the peace. They want everything to be without conflict but can tend to be complacent and minimize anything upsetting. They typically have problems with passivity and stubbornness. At their best, healthy Nines are indomitable and all-embracing; they are able to bring people together and heal conflicts.[43]

If you wish to identify your particular personality type you can either (1) take a self-scoring, computerized Enneagram test at http://www.enneagraminstitute.com or (2) refer to the book and complete the Enneagram questionnaire enclosed therein. The test on the website is called "The RHETI (Riso-Hudson Enneagram Type Indicator) Test," Version 2.5. It is said to be about 80% accurate and usually takes about 45 minutes to complete.

The surest way to improve our perceptions and relationships is to find out who we are, and the Enneagram is a powerful method through which we can do that quickly. When we see light within us, we see that light in others, and together we illuminate our pathway.

CHAPTER 4

LOVE RELATIONSHIPS

What is it that we search for in a relationship? We want validation, approval, acknowledgment, status, support, affection, kindness, compassion, respect, understanding, admiration, and forgiveness, and some of us also want passion, companionship, closeness, and devotion. These are the experiences that we humans by nature constantly desire, either consciously or unconsciously. What we think, feel, and do is usually a byproduct of a deeper need to have these experiences. The underlying essence that we are really searching for is Love, but the barrier that proves to be the most significant in obstructing our efforts to gain and keep Love is unrecognized and therefore unremedied.

Humans naturally seek Love, but don't know what it is. We *imagine* what it is and have expectations about it, and then become disillusioned when things don't work out. So, we end up learning and thinking that love equals pain, that love is sacrifice, and that love can turn to hate; this is what the world at large believes about love. The fundamental truth that the world has not yet realized is that *Love is*, period.

Love is Infinite. Love is ever-expanding, ever-extending. Love can never turn to hate. Love is Peaceful and Joyful. Love is all-encompassing; it excludes no one. Love knows no boundaries; it is universal; it is unconditional. Sparo Arika Vigil writes:

Real Love creates a feeling of Peace that deepens persistently, pervasively. Overwhelming feelings of love rise up from the core of our soul until there is no more understanding of "I" — there are waves of Love, Peace, Joy, all eternal; and a knowing of true comfort and security and beauty. There is a sense of your unique beauty, incredible gratitude for you, and a most extraordinary love for you. At the same time there is the sense of our absolute interconnectedness with each other, with the Source, with all humanity, with all the Infinite sparks. In the awareness of this eternal Love, gratitude and sharing is an expansive feeling of unlimited possibilities of limitless creation, Peace, Joy, and unimaginable adventures.[44]

The bottom line is that if we are not experiencing Love in the ways described above, then it is not because we don't deserve it or that we just haven't found the right partner, parents, children, family, or friends. If we are not living with Love daily, then only one barrier exists: *we don't know Love.* We don't yet recognize Love and we don't yet understand it fully. All our past references and conditioning have trained us to see what Love is not. If we don't know the thing we are searching for, how in the world will we ever find it? We search for a fictitious ego-love experience that has never satisfied, nor ever will satisfy, our deepest longing.

If we truly want this essence called "Love," our first recognition must be that we do not know what it is in the deepest sense, and, if we do not know what it is, we must also not know what it is for. Nor do we know how to access it. Love is not an emotion. It is not an experience. It is not something we gain. It is not something we earn. Love is a State of Being. This is our natural state of existence lying beneath the myriad layers of wrong-mindedness we accumulated through lifetimes of living through our false ego-self.

The first lesson in Love is to begin to understand that Love can only be known through its extension. This means that to know Love, we must *give* it. Love entails forgiving ego-error in others and ourselves. The conscious act of unconditional giving of our time, care, attention, forgiveness, and love is an expression of the State of Being we forgot eons ago at the time of the "separation."

The second lesson in Love is to begin to see that we *are* Love. Every one of us, regardless of what our ego-self has ever thought or done, *is* Love. And this is achieved through self-discovery and awareness.

Love cannot be known through seeking it because we already *are* it. If we search for it in our lovers, friends, parents, children, or family, we will not find it. However, if we give Love (without judgment or conditions) to the people in our life, consistently, we will not only find Love; we will also discover we *were* Love all along.

The striving, searching, and yearning that previously drove us to quest for an illusory image of love has ended. We have mistakenly confused conditional relating with real Love; then we labeled that pseudo-relating "love." Now we have the chance to embrace real Love by undoing, or unlearning, what it is not.

Specialness Pseudo-worthiness

The type of love we are most familiar with is "special" love, or the conditional variety of love. Our culture teaches us to equate love with feeling special; in fact, the motivating factor in all special love relationships is the need to feel *special*. This sounds harmless enough, but at the very seat of this *need* lies a more sinister agenda. If we were to dare to look more deeply into this matter, we would clearly see how this need to feel special has sabotaged so many of our relationships with almost all people with whom we interact. Some of the most at risk are those closest to us, including our children and parents, since specialness often presents as the need for approval and appreciation.

The need to feel special eventuates from the ego-self's separated state. Separation breeds an unnatural desire for our lost sense of worthiness that costs us plenty in life. The ego-self, being spiritually bankrupt, searches to leach out specialness in whatever form, good or bad, it can acquire, just as long as it can be set above others. And when we perceive that we are set above, we are also setting ourselves apart, which is a form of disconnection. Specialness in any form serves as a divider between us; it segregates and focuses not on our oneness or sameness, but on our differences. In Truth, specialness is a form of separation, and it cannot possibly ever give us a deep or lasting sense of worth.

Real worthiness comes from an eternal place within. It is innocence, Love, equality, extending, and trusting. Our sense of worth is not something we gain from outside; it is born from the recognition of who we are and is increased by the level of reverence we have for others. Being an inner well from which we draw our sustenance, approval, and appreciation, real worthiness never desires to stain its purity by seeking any type of specialness from outside. It understands that to set ourselves above, to be better than others, is to summon and increase guilt. The ego thrives on hidden guilt because it isolates us from others, ourselves, and The Source, thus making us more dependent on its empty promises. This ensures a dependency cycle where we crave "pseudo worthiness," yet the temporary satisfaction we derive from it separates us. Once we have achieved what the ego wanted, we feel a strange sense of emptiness and once again initiate the cycle of looking for this pseudo-worthiness elsewhere.

Any form of competition or comparison is a way of searching for specialness: to be the most intelligent, attractive, gifted, creative, popular, athletic, or even to be the sickest, ugliest, most victimized, most ostracized, most despised, most depressed, are all ego attempts at being set apart. Specialness in its undiluted form comes from the mass of guilt we acquired millennia ago when we believed we shattered Heaven and abandoned The Source. Projection was born from this thought, and we continue to project our guilt out into the world, seemingly acquiring two things: (1) our innocence (because *others* are to blame and not us); and (2) our retribution (our attack, which we judge to be justified because others persecuted us). This projection enables us to make and attain specialness.

Now we can differentiate between innocent victim and guilty perpetrator, or between winner and loser. What all this blaming and competing does is to reinforce our own unconscious guilt, confirm the illusion that our worthiness is gained externally, and ultimately set us up as separate.

At this time in our evolutionary development, we have certainly reached a point where life issues as base as pure survival and fight-or-flight fear are no longer perceived as daily threats and motivators. Once immediate survival issues dissipated, our civilization seemed to focus on the individual. Having more time and intelligence increased our desire for specialness, to be unique, original, distinctive, exclusive, and separate. We developed an adoration of, and desire for, individualization in our culture. We have unconsciously fed and nurtured this aggrandizing obsession for individual specialness through so many widely accepted areas of our lives, such as education, politics, sports, business, commercialism, fashion, music, movies, media, the arts, and computer/video games, to name just a few.

We encourage our children to be special, not recognizing the destructive ramifications such individualization has introduced to our culture. How many children plea beseechingly at home or at school for constant attention, recognition, and approval? The pressures "to become" and "to have" are core desires for specialness, or pseudo-worthiness, extracted from exterior sources. This then fuels the competitive ego to drive unconsciously toward an unnatural rivalry that deprives us of a sense of real inner worth and connectedness to "All That Is."

Throughout history we passionately pursued a race to mass individualism, which drew us ahead and outside of ourselves. Now, however, having attained our individual peak of the personal, original, exclusive, and separate, we find that we are not happy, and evolution is calling the world back to a state of

Oneness and Unity. Planetary consciousness is aligning itself with profound integration, eventually dissolving the idea of duality. In an article on "What Is Enlightenment," spiritual teacher Andrew Cohen explains,

> ...[as] for our postmodern selves, the painful experience of psychological and spiritual alienation has reached its historical apex [through individualism]. In our pursuit of personal, social, philosophical and spiritual freedom many of us have abandoned our great spiritual traditions and as a result have lost touch with our own individual and collective soul, unexpectedly ending up quite alone on the desert island of our own ego. For those of us who desperately want to move forward, who can't go back to the way things were before we had seen through the limitations of the familial, tribal, religious, and nationalistic notions of self—*where* are we to look?[45]

We have entered the next level of consciousness in evolution, going, as Cohen states it, "beyond what we could call personal realization to something else altogether: a profound awakening that transcends the individual."[46] Our true Liberation now rests in embracing Conscious Relationship as the vehicle for self-realization and planetary healing. Through this avenue, we relinquish destructive ego-limitations and expand into a realm of Unity and Oneness that is infinitely more liberating than anything we have ever known previously.

If we truly want Love, Peace, and a sense of wholeness, we must remember that these cannot be acquired through manufactured specialness. Love, Peace, and wholeness emerge from within us through our reverence of others and Loving What Is.

Conscious Love

One of the earliest exponents of the Enneagram was George

Ivanovich Gurdjieff. He depicted three kinds of love:

- *purely physical love*, as sexual attraction;
- *emotional love*, which often tends to transform itself into hate; and
- *conscious love* which leads to the perfection of both partners.

Nearly all of us are familiar with our culture's worship of the first two types of love: physical love as sexual attraction; and emotional love, which often turns to hate. However, the third and most powerful form of love, Conscious Love, is rarely ever recognized by mainstream media and is not even a topic open for discussion in most families! In fact, if we were to survey the general public, asking them to honestly depict "what love is," we would find that most of the feedback would be colored by sexual or emotional love, while Conscious Love would be sadly unrecognized and under-valued.

Conscious Love is eternal, not superficial or temporary. Conscious Love is really the primary goal in any physical, emotional, or platonic relationship. It means recalling that we are not separate, that we each project our own reality, and that any conflict seemingly caused by another is always an opportunity to heal our perception. Conscious Love emerges from the commitment to experiencing and sharing love for the highest good of all involved.

The reason so many relationships (romantic, family, and friends) fall apart is because they are based on the short-term, personal-gain agendas that drive most sexual or emotional relationships, that is, the ego's need for specialness. While emotions or sex can contribute a great deal to a relationship, they cannot sustain it without there being a true union in Conscious Love.

The three main ingredients of Conscious Love are:

- commitment to each other's growth, i.e., creation of a Unified Goal;
- complete personal responsibility, i.e., recognizing that we project our own reality; and
- seeing any conflict as an opportunity for us to heal our perception (undo the ego).

Conscious Love calls for enduring discipline. The area we most need to observe is the ego's addiction to separation, in other words, any form of judgment that isolates us from one another. We learn that Conscious Loving is the perfect vehicle for us to increase our daily experience of Joy, Love, acceptance, and enthusiasm. Being Love in action, it is always extending, not separating, and is most powerfully expressed through our giving of the following: forgiveness, acceptance, non-judgment, and gratitude.

The Unseen Child

When a parent is still predominantly ego-self identified, he or she will perceive the child through the eyes of the conditioned ego and not through the vision of the Unified Self. The child's pure Self is then unseen, and thus the formation of a stronger ego-identity is encouraged. This weakens the child's trust, both in The Source and in his or her own Unified Self, equating to a distrust of life.

Most of us learned our early ego conditioning primarily from our parents and families. Before the age of five, we had already developed a great need for ego specialness. Our fragile little egos were well on the way to becoming a mistaken identity through which we confused people, things, and circumstances with our sense of false self.

We learned to gain attention and approval by acting out certain behaviors and quickly adapted ego-survival techniques, such as judging, lying, pretending, denying, repressing, fanta-sizing, and projecting. "Giving to get" was high on our list of daily preoccupations, as was the desire to be special: the best, the worst, the most different, or the cutest. Because of our inability to establish a healthy boundary between our sense of self and the phenomena that occurred around us, we mistakenly learned that our happiness depended on getting our needs met externally. We formed a strong belief in a personal identity whose worth was based on having, owning, getting, becoming, doing, and achieving instead of on the pristine and unchangeable essence of our Unified Self. We were encouraged to acquire knowledge by observing and learning from people and experience; yet we were not taught how to observe our own thoughts and emotions or to question any limiting beliefs.

Our parents were conditioned to fabricate an ego-identity from which they established and ran their lives. The sad outcome for the child of a parent who still mistakes his ego as self is the very real possibility of not having been seen by the parent (Figure 4.1). The child will invariably lack true validation and recognition because the child has been evaluated through the parent's predominant perception, which is ego.

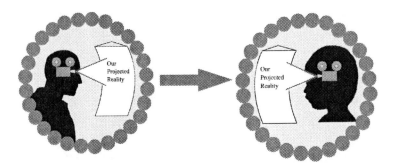

The parent's mistaken identity (ego) obscures the true perception of the child.

Figure 4.1: The Unseen Child

In order for any one of us to have gained a solid sense of our own sacred essence as children, our parents would have to have had some understanding of their own Unified Self. They would have been living examples of the joy of living within Conscious Love relationships. By example, they would have taught us the art of unconditional love, contemplation and observation, self-inquiry, and self-nurturing. Our parents would have imparted to us a deep sense of inner security that emerged from Absolute Trust in a Higher Order that always has our own best interests at heart. As children we would have reveled in wonder at the profound sense of interconnectedness that surrounded us.

Most of us were not raised in an enlightened environment, with the result that most likely our Unified Self was rarely, if ever, recognized or seen. As unseen adults, we are more likely to perpetuate the ego's dysfunctional specialness cycle within our romantic relationships and with our children. This is why it is so important for us now to engage wholeheartedly in the undoing of our dysfunctional belief systems.

The Quest for Love

"If You Love Me, You'll Do What I Want" is a section title in Byron Katie's book *I Need Your Love—Is That True?*[47] Katie explains that the launch of the quest for love and approval is initiated by our unquestioned thoughts about needs and wants. As children we emulated our parents, who rewarded us when we were good and punished us when we didn't comply with their needs.

Katie explains: "The child expects his playmate to want to play the games he wants to play. If not, there's a big fight, and they both stomp off to find an adult to complain to: 'He's not my friend anymore!' The belief that a friend is someone who will do what you want is already fully active in this child....His parents never questioned the thought that obedience is an expression of love, so why would he?"[48] This is why most of us enter into love relationships with the unconscious attitude that "loving me means you will meet my needs." No one ever taught us how to question what we want from love. And we haven't learned that questioning what we believe is the key to liberating us from the stranglehold of dysfunctional and unsatisfying relationships.

What Is a Special Relationship?

Unfortunately, most of our relationships are based on our seeking to support our own separate identity through an exclusive interaction with a significant person. This means our ego's only focus is to feed its own image through this interaction. It does not seek for communion and integration with everyone. Its plan is to use a select few with which to have a special relationship so it can inflate, embellish, and reinforce its grandiose image. Essentially what this does is fragment the psyche, teach that hate and love can co-exist, and attract an abundance of guilt in the process, causing utter chaos in our life. Put briefly, the type of love the ego seeks is not Love, but the recognition and reinforcement of its separated state. We say we want Love, but our egos unconsciously attract scarcity, attack, judgment, guilt, and fear. These all lead to separateness, which of course is exactly what the ego wants for us. Actually, at the top of its list of desires for us is really death, and it knows that separation and attack cause guilt and guilt creates fear. Deep unconscious guilt is the perfect illness and death "magnet."

So here we are, deeply yearning for real Love, a sense of worth, and communion with our significant others. However, our ego relentlessly sabotages our best efforts.

The ego is certain that love is dangerous, and this is always its central teaching. It never puts it this way; on the contrary, everyone who believes that the ego is salvation seems to be intensely engaged in the search for love. Yet the ego, though encouraging the search for love very actively, makes one proviso; do not find it. Its dictates, then, can be summed up simply as: "Seek and do *not* find." This is the one promise the ego holds out to you, and the one promise it will keep.[49]

There is huge conflict between the ego and the Unified Self on the subject of love. The ego, being a master illusionist, offers us a solution that looks like this: it delivers the promise of finding love, but it makes sure that it is *ego*-love. Ego-love is saturated with specialness, judgment, blame, and guilt. It involves sacrifice, projection, withholding, revenge, conditions, and obligation. The ultimate lure is to get your needs met, and it uses whatever devious means it takes to accomplish this. For example, if our partner lets us down, our ego projects anger, blame, and the withholding of love as punishment. Our partner's ego then perceives this as attack and responds with a counter-attack, either aggressively or passively. There is no order of wrong-mindedness. So the ego's offer of love lets us experience some fragments of love while making sure we suffer a large degree of blame, shame, and guilt.

Another dysfunctional aspect of special relationships is the ego's focus on the body while shunning the importance of the mind. It says bodies can join while minds cannot. Any thoughts or feelings we may have are private and are only considered real or a possible threat if they are acted out. "To the ego the mind is private, and only the body can be shared. Ideas are basically of no concern, except as they bring the body of another closer or farther."[50]

Through the ego, we tend to see our needs being met through the behavior of another: a smile, a favor, an embrace. In other words, it is really others' behavior that we want to meet our needs. We are attracted physically to a partner and expect the right words, touch, action, and behavior in order to satisfy our desire to be special. And they expect the same. Rarely do we ever see into someone's heart and soul and simply love them, not for what they can give to us, but truly for *who* they are—with no conditions.

Special Bargains

> By offering freedom you will be free. Freedom is the only gift you can offer to God's Sons, being an acknowledgment of what they are and what He is. Freedom is creation, because it is love. Whom you seek to imprison you do not love. Therefore, when you seek to imprison anyone, including yourself, you do not love him and you cannot identify with him. When you imprison yourself you are losing sight of your true identification with me and with the Father.[51]

The reason most of our special love relationships ultimately wane or collapse is because we unconsciously bargain. This may sound minor; however, it is poison to love. In order to gain the special love we seek, we need to engage in some sort of transaction or trade with the other person. This usually entails the giving of our financial support, usefulness, status, time, energy, attention, recognition, favors, love, or gifts, in exchange for what we desire. As innocent as this may seem, it certainly is not. If we want specialness in any form, then we have to sacrifice for it. We enter an unconscious agreement, in fact, a bargain that details what we are expected to give each other in exchange for what we receive. Without knowing it, we keep a secret tally on who's given what and who owes what. Under all this calculating is purely the desire to get, which always leads to guilt.

We are often not aware of the bargaining that takes place. It will always instill a sense of guilt in us, although it is most often hidden. For example, if I give something, such as my time, love, or a gift, my ego will unconsciously reason, "I gave, so now I have less. And now you not only have more than I, but you are responsible for what I lost in the transaction. And because of this, you are guilty until you give me something of equal or greater value in return." Even the expectation of a thank-you for a gift is a condition placed on our giving. This is the delusional bargaining cycle of the ego. We make the other responsible for what the ego perceives is our loss.

At the core of all this trading is the desire to trade each other's specialness. The ego always sees in someone else something special that it believes is lacking in itself and wants to take that part of him or her in order to supply what is missing in itself. The problem is that we then feel we need to pay for what we took or else we will feel guilty, and the cycle begins. All this endless "give-and-take" activity stems from our feeling woefully incomplete and inadequate on our own, and this is the ego's way of attempting to make itself Whole.

This situation often occurs in romantic love relationships when we unconsciously trade our hearts, bodies, and lives in exchange for our partner's seeming specialness. In searching for this false specialness to complete ourselves, we surreptitiously give our power over to our partner and our partner does the same. This causes resentment and eventually, through mutual disempowerment, blame and guilt are fired back and forth. We see here that this idea of giving and specialness is purely an ego trick to disguise hate as love. When so-called love induces anxiety, despair, fear, judgment, and attack, we can be sure that this is not love, but special ego attachment. The reason why so many of our relationships fail is because the fickle attraction we call "love" is based on the ego's rule of "giving to get." When this special love wears itself thin with one partner, we go looking for a substitute relationship through which we unconsciously reenact the entire special-love theme all over again.

The special relationship will never give us the sense of completeness, worth, belonging, and togetherness for which we long. In fact, it is literally guaranteed to lead us to scarcity and loneliness, both of which the ego thrives on.

Falling in Love
Falling in love is widely believed to be a manifestation of love.

However, the truth is that the experience of falling in love is not Love and is always a fleeting one. Psychiatrists talk about ego boundaries being formed at a young age. When a newborn baby arrives into the world, he cannot distinguish between his body and the environment around him. When his mother moves or talks, the baby thinks that he himself is moving and talking. All is one for the newborn because he has not yet acquired a sense of separateness or boundaries. As the baby grows, he learns that his mother is not him, that she is separate from him, sometimes attentive and sometimes not. Knowing now that he is a separate self existing outside of others, he begins to form a sense of identity. He knows his body, along with his voice, feelings, and thoughts, is his, and his alone. Ego boundaries represent the knowledge of these limits in our minds. These ego boundaries, which are considered so important to a healthy individual, are what actually imprison us and limit our experience of feeling whole, loved, worthy, and supported. Isolation and loneliness are by-products of the natural tendencies of our ego boundaries.

Occasionally in life we do take the risk of temporarily collapsing our solid ego boundaries and experience the euphoria and connectedness that invariably follow. In his insightful book *The Road Less Traveled*, M. Scott Peck, M.D., defines love thus:

> The experience of falling in love allows us this escape temporarily. The essence of the phenomenon of falling in love is a sudden collapse of a section of an individual's ego boundaries, permitting one to merge his or her identity with that of another person. The sudden release of oneself from oneself, the explosive pouring out of oneself into the beloved, and the dramatic surcease of loneliness accompanying this collapse of ego boundaries is experienced by most of us as ecstatic. We and our beloved are one! Loneliness is no more![52]

The blissful feeling of connectedness and oneness we once felt as a newborn baby returns, and we feel a sense of omnipotence, convincing us there are no problems that cannot be overcome now that we have come into possession of our missing half. We mistakenly believe we have found the savior who will complete us and make us whole and we will live happily after. The illusion of specialness has seriously clouded our perception; now we seek to trade our partner's specialness for ours, and the dysfunctional cycle of "giving to get" is initiated. After a relatively short period of bliss, the downward spiral sets in. Our ego boundaries snap back and we fall out of love as quickly as we fell in, having to face the reality that we are two separate individuals, and then decide whether or not to continue the relationship.

We can break the cycle of operating in special-love mode once and for all by making a conscious and wholehearted decision to work conscientiously at embracing and giving Conscious Love (see earlier section on "Conscious Love"). The feeling of falling in love may be romantic, but if we equate that situation with a real sense of loving, we are being deceived. Conscious Love eclipses the naïve notion that *feeling* love signifies True Love. As we grow emotionally and spiritually, we begin to realize that "real love often occurs in a context in which the feeling of love is lacking, when we act lovingly despite the fact that we don't feel loving....Falling in love is not an extension of one's limits or boundaries; it is a partial and temporary collapse of them. The extension of one's limits requires effort; falling in love is effortless....Real love is a permanently self-enlarging experience. Falling in love is not."[53] The act of falling in love is a self-limiting one that has nothing to do with cultivating and nurturing our spiritual development, except for the wonderful opportunity it presents for Undoing the ego.

Before falling in love.
Two separate egos

Falling in love.
A temporary collapse
of ego boundaries
creates the "illusion"
of real love.
However, both partners
do not see each other;
rather, they see the ego's
projected reality.

Falling out of love.
Unless both partners
commit to
conscious loving,
ego boundaries will
snap back
and love will
appear to cease.

Figure 4.2: Falling in Love

As we said, falling in love is the temporary collapse of a section
of our ego boundaries (Figure 4.2). It is not an experience of true,
unconditional Love. Therefore, the experience of euphoria is
bound to recede as each ego-boundary snaps back to its original
contracted wall. This type of love is called "special love," and,
because of its conditional quality, it is a contracted form of love
that unconsciously seeks to get rather than give, even though it is
ingeniously disguised as love and certainly looks like love to us.
Conscious Love, on the other hand, requires the unconditional

extension of oneself, giving for the sake of giving, with no strings attached.

Real Love Is Never Lost

When we think of a relationship, we rarely investigate truthfully as to its ultimate purpose. When we meet with our significant other, one of the last questions we consciously raise is, "What is the mutual goal of this relationship?" More often than not, we unconsciously deceive ourselves into believing that our mutual goal is Love, but rarely do we inquire as to the true meaning of the term "Love." The majority, if not all, of our relationships in the past were based on special ego-love, the unconscious "giving to get," or conditional, variety. For the most part, we are largely not familiar with real, conscious, unconditional Love.

The underlying goal of special relationships will always be mutually exclusive because each partner has an unconscious agenda of his own, which is to feel more special than the other. So, as each person seeks a personal goal of specialness, we have a partnership that has at its foundation two individuals, each with his own independent self-seeking goal. Added to this scenario is the complication of justifying our relationship by our seemingly mutual purpose, which is to be happy, start a family or business, or be successful. At the root of all this busy-ness is an unquenchable thirst for individual specialness, or pseudo-worthiness. Both incomplete persons join in an attempt to make themselves complete through the special attention they demand from the other. While on the surface it may appear that most relationships emanate a sense of togetherness, they will invariably conceal the hidden agendas behind their (uncon-scious) secret agreed-upon joint endeavor. Under all this pretense are two people who are dedicated to their very own special ego needs, and, if by chance one person's ego needs were to draw them away from meeting the special needs of their partner, then that partner will withdraw their love in retaliation.

Hence the common dilemma we experience with love appearing to be mixed with hate. How else could love turn to hate? Unless, of course, there were first a well-guarded, deeply hidden personal agenda that was wrought with superficial, self-aggrandizing intentions. How many so-called loving relationships (romantic, family, and friends) have we witnessed turn to bitter battles that leave us and maybe others scarred from their ugly conflict?

Real Love can never end; nothing in this world could possibly terminate it. If a relationship disintegrates beyond repair, then the truth is that there never was a relationship to begin with, only two egos competing for specialness. If it seems that love cements a relationship and later on it falls apart, one can be sure there was little love there in the first place. Love is eternal, constant, and ever-expanding. It is not possible to change Love. It is not possible to terminate it. However, it is quite possible to abort a special relationship that no longer sustains the pseudo-worthiness of its participants.

This may appear a harsh and cruel statement, but any relationship in which we thought we suffered from loss is nothing but the loss of our ego's specialness at its nucleus. Even childhood suffering, or for that matter *any* hurtful past experience, is still, at its absolute center, the frustration or desta-bilization of our specialness. Our Unified Self, the pure and innocent reality of who we are, is untouched and completely unharmed by any childhood suffering. All that was disabled was our ego's sense of specialness, and that is why we unconsciously search for special relationships as the remedy to our pain. In fact, psychologists know that we attract partners who display both the negative and positive tendencies of our parents. Although we are not aware of it, we attract specific qualities in partners that challenge us to heal our past. Unfortunately, because we are usually unaware of how to heal specialness, we invariably fall into the trap of special love. Any broken romances that began with what appeared as love and ended in hate were never truly loving in the first place, because real love, Conscious Love, cannot enter where specialness is made the goal. Nobody has ever lost Love because Love can never be lost. If we believe that we have ever lost Love, we deserve to see the truth that: what we lost was not Love, but specialness.

So many of us, caught in the illusory specialness of relationships, say we know the person we love or admire. Using logic and reason to see beyond the obvious, we can begin to grasp the likely possibility that we haven't even begun to discover this person's Ultimate Reality any more than they have discovered ours.

If, for example, most of us live and love oblivious to our ego's dictates, we will automatically cultivate special relationships rather than Unified ones because that is what egos do. Two egos join in a relationship that uses mutual benefits to obscure the fact that they each have a separate goal: to attract and maintain their own specialness at the cost of their partner. This they do totally, unconsciously justifying their giving to receive.

Specialness has been an unquestioned, unchallenged, and destructive concept that we have lived with since early childhood (or, better, since the "separation" eons ago). Put briefly, all persons who, since our birth, made a stain on our specialness remain as ghostly "shadow figures"[54]—shadows of the past—in our memory, and we unconsciously superimpose these unloving thoughts on our loved ones today.

When we meet someone, we don't see them as they really are; what we see is an image that might be able to meet our special needs, a jumbled sum of our past shadows that is superimposed over this person's Reality. We literally perceive the past when we are with people. Rarely do we enter a completely pure now moment to see the loving Truth beyond our ego's projection. To consciously suspend our ego's judgment on another, to withhold any past perception and enter the present moment with them, clean and clear, is to give and receive the greatest, most magnificent gift imaginable. This is Love, real innocent Truth, recognizable by the immense Peace and Joy that accompanies this moment.

The Unified Relationship: A Unified Goal

As we may have suspected by now, the one distinguishing characteristic of a Conscious Love relationship that ensures its deep and eternal value is joining in a common goal, not a superficial goal, but one that allows extension of Love rather than separation. Peck explains this beautifully:

> I define love thus: The will to extend one's self for the purpose of nurturing one's own or another's spiritual growth....the behavior is defined in terms of the goal or purpose it seems to serve—in this case, spiritual growth....When one has successfully extended one's limits, one has then grown into a larger state of being. Thus the act of loving is an act of self-evolution even when the purpose of the act is someone else's growth. It is through reaching toward evolution that we evolve.[55]

Transforming a special ego relationship to a Unified one requires that we join in one shared goal. Through disciplined awareness, we consciously have our partner's best interests at heart and at all times focus our attention on the goal, which ultimately is the healing of both partners.

This Unified Goal asks that we make a commitment to be 100% personally responsible for all our thoughts, feelings, and actions. Once we realize that what we see in others is a projection of our own and not Truth, we will also realize that our liberation in this lifetime depends upon our absolute agreement to re-learn what Love is. We would acknowledge that we know nothing about Love and openheartedly request the Universal Inspiration to reveal Truth to us through our Unified Self and our partner.

We would remember that any attack or judgment is a disguised call for Love and that there is no justification for counterattack. These are all mistakes. And we would learn to embrace and trust the concept that all giving *is* receiving. Along with all of this, we would be thoroughly committed to openly investigating every limiting belief or thought we held, with the certainty that upon their dismantling we would find them to be untrue, finally revealing the Loving Truth that they concealed from us.

Entering a Unified Relationship is literally the process of reversing the dysfunctional stranglehold of separation that has haunted humanity since the beginning of time. It is the most monumental leap of advancement any one of us could possibly take at this time in evolution. Sharing the goal of Unity means we share the same purpose. This means we *will* that our intent becomes united and that we direct our efforts in the same direction. What we do becomes the means to the same end, and we will see the same meaning in everything. We will share one purpose, bringing our minds into unity and healing. Sparo Arika Vigil writes:

"Isn't there a better way?"...when you've come to the realization that the only kind of relationships you want are Unified Relationships, how is that actually achieved? How do we meet each new relationship with another person with Truth and a Unified goal? How do we transform each existing relationship we have into one that is open to the limitless possibilities of Love? They can all be changed by a simple question, "Isn't there a better way?" "Yes....Perhaps....I don't know." When you allow your own Truth and conviction to gently surface by saying, "I'm sure there is a better way, let's find it together," you set into motion a miraculous transformation in the relationship and healing begins.[56]

Window to Love

The most powerful tool we have for initiating the immediate healing of specialness is the now moment, a topic we'll explore in even more detail in Chapter 7. Earlier, we explained how our ego-self is preoccupied by either thoughts of the past or expectations of the future. It cannot exist in the here and now because, when we dissolve into the very present moment, we escape time and enter into eternity. In this moment there are no thoughts of the past, of grievances and limitations. There is no superimposing of projection on another; in this precious instant, we are free from judgment. Being in the now moment is entering a transcendental realm.

How would we be to others and ourselves if all negative thoughts, fears, and beliefs did not exist in our minds? What would we be without any fear, any thoughts of pain, anger, or frustration? The truth is that our thoughts and beliefs are not who we are; we, in our ego-self state, projected this reality, and none of it is real. If we want so badly to be free from suffering, we must realize that all of it was unconsciously manifested by our ego's thinking and subsequent beliefs. They have seemed so real and true because our beliefs are immediately mirrored back to us by the seeming outside world. This has been our cycle, our reality. Finally, we think we see the confirmation that our reality is true, but none of it is true! The truth here is that we, through our distorted thoughts and beliefs, project whatever suffering we perceive as existing in our reality today, either personally or collectively.

To reverse this insanity, we need to learn to enter into now-moment awareness because it is in this place where we gain a wonderful sense of sincere humility and Oneness. None of our past reference points remain, and we are literally free from limitation; hence, no judging enters. Because the ego is silenced, our minds are free to open to a new perspective. Nothing we look upon is tarnished with the past or the future; all is fresh and alive. The next time we are with the ones we love, we may choose to enter into a moment of total awareness, seeing them without any form of past referencing. We may see them without any thoughts or judgments, just allowing their Unified Self to reveal its luminous reflection of Truth that was for so long concealed by our distorted perception. *A Course in Miracles* states:

> When you have learned to look on everyone with no reference at all to the past, either his or yours as you perceived it, you will be able to learn from what you see *now* [his past has no reality in the present, so you cannot see it]....The miracle enables you to see your brother without his past, and so perceive him as born again. His errors are all past, and by perceiving him without them you are releasing him. And since his past is yours, you share in this release.[57]

And when we fully enter the now instant we will experience "...the lifting of the barriers of time and space, the sudden experience of peace and joy, and, above all, the lack of awareness of the body..."[58]

Decision to Transform Our Relationship

Often, we will decide to commit ourselves to transforming our special relationships with the ones we love while they are not yet aware or desirous of the need for transformation. If this is our challenge, that we desire change and they do not, it is wise for us to be patient. Any pushing or pulling on our part may just add to our partner's resistance and cause them fear. The truth is that all we need do is literally place our heartfelt intent for a Unified Relationship with the Universal Inspiration. The instant we request Wholeness is the instant our request is embraced and transformation initiated. Every relationship will have its own way of finding an integrated goal to which the Unified Relationship will progress. If we are sincere and patient, we will work on our own goal, investigating our mind's destructive thoughts and limiting beliefs, and apply ourselves diligently to the task of removing the blocks to the awareness of Love's presence. Be patient, and look upon this as an opportunity to be a teacher of Love and acceptance by demonstration. Our changing for the better is an open invitation to our partner to join us in this Unified Goal to Infinite Love.

Sometimes, when two people are faced with changing the relationship's goal from a special one to a Unified Goal, the outcome may not be what we expected. Occasionally, one or both partners decide to give up on the transformation, preferring to cling to the conditional form of special love. There may be an inability or unwillingness to commit to the degree necessary for true loving reform to occur. If this eventuates, the relationship either stagnates in its old form or, as often happens, falls apart, with one or both partners seeking the old goal within another special relationship.

When a romantic relationship breaks up, it is often very sad and distressing, even more so when there has been an attempt to transform it from a special to a Unified Relationship. In this case, it is important to realize that the break-up eventuated from not enough real Love being extended between partners. Real Love can only be increased by extending it. We do this through forgiveness (overlooking ego-error in one's self and partner), gratitude, patience, unconditional giving, listening, communicating honestly, with no conditions, meaning absolutely no hidden agendas to receive anything in return. The miracle of Conscious Love is known through its unconditional extension, and initially this may require extreme patience and tolerance in the early part of relationship transition.

Intimacy

While initiating or transforming a relationship to a Unified relationship, it is helpful to keep in mind that this is a radical shift into largely uncharted waters. While our goal is to attain a consistent and irreversible Love that cannot be threatened by anyone or anything, we are being asked to work at dropping all attack, including our ego defenses, judgments, excuses, justifications, projections, denials, resentments, blame, criticism, and neediness. If what we truly yearn for is a deep and eternal Love, then we must be prepared to help remove the blocks to the awareness of its presence in others and also in ourselves. This means learning that true intimacy goes far beyond sex and being physically and emotionally close.

Authentic intimacy, that is, the meeting of minds with the shared goal of becoming Whole, begins with learning to relinquish our defenses. It's through opening up and daring to be honest and vulnerable with our loved ones that we unlock the doorway to Love. Through this openness, we gain self-knowledge and self-love. We learn to trust ourselves and The Source. Lasting authentic intimacy comes from learning to access our own true nature. However, what many of us do instead is get caught up in a cyclic futile search for intimacy in brief encounters of sex and either emotional or physical closeness. We mistakenly believe these behavioral encounters with another person will give us what we yearn for, but they cannot give to us what we must eventually find within ourselves. That is why so many of us feel that love seems to wane over time.

Finding intimacy within is achieved by exercising love without defense. Whatever we mistakenly think we need to defend, hide, or deny in ourselves will end up denying us the Love we so strongly desire. Jett Psaris and Marlena S. Lyons talk about intimacy in their book *Undefended Love*:

> We long to surpass our routine, passionless, or conflict-driven relationships, but we are afraid to take the personal risks necessary to break free from our old, self-protective ways of being. Instead, we choose to stay emotionally safe,

comfortable, and in control. Once we recognize that all our efforts to change our partner's behavior, or to find a "better" partner, have failed to provide us with what we most desire in relationship, only then do we begin the challenging *self*-exploration that is necessary for a deep and nourishing connection with another.

In the process of learning to tolerate our fears, interrupt old defensive patterns, and let go of our attempts to manipulate our partners, we focus our attention on increasing our awareness of deeper layers of our experience. Finding intimacy begins with discovering ourselves, not with fixing or controlling ourselves or our partners. We have to be visible before we can be seen. We have to be available before our hearts can be affected. And we have to be present before we can be intimate. When we can drop all pretenses and relate with a heart that is undefended, we can finally discover the unmistakable connection we long to have with our authentic selves and with our partners.[59]

Conflict Resolution

Shifting our limited special relationship to a Unified Relationship involves initial changes, and these changes can seem unloving at first. We are so accustomed to wanting to be separate and special that, when we or our partners withdraw this specialness, it appears that Love itself is being withdrawn. For so long we have over-identified with pseudo-love and have not yet seen and felt the enormous benefits gained by learning to relate truthfully through the Unified Relationship.

Solving any form of conflict based on resentment, anger, or judgment requires a completely different approach from that which we usually took in the past. At the first sign of loss of peace, there is the opportunity to meet the goal of our renewed relationship. Instead of reacting dysfunctionally, we may choose to take these simple, yet profoundly transformative steps:

- Instantly interpret this loss of peace as an opportunity to consciously remember our shared goal.
- Ask yourself, "What do I want to come from this? What is it for?"
- Remind yourself that this situation's only real purpose is in providing yet another opportunity to overlook the ego, which means not making it real.
- Decide willingly to not give offense or take offense.
- Call on the now moment and be acutely aware that none of this conflict will obscure your partner's Unified Self or your joined Unified Goal.
- Ask to see Truth and nothing other than this.

Conflict cannot be healed by solving it at its ego-level. Approaching it in the usual way only exacerbates the cause of the problem. This calls for a conscious mind-shift the minute we identify the signs of loss of peace (see section, "May the Conditions That Cause My Fear Be Removed" in Chapter 6), remembering to see every challenge to peace as an opportunity to stick to the goals of Peace, Unity, forgiveness, and overlooking error. We ask ourselves the simple question:

- Do I want peace, or do I want the chaos that comes from letting my ego think it is right?

If we follow this process, we are able to:

- heal all conflict because we are conscious of, and dedicated to, relinquishing the ego's addiction to conflict;
- remember that all conflict is emerging from our own submerged guilt while being projected outside us;
- impersonalize our initial reaction and overlook the trivial details of the situation; and
- decide to choose peace, knowing that the real source of the

perceived problem is never outside of us.

What is required is that whoever is more sane at the time of conflict remembers the goal and enters the now moment, asking for transformation at that point. This is done on behalf of both ourselves and our partners. We are urged to undertake this resolution process many times until we undo the belief that separation and conflict lie outside us.

The goal of a Unified Relationship is to liberate each other. By the word "liberate," we mean to free each other from the false perception that we are mere dualistic humans existing in an insecure environment. In this relationship we learn that our partner is not separate—that he or she *is* us. By consistently overlooking the ego we finally convince our partner that he or she is the Infinite and Unified Self. Our partner will awaken to this truth and live up to the perception we have communicated. This person, having been loved unconditionally by us, returns to us the gift of our Unified Self perception. Together, we discover that we are One.

Commit in Advance to Truth

Have you noticed that, when we interact with one another, we almost always let the conversation determine the outcome? For example, if we find ourselves in the midst of an emotionally charged conversation, what are our usual thoughts? Because the ego wants its needs met, we will protect any beliefs, values, and opinions we have. And what happens as a result of the ego's direction? The outcome will always be random. The result will appear to be good if the ego's needs are met, but, if not, then the outcome is attack, blame, and guilt.

The ego has its own hidden agendas in communication and always allows the situation itself to determine the outcome according to its likes and dislikes. This process leads to separation because the outcome of our interaction could be anything at all. When we are communicating, we really need to reverse the ego's procedure by first introducing a positive goal for all our interactions. Whenever we are about to engage in conversation, particularly if it could press our buttons, we need to remind ourselves of the interaction's *goal*, which is Peace, no matter what happens. When we realize our goal is Peace, we can decide in advance what we want to happen; then we see the situation as a means to *make* it happen!

Don't let the ego produce a failed interaction with another just because it has allowed the "content" of specialness to determine the outcome. It is up to you to make the decision to commit in advance to Truth. And if you feel you have failed, forgive yourself and start over.

Confusing the Body with Truth

In romantic relationships, we will be challenged to shift our perception from the body (the cocoon) to the Self (the butterfly) within it. Our culture focuses on the body to the nth degree, to the exclusion of our True essence and purpose. In the above section on "What is a Special Relationship?," we discussed how we are largely hooked into specialness. That is, because of the nature of the ego, we unconsciously seek to gain, rather than give unconditionally.

The body, like the ego, is an illusion, and when we mistakenly identify with it, believing it is the means by which we gain our satisfaction, we invite separation and chaos. Like a cocoon, the body is literally just a shell, temporary and ever-changing. Its single purpose in this world is to facilitate communication — loving communication. Using it to attack or judge is abusing it. To mistake the cocoon as the butterfly is a serious misperception. Yet, any failed romantic relationship is the resulting legacy caused by mistaking the cocoon for the butterfly.

We are not cocoons interacting with each other; our quest is to see beyond the shell and set the butterfly free, both for our partner and ourselves. In fact, every person we come in contact with is seen by us as either the essence or the cocoon. In seeing them we see ourselves. Every day we encounter people, on the street, at work, in buses, everywhere. These encounters are never random. All of these encounters are opportunities to see either the ego or the Unified Self. What we see is what we increase in our own perception. As we see beyond the ego to the Infinite Perfection of every person, the Infinite Perfection of our own Unified Self is reflected back to us. A simple smile from the heart, filled with Infinite Love, will have a profound effect. Whatever we give, we receive.

Quantum Forgiveness

Probably the most valuable gift we can ever use to transform our special relationships into a Unified one is the willingness to forgive. Real forgiveness has an entirely different meaning from the conventional understanding we have of the word. The usual interpretation is seen from the ego's perspective: we see firstly that a person has sinned and is worthy of condemnation and punishment. However, we decide to forgive and release them from condemnation. Secondly, because of this sin, we see ourselves as more special, or superior.

The problem with the ego's perspective is that it inevitably accuses the perpetrator of the sin and makes it real. Then, by forgiving it, it sets us up in a superior light for being perceived as the helpless and innocent victim. Once again, the ego separates and judges. This is ego forgiveness.

"Quantum Forgiveness" is a term used by Gary Renard to describe the immensely transformative experience of a new interpretation of forgiveness.[60] This form of forgiveness is a miraculous dynamic with the power of the Universal Inspiration within it. If just one little thought could evaporate many years of painful evolution and bring us immediately to a permanent State of Oneness, it would be true forgiveness.

When we practice Quantum Forgiveness, we remember that there are only two possible responses in our reality: one is an expression of love and the other a call for it. The latter will usually present outwardly as someone attacking in some way. Quantum Forgiveness sees beyond ego illusion and acknowledges the only reality, that the so-called sin is a call for love and, as such, deserves a loving response. This demands the perception that no sin had been committed in the first place. There is no such thing as sin, only mistakes caused by egoic ignorance. The solution is not to reinforce the mistake by making it real; it is to overlook the mistake and ask the Universal Inspiration to stand between us and any fantasies of recrimination or judgment that our ego might be entertaining.

In the event that your partner or someone else casts judgment on you, remember this important truth: any judgment you react to is always your own *self*-judgment that is being mirrored back to you through the antagonistic accusation of another. If you can overlook this ego-error in the other person, you are, in Truth, forgiving and healing your *own* unconscious guilt. When you rightly see the other person's judgment as only *a call for Love*, then you're healing your own subconscious guilt as well as theirs. And if we can truly put our ego aside for an instant, we will be able to glimpse that there really is no *other*; we are *One*.

This is where the power of the precious now moment is called upon. It requires us to consciously *will* peace and clarity, even amid anger or disappointment. In this precious moment, ask for help in stepping aside from all past feelings, thoughts, and beliefs, and desire to see this person entirely free of the past. See this person as new, without mistakes. Then focus on Peace, Love, and total connectedness. In this instant, as you see this person without judgment, so too will you be released from layer upon layer of judgment. Your gift in this moment will free you both, forever. Their release is also yours.

This relationship, in the highest sense, is given us for the implicit purpose of forgiveness. It is a personal classroom in which we will find daily opportunities to fulfill our study quota and reach our final goal of graduation. It requires our undivided allegiance, particularly in focusing on the goal, which is always peace, during times of temptation to give or take offense. When we realize this, we may also see that every frustrating interaction we experience is not ever what it seems. Rather, it gives us the chance to reinterpret fault and choose happiness and peace instead, because in truth our happiness and liberation depend upon seeing any perceived attack as an opportunity to forgive.

Engaging in Quantum Forgiveness means overlooking the ego reactions of another and cultivating the ability to see straight through the fragile transparency of the illusory self. This means learning not to take things personally, because to do so implicates our own ego and not the Unified Self as the identity responsible for interpreting the situation. Remember, there is no order of illusions, and therefore it is just as great a mistake to take offense as it is to give it.

If we are committed to undoing the ego, then Quantum Forgiveness offers us the quickest route to Liberation. Having a significant other with whom we can interact presents us with the perfect opportunity to practice forgiveness. While we may get many chances to forgive, we may also be challenged by a common frustration. We may offer forgiveness by overlooking the other person's ego-error, and yet we may not feel forgiving. At first it feels like a mechanical process, all done in the mind through our intent to forgive. Yet, it is a decision made with the Universal Inspiration, which may or may not involve the immediate awareness of Peace. Sometimes we may offer Quantum Forgiveness for another's apparent attack, feeling free as a consequence, only to find that later down the track our anger or hurt reappears. We may well think that our previous offer of forgiveness did not work. Yet, it did; it always does. When anger or hurt arises in us, all we need do is surrender it to the Universal Inspiration. Our conscious intent to overlook error is a continuous process, and in the beginning sometimes we just have to "fake it 'til we make it." Rest assured that your offer of Quantum Forgiveness always works. You may not feel it at the time, but its miraculous rewards will reveal themselves as you learn to trust the process.

Helpful Visualization

Imagine for a moment that you once belonged in an absolutely ecstatic and blissful state where you and Love were inseparable. Then in one crashing moment, chaos exploded and you were suddenly catapulted into an unknown, unsafe, lonely, and pre-historic environment where the language of Love is a foreign one. You spend the next fourteen billion years there, struggling through the process of evolution only to come to this point right here, right now. In this moment, a flash of recognition ignites an ancient memory of your original state of bliss, and you fully realize that this is what you have so yearned for, since the beginning of time. You turn around and glance at a familiar face and recognize this person as the embodiment of your final liberation in this very lifetime. Beneath the thin veil of ego lies a brilliant, undisturbed, innocent extension of Love. This soul is here for *one* purpose only: to free you both.

Your freedom depends on your seeing Truth, where before you saw illusion (Figure 4.3). What immense gratitude could you have for this immaculate mirror of your Unified Self in the form of your partner!

> You and your brother are coming home together, after a long and meaningless journey that you undertook apart, and that led nowhere. You have found your brother, and you will light each other's way....A holy relationship is a means of saving time. One instant spent together with your brother restores

the universe to both of you....Time has been saved for you because you and your brother are together.[61]

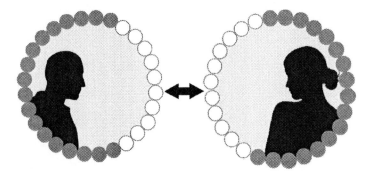

Overlooking ego error:
Every time we forgive we heal a part of the ego bracelet
and one more bead is made translucent.
Light, love, peace and joy are the result of becoming more translucent.

Figure 4.3: Undoing the Ego

The Unified Relationship: Our Relationship Goal

To create a Unified Relationship requires only one (you!) because this is *your* dream—you alone are the dreamer of your dream. You alone are responsible for making a decision for the thought system of the Universal Inspiration. Therefore, to enter a Unified Relationship does not mean that the persons in your life may necessarily even be aware of your conscious decision to embark on a journey to the Unified Self. It does not mean preaching and correcting anyone's error. All the work is done in the mind. A Unified Relationship occurs when, in any encounter or relationship, you recognize your self in the other.

The initiation of such a Unified Relationship can occur in just an instant (a precious now moment). In that instant, the energy of the Universal Inspiration enters and begins Its work of removing the existing blocks to the awareness of Love's presence.

A Unified Relationship can be initiated with anyone, of any

age, at any time, regardless of their particular attitudes and beliefs. The essential ingredient required on our part is the absolute willingness and readiness to enter and transform the relationship. And when we are truly ready, the person and the opportunity will miraculously appear. It can be with a parent, child, friend, lover, or even a stranger. If we are the initiator, then it may be that we work solely on our own delusional beliefs first, learning how to forgive the errors of our partners. It may seem that we do most of the work at first, but in truth we are getting more practice, and for that we can be thankful. In the same way that being on a sports team requires regular training sessions, we need not view these training sessions as extra work. We appreciate that, without them, we could not reach our goal. When we perceive this way, the task instills in us a sense of gratitude. Our training then is the ongoing learning of forgiveness, and through practicing it, we quite literally teach it. We teach by demonstration, not by judgment and correction. And what we teach we in fact learn, and whatever we learn we teach.

At first, when we relinquish the special relationship and mutually enter a Unified Relationship, we will often encounter a difficult entry phase that seems full of inconsistencies and conflict. The reason for this is that the previous divided goal of specialness is instantly replaced by its opposite, the mutual goal of joining in a Unified Relationship. As discussed in "Conflict Resolution" above, as the relationship dynamics change, our previous roles will no longer exist, and this will be rather unsettling at first. There will be a time where our old special behavior patterns clash with our new commitment to a Unified Goal. This entry phase is a period of fairly radical mind-shift that can feel exceedingly uncomfortable at times. We must remember that what we have invited in is diametrically opposed to the ego's thought system, and that there are bound to be times of confusion. To learn more about the evolution of relating, refer to the section on "The Six Stages in Developing Trust" in Chapter 5, which follows, particularly stages one to four. By the time we arrive at stage four, we have acquired, or are in the process of acquiring, Unified Relationships.

Undoing the Ego in Isolation

While perhaps the quickest route to undoing the ego is within a Unified Relationship, there may be circumstances that prevent you from having a significant other with whom you can join in this sacred process. If you are alone for any reason, you can still undo the only obstacle to peace, the ego. Very simply, practice the PIQ formula (Presence, Inquiry and Quantum Forgiveness) on your own whenever your peace of mind is threatened (see Chapter 5). You may find that your particular forgiveness opportunities center on the past, yourself, God, and your situation or circumstances. Above all, remember that you are never alone. The Universal Inspiration is with you quite literally. You need only "listen" and feel your fear or doubt dissolve. This is Truth.

The Greatest Gift Imaginable

To be on the giving or receiving end of an absolutely unconditional love exchange between two people is probably the closest we can come to knowing The Source while in a body. When we are able to overlook an ego reaction and see the deeper reality that another's "real" needs are truly our own, that is when the miracle meets both our needs at once; we both receive a significant undoing of ego perception, and the memory of our immaculate guiltless state returns. One more obstruction to the awareness of Love's presence is dissolved.

Many of us have had some kind of mystical experience, maybe a visionary dream or an awakening through meditation; yet, any mystical experience is really just a "state" that is purely temporary. Such a state rarely enhances the actual "stage" of spiritual development that we may presently be at. With the surge of New Age teachings that abound, we have grown accustomed to believing that there is value in pursuing certain "spiritual states." While having these spiritual experiences gives us a "high" and a sense of accomplishment, they are purely temporary—and therefore illusory—and do little to further our daily forgiveness lessons.

We could spend days, months or even years in one of these "states." Yet, one day we would still have to come back "down to earth" and live through the particular lessons that our spiritual stage of development requires of us. There is no escaping this one requirement; we can only delay the inevitable through the distraction tactics of the ego, ensuring more suffering as well. *There can be no escape from the birth-and-death cycle other than through the relinquishment of the ego*, and this freedom is realized only by entering the relationships and situations that life has masterfully placed before us so that we can learn the lessons they present. There are no accidents, there are no problems, and there is no one whom you are not meant to meet.

There is only One in and beyond this Universe, and you are that one, except that you do not know it yet. The healing of yourself and the Universe comes from your consistent recognition of, and response to, the fact that every single person who seems to appear in your life *is* you!

Have you ever been loved, loved without any expectation, without any judgment? Have you been loved to the extent that, no matter how many mistakes you made, you were still accepted without blame? Have you ever been truly seen, truly recognized as a pure reflection of immaculate Love by another, knowing all the while that they are happy to simply love you without the slightest demand on you? If you are absolutely honest, you will probably have to say "no." Most of us have not yet received this level of Conscious Love, nor are we familiar with extending it. That's precisely why we don't experience it: it is *because* we don't give it!

The ego believes that to "give all" and "forgive all" with no strings attached means we will lose. We would be sacrificing and giving up a great deal. The ego thinks we are all separate, and that if you "give all" and "forgive all," then at best you will be left with less and at worst you will be left with nothing because you gave everything away. And herein lies the opportunity for a complete turn-around, a miraculous change in perception. Just one change is required for you to invite the highly valuable experience of unconditional love with another, one that would go on to last forever and cement a relationship whose Holy goal is the healing of you both. If this level of Love is your desire, then only one change is necessary in your perception: to see that there *is* no other. You are it. Whatever you give—all the love, forgiveness, patience, trust, allowing, accepting, and non-judgment—comes back to you. Because in the end there's only *you* reflected in every single interaction you have with another.

Do not believe the ego for one more moment! If you have ever fully taken the risk of "giving all" and "forgiving all," then you will know the utter Joy of being loved by another who truly sees You, beyond the superficial ego-identity. To be graced through the loving eyes of the forgiven is to know that we ourselves are forgiven and therefore loved beyond our wildest imaginings. When you fall into this kind of Conscious Love, you will never again settle for the ego's counterfeit variety of love, and your life will mirror your unconditional love for all.

There is no other love. Whatever we give away, we give to ourselves, and what we see, we strengthen. This is the mindset that will undo the ego and return us to the magnificently loving existence to which we belong. This particular perception, with its practical application, is our fastest road Home. Do you really want to delay?

Your Unified relationship is your greatest catalyst for bringing Heaven to earth, both personally and collectively. There is a mystical transference that takes place within this union of two minds, each dedicated in advance to seeing only Truth in each other. Any perceived ailment can be healed through the extension of this level of Conscious Love. Many previous addictions are willingly and effortlessly relinquished. In fact, addictions seemingly relinquish you rather than the other way around.

Perhaps everything we desire, everything we do, and everything we live for, is a gigantic cover-up for the one thing that will unequivocally meet all our needs. Every need we have to exist in this form, in time, will be revealed by the one Answer, and that is the Love we will find ourselves to be. And this, we will discover, is the greatest gift imaginable.

CHAPTER 5

THE DEVELOPMENT OF TRUST: UNDOING THE EGO

Trust in The Source is the most important function that is required of us in order to reach our goal of awakening to the Unified Self. In the early stages of spiritual development, the majority of our trust is still invested in the ego-self. The journey to Wholeness is one whereby the trust we had in ego-self is withdrawn and shifted to The Source. As we said earlier, awakening is a process, usually achieved gradually in stages over time.

When we realize that spiritual growth in its most basic form is learning to trust in the Unified Self instead of the ego-self, we are better prepared to move through the process. Whatever has been holding us back or blocking our way will be transformed or removed, and this is often revealed to us through contrast. Without *contrast*, how can we learn to distinguish between what is truly valuable and what is not?

Trusting in The Source is definitely not naïve blind faith. This Trust is a finely attuned balance between personal responsibility and Absolute Certainty. It comes from recognition of egoic inner conflict and a willingness to surrender to The Source, Who *always* has our best interests at heart. In times of turmoil or disappointment, Trust illuminates the situation, reminding us that, no matter what happens, it is always for the highest good. The wisdom in knowing that everything is always perfect comes from trusting that we will always be given what we need, which, however, may not necessarily conform with what the ego-self wants (see Figure 6.1: "Needs and Wants" in Chapter 6). We must be diligent about reminding ourselves that we do not know our own best interests; only the Universal Inspiration knows.

The only way we can develop the incredibly liberating certainty of Trust is through the surrender of our ego-self. In the development of Trust, we must acknowledge that we are like little children who do not understand what they perceive and constantly ask questions like "What is that for?" or "What does it mean?" As we begin to question our former way of looking at things, we need only remind ourselves that the Universal Inspiration is our ever-present internal Guide and always responds to our call for help in perceiving things in a new light.

We simply *do not know our own best interests!* So at the very first moment we acknowledge this truth, we must consistently commit ourselves to offering over what *we* think are our best interests to the Universal Inspiration for guidance. Only then can we progress through the stages of Trust without resistance. *A Course in Miracles* offers a wonderful analogy to help us embrace the shift from the child-like perception of ego-self to the integrated Unified Self, as follows:

> Children perceive frightening ghosts and monsters and dragons, and they are terrified. Yet if they ask someone they trust for the meaning of what they perceive, and are willing to let their own interpretations go in favor of reality, their fear goes with them. When a child is helped to translate his "ghost" into a curtain, his "monster" into a shadow, and his "dragon" into a dream he is no longer afraid, and laughs happily at his own fear....For fear lies not in reality, but in the minds of children who do not understand reality. It is only their lack of understanding that frightens them, and when they learn to perceive truly they are not afraid.[62]

The Development of Trust: The Process
Here we describe the various stages in the development of Trust through the process of undoing the ego. This information is

based on the "Development of Trust" section in *A Course in Miracles, Manual for Teachers*.[63]

The "Development of Trust" section is a guide to help us remove the blocks to the awareness of Love's presence, the door through which Trust can enter, enabling us to release the ego with less fear. This guide is meant to assist us in understanding the ongoing process that we call "the Undoing." The more we learn to place our Trust in the The Source, the more the ego is undone.

Each of these stages brings about an increasingly wide and clear perception. The more we advance, the less we invest in the ego's perception of duality, such as good behavior versus bad behavior. And the more we advance, the more we come to perceive "good" as anything that brings us closer to Truth and "bad" as anything that pulls us away from it. Ultimately, of course, upon awakening, all such distinctions disappear completely.

There will be overlap in each of the stages. For instance, you may be experiencing many insights from stage four while still struggling with stage three. Getting caught up in repetitive cycles can sometimes occur, especially, for example, with the ego-self's temptation to perceive sacrifice during the first three stages. We sometimes get caught up with repeating other old patterns, thinking we are working the steps, while all the while our old hidden agenda becomes reinforced.

At each stage in the process of developing Trust, our perception of reality will shift and evolve as we release the ego with the Universal Inspiration's guidance. For example, two individuals experiencing the same event will perceive their surroundings differently from each other, depending upon their stage of development. For example, someone in stage one takes offense when he or she experiences a stage-five person being authentic (in line with the Universal Order). In other words, sometimes the authentic actions and truthful speech of a person who is at least in stage five and has overcome false-humility and the notion of sacrifice are misinterpreted as uncaring, irreverent, or offensive to the ego of the person who is at the beginning of his or her Undoing.

Spiritual evolvement has little to do with "good" behavior in itself, from the ego's perspective (such as doing good deeds), and everything to do with being authentic, that is, coming from a place of Peace within the thought system of the Universal Inspiration. The accomplishment of ego-release eradicates fear, limitation, and chaos. Once these are relinquished, we awaken to miracles.

The PIQ Formula for Undoing the Ego

The PIQ "formula" is simply a mind-referencing tool to help us quickly return to a state of peace whenever that peace is threatened. You will find this theme discussed in many ways throughout this book. Spiritual growth includes acquiring self-knowledge, and the PIQ formula is also designed to help you gain insight into why and how you react to the world around you and it highlights the issues that are troublesome to you.

PIQ represents:

- **Presence**: the return of your mind from thoughts of the past or future to "the now moment," or the present moment, the only moment that's real and therefore the only moment you need concern yourself with.
- **Inquiry**: a vigorous and radical self-examination, during which you bring your thoughts and beliefs into question, while reminding yourself of the "source," or cause, of the uncomfortable effect of projection. For example, you might ask yourself: "What is reality presenting at this moment? Am I resisting *what is*? Why?" While the cause of your loss of peace and upset might *appear* to be another person, circum-

stance, thing, or situation "out there," it is really caused by your own mind's interpretation of it. Take full responsibility for those thoughts and offer them to the Universal Inspiration for reinterpretation. This reminds you that the world is being done *by* you and not *to* you. You alone have the power to change any thought; nothing "out there" has power over your mind.

- **Quantum Forgiveness**: the choice for overlooking our own or another's error instead of judging and condemning. You remind yourself that whatever you forgive in another is also forgiven in you. What you give, you receive. This gradually erases the mass of unconscious guilt in your mind, thereby undoing the ego while the Universal Inspiration works Its miraculous transformation in your life.

We develop Trust in our Unified Self as we unlearn our allegiance to the ego-self. This entire process is literally the reversal of what we have been thoroughly trained to believe as true and real. Whatever obstacles limited our ability to perceive Love, Trust, Peace, Joy and abundance of spirit will be undone. This is an experience of de-programming, re-training, and re-education. It is a six-stage process quite literally aimed at helping us to dis-identify with the ego. The only part of this entire journey that will cause discomfort is our resistance to *what is*. We unconsciously cling to whatever is familiar to us. Because we have existed (personally and globally) for eons in the ego's extremely constricted and upside-down belief system, that belief system, then, is what we cling to, whether or not it is detrimental to us and whether or not it makes sense. In other words, we do not know our own best interests; therefore, asking for Higher Guidance is essential.

If we have an open mind that is wholly willing to acknowledge that the ego's "knowledge" is meaningless—that we know *nothing* about the Universal Order of Reality—and wholeheartedly trust the process, we will move through fear to Love with little resistance. Unfortunately, resistance is high, particularly at the beginning of Undoing, because we are afraid to let go of that all-too-familiar "friend" of ours, the ego. Understanding ahead of time what may be the most likely reasons for our resistance will alert us to those obstacles and assist us in increasing Trust.

The Six Stages in Developing Trust: An Overview
This guide to the various stages in the process of developing Trust is designed to provide you with an approximate road map that will light your way through each step. It is meant to encourage and support you as you progress on your journey to discovering your Unified Self within.

1. Undoing

"First, they [teachers of God, you] must go through what might be called 'a period of undoing.' This need not be painful, but it usually is so experienced. It seems as if things are being taken away, and it is rarely understood initially that their lack of value is merely being recognized. How can lack of value be perceived unless the perceiver is in a position where he must see things in a different light? He is not yet at a point at which he can make the shift entirely internally. And so the plan will sometimes call for changes in what seem to be external circumstances. These changes are always helpful. When the teacher of God has learned that much, he goes on to the second stage."[64]

This first stage is usually precipitated by a wake-up call, a disillusionment, such as a relationship break-up, accident, collapse of career, financial disaster, a threat to one's identity, or somebody's death. This crisis point marks a turn towards our seeking a different direction in life and is our invitation to the Universal Inspiration, a momentous decision that initiates the

Undoing process within our perception. Occasionally this stage can be brought about by a spiritual experience that is strongly contrasted to the meaninglessness of our life to date, thus motivating us to pursue a Higher Pathway from here on.

The notions that we are personally responsible for all our own discomfort and upset and that we do in fact create our own reality begin to dawn on us. Resistance to the new thought system quickly follows, exposing the internal conflict inherent in the ego-self belief system, making that conflict seem greater than ever.

2. Sorting Out

"Next, the teacher of God must go through 'a period of sorting out.' This is always somewhat difficult because, having learned that the changes in his life are always helpful, he must now decide all things on the basis of whether they increase the helpfulness or hamper it. He will find that many, if not most, of the things he valued before will merely hinder his ability to transfer what he has learned to new situations as they arise. Because he has valued what is really valueless, he will not generalize the lesson for fear of loss and sacrifice. It takes great learning to understand that all things, events, encounters and circumstances are helpful. It is only to the extent to which they are helpful that any degree of reality should be accorded them in this world of illusion. The word 'value' can apply to nothing else."[65]

At this point we begin to learn that changes, no matter how insignificant or severely disruptive they may seem to be, are always helpful lessons to be learned. We begin to sort out the valueless and the valuable, relinquishing the former and retaining the latter, although there is still fear of loss and sacrifice. In that regard, there is overlap here with the first stage.

3. Relinquishment

"The third stage through which the teacher of God must go can be called 'a period of relinquishment.' If this is interpreted as giving up the desirable, it will engender enormous conflict. Few teachers of God escape this distress entirely. There is, however, no point in sorting out the valuable from the valueless unless the next obvious step is taken. Therefore, the period of overlap is apt to be one in which the teacher of God feels called upon to sacrifice his own best interests on behalf of truth. He has not realized as yet how wholly impossible such a demand would be. He can learn this only as he actually does give up the valueless. Through this, he learns that where he anticipated grief, he finds a happy lightheartedness instead; where he thought something was asked of him, he finds a gift bestowed on him."[66]

Here we learn to relinquish the dysfunctional aspects of the ego's special relationships. This period may be perceived as one in which we feel "called upon to sacrifice our best interests [the desirable and valuable, in the eyes of the ego] on behalf of truth."[67] If so, then enormous conflict will result. But in the process of relinquishing what we learn to be value*less*, we realize that we are experiencing happiness and lightheartedness instead of the grief that we previously anticipated.

4. Settling Down

"Now comes 'a period of settling down.' This is a quiet time, in which the teacher of God rests a while in reasonable peace. Now he consolidates his learning. Now he begins to see the transfer value of what he has learned. Its potential is literally staggering, and the teacher of God is now at the point in his progress at which he sees in it his whole way out. 'Give up what you do not want, and keep what you do.' How simple is the obvious! And how easy to do! The teacher of God needs this period of respite. He has not yet come as far as he thinks. Yet when he is ready to go on, he goes with mighty companions beside him. Now he rests a while, and gathers them before going on. He will not go on from here alone."[68]

This is a time of consolidation where we have learned there really is no sacrifice in relinquishing the valueless—and therefore no conflict. We recognize the power of this new thought system and can see our way clear of all obstacles. This can be a euphoric period because of its stark contrast to the enormous pain that always resulted from the old way of thinking. Peace is restored. This is when we usually gather "mighty companions" through establishing Unified (Holy) Relationships, and we go on from here *with them*. In other words, as we begin to see others as one with us, that they *are* us, we begin to see them as our companions on the journey Home. Or if we are alone, we may find our mighty companions emerging as the Universal Inspiration through Quantum Forgiveness.

5. Unsettling

"The next stage is indeed 'a period of unsettling.' Now must the teacher of God understand that he did not really know what was valuable and what was valueless. All that he really learned so far was that he did not want the valueless, and that he did want the valuable. Yet his own sorting out was meaningless in teaching him the difference. The idea of sacrifice, so central to his own thought system, had made it impossible for him to judge. He thought he learned willingness, but now he sees that he does not know what the willingness is for. And now he must attain a state that may remain impossible to reach for a long, long time. He must learn to lay all judgment aside, and ask only what he really wants in every circumstance. Were not each step in this direction so heavily reinforced, it would be hard indeed!"[69]

Here we learn to lay aside *all* judgment, including determining for ourselves what we want (what our own best interests are) instead of asking the Universal Inspiration to reveal to us what it is that we really want. The unsettling comes from the endless amount of time it seems to take to learn to apply this principle to every single circumstance that presents itself to us. This is where we finally surrender completely to the Universal Inspiration's Will and let go of any previous investment in the ego-self will. Great vigilance and perseverance is necessary to complete this stage.

6. Achievement

"And finally, there is 'a period of achievement.' It is here that learning is consolidated. Now what was seen as merely shadows before become solid gains, to be counted on in all 'emergencies' as well as tranquil times. Indeed, the tranquility is their result; the outcome of honest learning, consistency of thought and full transfer. This is the stage of real peace, for here is Heaven's state fully reflected. From here, the way to Heaven is open and easy. In fact, it is here. Who would 'go' anywhere, if peace of mind is already complete? And who would seek to change tranquility for something more desirable? What could be more desirable than this?"[70]

Figure 5.1 below indicates the amount of ego-release—the release of mistaken identity—that might be expected with each stage in the process of developing Trust. In other words, the amount of missing beads corresponds with the amount of ego-release, that is, the greater the opening in the bracelet, the more likely it is that ego-release has occurred. One could also say that the opening in the bracelet relates to the degree of withdrawal of projection.

The extent to which the mistaken-identity bracelet is closed represents the degree to which we experience any of the following:

- a perception of ourselves as separate from The Source, separate and different from others, and, therefore, separate from the Unified Self;
- a perception of duality, that is, you versus me, good versus bad, fear in all its forms, including paranoia of others; conflict in all its forms;
- an inability to see past the ego-self, the darkness (unconscious guilt) caused by ego (resistance, attachment, and judgment);
- trust in ego-self and illusion (personal and global identification);
- a sense of feeling dominated by ego-beliefs (separation, personal identity, guilt, etc.);
- a sense of being dominated by time, thought, emotion, having, and becoming;
- limitation of one's potential;
- a sense of victimization (by the seeming external world, self, and others);
- a sense of scarcity of financial wellbeing, love, good health, vitality, and abundance;
- random chaos, conflict, sacrifice, and struggle;
- uncertainty and need for pseudo-security;
- specialness, pseudo-worthiness, and relationship limitations;
- special love and/or hate (conditional love); and
- dependence on others or external influences to bring happiness.

STAGE 1: THE UNDOING

STAGE 2: SORTING OUT

STAGE 3: RELINQUISHMENT

STAGE 4: SETTLING DOWN

STAGE 5: UNSETTLING

STAGE 6: ACHIEVEMENT

Figure 5.1: Six Stages of Ego-release

The extent to which the mistaken-identity bracelet is open represents the degree to which we experience any of the following:

- the ability to see and embrace the Unified Self and The Source and the corresponding freedom therein;
- acceptance of *what is*, enjoyment, and enthusiasm;
- personal responsibility for what we perceive (the reality we create personally and collectively);
- an ability to co-create our reality;
- Trust in The Source and our Unified Self (Truth);
- an ability to practice Quantum Forgiveness and overlook ego-error in others;
- receptivity to, and integration with, the Unified Will (intuition);
- Love, Peace, Joy, and abundance of spirit;
- liberation from suffering, control, and planning the future;
- liberation from emotional turbulence, compulsive thought, and the need to have what we do not have or want, or to become what we are not;
- freedom from the constraints of time;
- freedom in every aspect of life;
- an ability to heal the minds of others through extension of Love;
- fulfillment of life purpose;
- integration between real needs and ego desires;
- open-mindedness, flexibility, honesty, kindness, gentleness, tolerance, patience, defenselessness, Trust, and generosity of Love; and
- alertness, creativity, and passion for life.

Undoing the Ego

For most of us, the ego-release process takes time, and we need this time to undo the beliefs and conditioning that made up our separated self. Unlearning is a mandatory step to the unveiling of our Infinite Unified Self. We cannot live peacefully or productively while we value some ego illusions over Truth. "For truth is true, and nothing else is true,"[71] is what we find more and more as we discard the heavy binding chains of the ego, which have so limited us.

In the introduction to this chapter, we talk about the stages in the development of Trust as being a process of ego dis-identification through which we gradually realize the one source of all our suffering and limitation. As we progress, we usually have little or no recognition of our own best interests, because until now our ego has controlled what we perceived as important. The ego-self is inherently incapable of recognizing the truly valuable. As a consequence, it frequently attempts to convince us to value meaninglessness, because that error fuels the idea of separation.

The most important attitudes that we need to cultivate and consistently practice are, "I do not perceive my own best interests" and "I do not know what anything is for."[72] This idea is very important to embrace because our ego's perception is literally upside down in relation to Truth; thus it believes and sees an illusory reality.

Humility and open-mindedness are precious attributes. The journey to ego-release takes us headlong into a dimension of not-knowing, the absolute opposite of the ego's compulsive need to know and to control. The ego has no core of truth on which to rely. Its compulsion for separation and specialness feeds its pseudo-worthiness and false sense of security. Our Unified Self, on the other hand, trusts implicitly that all changes are necessarily beneficial, no matter how uncomfortable they may be initially. It knows it is infinitely safe, secure, and worthy; hence it has no need for our familiar obsession with the compulsion to control and the need to be loved and protected by outside sources. It realizes that acknowledging *not*-knowing provides the space from which Truth reveals itself. Universal Intelligence in the Universal Order, or True Knowledge, is realized in direct proportion to the degree of our release from the ego's "intelligence." It is a paradox that can only be truly accepted when we plunge into the waters of not not-knowing and now-moment awareness; suddenly Truth reveals Itself, and Infinite Knowledge—true Wisdom—is remembered.

The acknowledgement of not-knowing is a prerequisite for True Knowledge because 99.9% of the reality we have believed to be true is not true at all. The modern-day field of quantum physics seems to verify, support, and give credence to the idea of the illusory nature of the world. Quantum physicists have reported their findings that 99.9% of solid matter, e.g., our bodies, furniture, cars, and buildings, is empty space. It is actually oscillating energy and not solid at all! Yet we are conditioned to believe the opposite, that we and everything in this universe are rock-solid real.

That just about sums up how much false information we need to unlearn, or dis-identify with, through the ego-release process. We don't say this in order to alarm anyone or cause despondency. On the contrary, the path is made easier if we openly admit to not-knowing. It is a simple truth that we begin this Undoing journey as largely ignorant. This attitude will reduce much of our resistance, which in turn will diminish our fear and doubt.

There are two very valuable tools that we can use during this time: The first is the PIQ formula: Presence-Inquiry-Quantum Forgiveness (see the section above). The second is the Enneagram (see the section "Powerful Tool for Self-discovery: The Enneagram" in Chapter 3), which identifies the particular way we perceive and react to our reality and how to overcome the issues that limit our potential. Through practice, we grow with Absolute Certainty in our perfect alignment with the Unified Self.

Possible Side Effects of Undoing Ego

As we will explain in Chapter 6, during our practice of the six stages in the development of Trust, ego-release can be fraught with conflict, particularly at the first and second stages. This condition can be attributed to the introduction of a new thought system diametrically opposed to that of the ego. When we begin to adopt the Unified-Self thought system, our ego tends to put up a fight, and the ensuing conflict is often felt within us, but can also be mirrored outside us as well.

One of the first obvious impacts made in our lives will be within established close relationships, when we make the shift from a special (conditional) relationship to the ideal Unified (unconditional) relationship. The initial change usually produces confusion, misunderstandings, and blame through the projection of our ego-self's guilt. Also, fear seems to be intensified in the beginning, but discord will dissipate as understanding and Trust deepen. Working through the challenges of ego-release takes time, commitment, tolerance, patience, kindness, gentleness, and Love.

Ego-release can be a challenging prospect for anyone wanting to embrace spiritual transformation, although this need not be so. Relinquishing the ego is not about renouncing, or denying, the world and all its distractions, but about discerning and re-assigning its value in part and as a whole. It is the journey we undertake in order to discover our Infinite potential.

In the past, ego-release was often referred to in Christianity as mystic death and mostly reserved for the great saints and mystics of the day. Now, however, we have entered an era of heightened consciousness, and the responsibility of saving mankind and the earth we live upon rests with the masses and not with only a chosen few. This being the case, it is now imperative that we embrace ego-relinquishment and therefore heal ourselves and our planet. To this end, we will discover and realize that our *only* earthly purpose is in fact a spiritual one. Coming home to our Infinite nature, our Unified Self, is the most powerful and beneficial act that anyone can accomplish in his/her lifetime. To be self-realized is to be liberated, to live fully in Joy, Love, Peace and abundance of spirit. From this state, nothing is impossible, and, because all minds are joined, miracles follow.

This transformative process is one of release, of undoing the finite and the limited; it is the letting go of all that hampers our potential. No one can integrate and heal himself without undoing the ego. Many have tried and many are still trying to find shortcuts to avoid ego-release. We all attempt spiritual bypassing at times, but it will eventually lead us back to yet more and even greater suffering, whereupon humility softens our resistance to the experience. We start over, with a deeper understanding of what is valuable and what is not.

The whole ego-release experience brings about the following:

- We are able to discern Truth.
- We have the ability to distinguish between the valuable and the valueless.
- The Unified Self directs all thoughts, feelings, and actions.
- We become pro-active and are no longer reactive.
- We no longer perceive duality, as in good versus evil.
- We are no longer driven by compulsive sensory appetites, physical, mental, and emotional (the end of the cycle of pursuing happiness while trying to avoid pain).
- The state of Being is now integrated with doing. Peace becomes the objective.
- We become living Co-creators.

The Undoing learning—or, more accurately, *un*-learning— program presents many tests and assignments that encourage us to withdraw our previous investment in the illusion of ego-self. At the precise moment we ask for more Light in our life, the Universal Inspiration answers and we begin the ego-release journey to Liberation.

Now we learn to surrender the beliefs and attachments that have seriously impaired our perception and potential. Any dysfunctional beliefs will be challenged. Any misidentification with objects, people, status, or places will surface to be transformed. A time of restructuring hastens and intensifies during the ego-release phase. It may be helpful to remember that this phase is highly beneficial in helping to reveal deep-seated or core wounds that have, until now, unconsciously directed our life. This is the time to drop defenses, denial, and old avoidance habits and ask to embrace Truth. Any emotional or mental baggage, conscious and unconscious, will surface to be acknowledged and transformed within the confines of a special relationship. The triggers that press your buttons are usually people or circumstances that elicit feelings associated with your core wounding. Feeling attacked, betrayed, abandoned, humiliated, invalidated, or unworthy is common during this phase.

During this period, especially when we feel lost and alone, try to see the bigger picture by remembering that the adversity we may be experiencing is always a blessing in disguise. Any person, thing, or circumstance that bothers us is a *gift*, inviting us to respond differently from how we would have in the past. It is teaching us to see, value, and behave in more empowering ways.

If we find ourselves resisting, denying, judging, defending, comparing, criticizing, or accusing others, we catch ourselves as soon as we can. Mentally walk through the steps that identify the truth behind each encounter. We might ask ourselves: "What beliefs am I holding," and "How have they affected my feelings and behavior?" All we need do now is to choose again. Choose to look at it differently this time. As we mentioned before, cultivating an acute sense of awareness by being in the "now" moment, when we observe our thoughts and emotions, will help us immensely.

Any striving and seeking that may frustrate us is usually a sign that the ego itself believes it is doing the "hard work." Any sense of having to expend effort is ego, and ego is illusion. We are embracing the process of the removal of existing blocks to the awareness of Love's presence, not striving for enlightenment. It is important to keep in mind that striving is pressure, and pressure is of the ego. We are *already* our Unified Self, in pristine perfection; all we are doing here is removing the layers that have concealed that Self. To reduce the risk of more ego identification, it is wise to remind ourselves that our daily mission is to be a servant of The Source rather than to gain enlightenment.

What we need is the willingness of humility, fully realizing that the ego's knowledge is a trap to keep us limited in this bodily form. Transcending ego is letting go of the known in order to behold Truth. We don't have to strive, acquire, and attain Truth. It already is. We just need to drop all our defenses to it, all our resistance to *what is*. Surrender the known and the finite and we begin to see Truth. As we see it, we begin to live it, and then we come to realize we *are* It.

The onset of ego-release often presents as a spiritual healing crisis. It is an undoing process, urging us to break away from mass consciousness, collective conditioning, and our own long-held self-limitations. It really is a kind of separation from the known (familiar) and restricted in order to embrace the unknown and unlimited, or absolute. Instead of living in illusory pseudo-security of the ego, we learn to trust the absolute freedom of not-knowing. So much liberation is restored when we surrender to this process of undoing! By embracing not-knowing, *true* knowing becomes available to us as each moment unfolds. This is when we really learn the value of not-knowing and not-planning. However, because we are so uncomfortable with not-knowing, we tend to resist it. This resistance is more intense in the earlier phase, which can seem to intensify discomfort due to change and transformation. Resistance always creates inner conflict, which can lead to depression. If depression does occur in this instance, then more than likely this will be a spiritual healing crisis rather than psychological clinical depression.

This type of healing crisis differs from other healing crises in that we recognize that we are not a victim of this process and therefore are not helpless. At our core, we know that we invited Truth and Love to be revealed within ourselves and our life. We consciously acknowledge that doing so may involve transformation which, at times, can be challenging. We realize that we are in the process of releasing our ego-self. Trust is called for when despondency sets in. Faith and courage are required so as not to fall victim to our ego's feelings of helplessness. Remember: all will be revealed in perfect Unified Order. All that is required of us to fulfill our part is self-honesty, now-moment awareness, and commitment to our goal.

Social Isolation: Cause and Effect

By now we realize that spiritual growth means taking personal responsibility for all our thoughts, emotions, and actions. We understand that we ourselves are the cause of our life from our first thoughts down to our last action. We are responsible for how we see the world. And we know that all effects are born from our perception. Only with this knowledge can anyone ever attain progress toward spiritual enlightenment. Social isolation develops when we refuse to gather with the mass mind, which takes no personal responsibility. Most people, at the fundamental level, remain victims of the world, because they honestly have no clue where the cause of all their suffering lies. Nor do they think to question the cause of their misery. It's as though a mass unconsciousness overtook them and they believe all bad effects come from random chaos and all good effects are random rewards.

The notion that we individually project our own reality because we are the cause of it is a relatively new concept that can seem quite threatening to many people. Socializing and engaging in everyday conversation often reveals a striking contrast of beliefs and values in the early stages of Undoing. We may suddenly find that, because of this fundamental change taking place in our perception, we cannot engage in meaningless conversation that we find to be largely disempowering and, quite honestly, a waste of time and energy. We no longer want to be inauthentic, untrue to our Self. Therefore, we find that we want to disengage from any social contact that depletes us at this time.

In close relationships, a potential challenge may lie in having to change our style of relating to align more with our new-found Unified thought system of awareness and authenticity. If this relationship was previously conditional, our challenge is to bring Truth into it without attack, judgment, or guilt. Sometimes, bringing in Truth appears to the other person as if we are withdrawing love. Most of us are addicted to "ego-stroking" and mistake it for love. Withdrawing "ego-stroking" can bring about much insecurity that is usually expressed through bouts of anger and projection. If "nothing real can be threatened," then the possible transformation brought about by our relating authentically now will effect a positive change. If the other person refuses that change, then there wasn't enough real respect and love to hold the relationship together in the first place.

If we find that we are mostly alone with our empowering beliefs and perhaps feel unsupported by others, we may undergo a period where we sincerely question ourselves and our seemingly alienating beliefs. We encourage you to remember the original commitment you made and to realize that, at this point in time, you are a pioneer in spiritual terms and that you must be fully capable or you wouldn't have heard the *Call* to awakening in your heart in the first place. Our freedom lies in our consistent response to that *Call* and the memory of our Unified Self.

Job, Career, and Interests

Sometimes, we may be faced with major decisions concerning our job or career. Becoming more aligned with our Unified Self's authenticity will present us with tests that challenge the ego's attachment to the pseudo-benefits of illusory sacrifice and specialness. If, before ego-release, our job or career involved unhealthy sacrifice and inner conflict, we will most surely be faced with change, but it is always empowering change. Part of this process is learning to identify any inner conflict and address all issues in our life that feed that flame.

Any areas of our life that are largely fear-based will be highlighted in order for us to reevaluate them. Occasionally, previous hobbies, interests, or even passions, too, can diminish in importance now. When this change occurs, its purpose is always to assist us, and the Wisdom involved will not reveal itself until further down the track. Anything that previously gave us a false sense of identity or security will require transformation or elimination.

In the advanced stages of ego-release, holding down a normal job that is not conducive to our present needs is likely to be difficult, as the two realities are mutually exclusive. This intense period is usually best spent with like-minded people who respect and understand the immense value of undergoing the ego-release process.

The Body

Occasionally it is our bodies that seem to react to our renouncing of ego-self and they may do so by getting sick. If this occurs, it is helpful to know and remember that the body is only responding to the ego's directive, even if unconsciously doing so. In any instance where the body suffers, it is always wise to cultivate now-moment awareness and ask your Unified Self, "What is my body telling me? What inner conflict am I experiencing?" and "How can I return to Peace?"

Ask for clarity and never settle for the mass conscious ego belief that sickness is random. There can be great wisdom and learning behind sickness, as long as we have a need to experience it. As we mentioned earlier, in any area where we may be overly identified with the ego (such as the body and the pleasures and addictions of the body), we can expect transformation. For example, during a healing crisis, sickness may lead to a positive outcome, such as quitting smoking, losing weight, or committing to a healthy lifestyle once and for all. As we gain greater Trust in our Unified Self and more fully release our ego, we learn to see the perfection and unity of every person beyond the limitations of their body.

Who Are Our Greatest Teachers?

Our ego-self, desiring pleasure and avoiding pain, will tell us that our greatest teachers are those who give us its version of love and support. It will not voluntarily identify those people who challenge us and bring out either defensive or offensive behavior in us. We can recognize those persons by our response to them, which may include feelings of embarrassment, righteousness, and anger. Some of our greatest teachers are those who frustrate, anger, hurt, confuse, or abandon us. They may be partners, family, friends, colleagues, parents, children, or strangers. These people all have the ability to de-stabilize us, prompting a range of reactions. These "irritating" people, who seem to torture us at times, hold powerful keys to our personal freedom and liberation. Without these challenging behaviors, it is easy for our ego to become blissfully complacent, growing eventually into a monster of gigantic proportions, intent on our annihilation. Without these great teachers, it is so much more difficult to become aware of our ego's existence. Through all our encounters, then, we learn so much from the contrasts offered by our teachers' "offensive" behavior. As we proceed along our journey, with our growing awareness, we have the opportunity to recognize the value of these people in our lives.

While many of our greatest teachers impart knowledge through the experience of conflict, occasionally we find teachers who teach through Love. These are the extraordinary people in our lives who choose to forgive us and overlook our mistakes.

They are the ones who have loved and continue to love us, regardless of all our human errors.

Any person in our life who demonstrates unconditional love is perhaps the greatest of all teachers. Consistent loving without ego conditions is a fairly rare experience. We all yearn for unconditional acceptance and forgiveness. And we know that incredibly liberating feeling of being forgiven. The act of forgiveness has a great and positive impact on both the giver and the receiver. Overlooking error in others is the most powerful transformational gift, which has the potential to teach Love in its purest form. It does this by removing the blocks to the awareness of Love's presence. At the core of each and every human being is the desire to be loved unconditionally. This is never possible through the ego-self and its values.

It only takes one person to transcend the ego-self and suspend doubt, by overlooking error in another, in order to initiate a Miracle. The Miracle of forgiveness is the greatest of all available teaching tools; yet it seems to be the hardest to embrace, from the ego-self's standpoint. Great teachers are those who resist little and extend a great deal. They don't defend, yet they are strongly committed to Truth. They offer guidance without the need to control and criticize, or gain allegiance, superiority, recognition, or love. Knowing that "nothing real can be threatened,"[73] they have nothing to defend or protect, thereby affirming our own Unified Self and Perfection.

Many seekers-turned-teachers have traveled the journey of undoing from awakening, right up to the doorway of ego-release, and there they stop. Because they perceive enormous sacrifice involved in enduring ego-release, they resist and tend to stay in a fairly limited and controlled state at that doorway for a long time.

We can find hundreds or even thousands of these spiritual teachers, unwilling to cross the threshold of their personal ego death, yet professing a myriad of transformational information.

This point is highlighted only to caution that, unless the teacher is embracing their own ego-relinquishment, there is always the risk of the teacher's ego-self intruding, causing delay to their students' progress.

A healed teacher, however, has embraced ego-release, and his or her humility testifies to this. This person teaches through example and cannot be tempted because of heightened awareness of the ego's ways. Therefore, a healed teacher is like a clean mirror reflecting only the Absolute Trust that remains to be shared and embraced.

A warm, kind, gentle, and encouraging person would be the type of person that most seekers would more typically desire as their ideal teacher. The most envied learning environments and situations are those that are suffused with ethereal beauty and nurturing conditions. However, for most of us, embarking on the Undoing journey necessitates the appearance of radical and sometimes even atrocious situations and people, all with the one goal. And that is to shake, rattle, and shatter our ego-self until we willingly ask the Universal Inspiration to take over and correct our perception.

It takes outrageous and even shocking people and circumstances to crack most ego illusions! The ego-self sometimes calls for extreme confrontation on many fronts, but it is those very situations that present the best opportunity for undoing the ego's grip and allowing true perception in. Unless we invite the Universal Inspiration into our awareness, the ego keeps us living in a heavily sedated sleep where daily nightmares appear to threaten us. We are ingeniously deceived and severely restricted by its perception of worldly conditions, laws, and day-to-day fears, created by ourselves and those around us. This is like a dense and heavy fog in which we attempt to endure and survive. Most of us are unaware of this heavy fog and call it "life." Being reborn into Life, and living outside the sedated sleep of ego existence, can only occur through dis-identification with the ego.

The greatest of all possible challenges, and the one in which our entire liberation rests, is ego-release. It is the mightiest of all human accomplishments, and through it we become a magnificent co-creator, victorious in our capacity for miraculous transformation.

Perhaps we already realize that transcending ego is the sole reason why we were born and that, until it is embraced, our life is a cycle of illusion. If we can see this, then we will also see adversity and harsh teachers as valuable vehicles of learning. In this mindset, we can disarm resistance and hasten our own transformation. Until we surrender egoic perception, we're under a spell that literally controls our life through our thoughts, beliefs, and feelings, right through to all their manifestations, such as accidents, conflicts, disease, and devastation.

The objective of undoing the ego is to recognize, embrace, and value Love fully; to accomplish this goal, we must finally surrender all obsession with fear and guilt along with all its illusions. Only then can we know and receive Love fully. Through this transmutation process, the seed, powerhouse of our Unified Self, cracks open the hard outer shell of ego and bursts into full bloom and is set free. It surges upward to the earth's surface and is born anew, into the world of Light and beauty. Only when that occurs can the seed, free of the husk of ego, germinate and blossom fully, to its greatest potential.

The process of ego-release brings us to the point of Absolute Trust in the Voice of the Universal Inspiration, our Unified Self. We learn there is no other voice that soothes us. We align all our thoughts and intentions with this power and consult it not just daily, but minute to minute. No effort is required.

When we flow with this Unified Self, our life becomes a miraculous reflection of that alignment. There is profound Peace in knowing that all people, things, and circumstances are also under the influence of Unified Alignment. The surrendering of ego-self is not sacrifice. How could it be? If you traded hell for

Heaven on earth, would you call that sacrifice?

Now that we are ready, a useful prayer might be to ask, "Free me from illusion and bring me right-mindedness." This very simple request, if asked with great sincerity and passion, will be fulfilled. Through this prayer, our destination is assured and guidance will be provided to us every minute of our journey Home. Once through ego-release, we then receive wonderful gifts without being attached to them. All that we thought we would lose through ego-release is returned to us in all its purity, divested of its previous illusion.

Ego-self Esteem: The Illusion

The driving force behind our need for self-esteem is, unfortunately but not surprisingly, the ego. As we explained earlier, this illusory self thrives on separation and the need to be special, or set apart. Any areas of our life that are suffused in illusory specialness will be called upon for reevaluation and correction. Any unhealthy props that are keeping the glue of our ego together will require dismantling.

> "Self-esteem" in ego terms means nothing more than that the ego has deluded itself into accepting its reality, and is therefore temporarily less predatory. This "self-esteem" is always vulnerable to stress, a term which refers to any perceived threat to the ego's existence....The ego is the mind's belief that it is completely on its own....it [the ego] does perceive itself as being rejected by something greater than itself [the Source]. This is why self-esteem in ego terms must be delusional.[74]

Enlightenment is the biggest threat that there could possibly be to the world. But in the modern spiritual marketplace, this all important fact too often seems to be overlooked. Indeed, in the name of spiritual transformation, many of us are devoting a lot of time and attention to improving ourselves, without questioning the ultimate validity of the self that's being improved, or even beginning to question the entire worldview within which that self exists.[75]

The ego-self is always seeking ways to improve, inflate, and satisfy itself. It does these things to shore up pseudo-self worth, attempting to make itself into a meaningful and valuable image. But image it is, and certainly not Truth. Truth reveals that nothing real can be threatened; therefore, nothing that is *real* has any need to be improved, built up, or satisfied. In this world of ego illusion, all that is required of our Unified Self is the objective of ego-release. This clears away the last vestiges of ego identification, revealing only one True Will, being the Unified Will, and we realize it as our own.

Cultivating Ego-self Doubt

All the ego areas that we invested in will usually be challenged and transformed. Ego qualities relating to abilities, relationships, material objects, status, and the physical body will all be highlighted for healing and transformation. An ego-release prerequisite is self-doubt in almost every area of our life. Cultivating doubt and skepticism for all the illusory aspects of our life, beliefs, and values is definitely helpful in this instance. The more often we can say, "I know nothing," the closer we are to our Unified Self. Again, "I do not perceive my own best interests" is also an excellent affirmation that greatly assists us. The only doubt that should be avoided at all costs is Unified Self doubt. This is doubt in The Source and lack of Universal Trust that all people and circumstances are helpful in teaching what is valuable and what is not.

The ego-release experience teaches us that self-esteem is absolutely meaningless and a pure distraction from Truth. We really learn this through direct experience of the loss or transformation of all the ego has invested in. That is why self-esteem as we know it seems to be threatened or annihilated by ego-release. Once all ego props and crutches, including ego (false) self-esteem, are stripped away and we are no longer identified with illusions, we are born anew. Now we have inner Peace, Infinite Trust, and miraculously enhanced abilities.

Remember this: if we are embracing the concept of undoing the ego, then almost certainly the people closest to us will also be affected. Because the ego-self feels threatened by change, we may encounter resistance from them. This is common. Breaking away from the collective mindset can reveal helpful insights into many of our relationships, and some of these insights call for new adjustments to be made.

For example, a longtime friend may exhibit a pattern of being a victim of life, and we realize that we unwittingly have been disempowering our friend by supporting her or his ego-self's image. Realizing this, we withdraw dysfunctional support and offer a new more empowering one, perhaps teaching the concept of personal responsibility by demonstrative Love. Our friend now has to choose which is more valuable, the friendship or the victim identity.

Embracing ego-release can bring change to nearly every area of our life. A type of social isolation is often a temporary product of this phase because we are breaking away from mass ego beliefs and values.

CHAPTER 6

THE SIX STAGES OF UNDOING EGO

During the process of Undoing the ego, we pass through several stages of spiritual growth. *A Course in Miracles* identifies six stages in developing Trust[76] in the Universal Order of things and in the unfailing presence and guidance of the Universal Inspiration during this crucial time of profound transformation in our perception. In Chapter 5, we provided an outline of the six stages. This chapter describes the six stages in depth and serves as a guide to some of the experiences we might expect to have as we progress along the way. Furthermore, this chapter also provides helpful insights about the changes that typically occur within ourselves and in our relationships with others during this critical time. Being forewarned about these possible experiences and changes, some of which can be rather unsettling, can be helpful in assuaging any misgivings we might have regarding whether or not this path is the right one for us.

The decision to make a radical shift in the direction of our life and to undergo the process of Undoing the ego is often precipitated by disillusionment or a crisis of some sort. We might, for example, experience a personal tragedy, such as the sudden death of a loved one. The decision can also result from a peak of over-saturation in ego-self identification, followed by loss of, or change in, for example:

- relationship, either romantic or family;
- status in career, family, or society;
- material wealth or possessions;
- image, body (such as aging), or personality; or
- health, both physical and mental (including prolonged

depression or dispiritedness).

A life crisis, then, often serves as a type of wake-up call to get our attention, urging us to question all our beliefs and values and insisting that we change and find a better way of conducting our lives and looking at things. We live our lives largely unconsciously, learning to cope with our fears and conflicts in various ways, until we are faced with disappointment, loss, or life-altering change, and the pain becomes intolerable. Such pain serves to dehypnotize and motivate us into action, ultimately leading to our awakening to the *true* purpose of our life.

Stage 1: Undoing

In this first stage, we are frequently not yet aware of our displaced loyalty. Up until now, our world perception was based on separation, and we relied on our ego-self for answers to all our problems; "order" seemed to reign in our chaotic lives. The disillusionment phase awakens us to the yearning for deeper meaning in our lives. Now we seek new guidance and a different answer to the difficulties we are facing. It is here, especially during this initial time, where fear, confusion, and chaos seem to *intensify*. However, this phase is really one of great opportunity. Not until we feel vulnerable and threatened with annihilation do we begin to soul search and call out to The Source and the Universal Inspiration and ask for help from a pure intent. Our vulnerability becomes our strength as our ego-self is temporarily set aside and Truth is sincerely requested.

The First Step
The first step towards self-realization involves willingness and commitment to:

• Acknowledge that we know nothing in terms of Truth.

- Demolish any barrier we have towards learning Truth.
- Unlearn almost everything we thought was reality, including our own limited identity and our beliefs.
- Take full responsibility for our life, acknowledging that we alone create our reality daily. There is no room here for helplessness.
- Accept the fact that the initial phase of the process is likely to raise many fears and face those fears rather than avoid them.
- Accept the fact that *all* change in the direction of self-realization is beneficial, even if uncomfortable, painful, or fearful at the time.

A word of caution: Many, if not most, spiritual seekers and teachers have not yet taken the first step. They have, perhaps, accumulated an astonishing amount of spiritual knowledge; however, their egos are still intact. The ploys of the ego are absolutely astounding. The ego will immediately develop a means by which to appear enlightened, through searching for and collecting more spiritual information. The ego can hoard so much spiritual information that it can bluff almost anyone, including its owner, into believing that it is enlightened. The "enlightened" ego, however, has not even commenced the Undoing; in fact, it has run in the opposite direction by gathering even more beliefs that will later require dismantling! So beware of the ego's obsession to keep searching outside for wisdom. Wisdom is revealed through *undoing*, not through amassing further intellectual information.

Taking the first step initiates the unlearning and undoing of the ego. The method is to peel away the layers of self-deception, eventually revealing the truth of who we are. We begin to learn what is really valuable in Truth and what is not by questioning all our beliefs, values, perception, and relationships. This is where we gain our first glimpses of the Universal Order in our lives, and we are urged to trust in the changes that this Universal

Intelligence presents. There is no room here for helplessness or feeling a victim; to do so cancels out the opportunity to embrace Trust.

One of the objectives of this phase is to help us understand and accept the fact that all change is beneficial, even if it is uncomfortable. At all times, it is wise to remind ourselves that we are involved in the process of Undoing, and that it is leading us closer to freedom and peace of mind.

It is important to realize that, by undertaking these steps, we will most certainly be challenged with a great deal of inner conflict, resulting from the collision of two opposing thought systems, that of the ego-self and that of our Unified Self. We are heavily entrenched with helplessness, limitation, and judgment from years of guarding and grooming our ego-self, and then suddenly we introduce an alien concept that seems to be destabilizing the very foundation of our existence. The ego-self is outraged that we are embracing its ultimate enemy and that we have come into the knowledge that we alone are wholly responsible for creating our own reality. Can you imagine its hostility? After all, its very life-blood is drawn from our belief in the illusion that we are victims of the world we see, that other people can attack us, that guilt and punishment are warranted, and that giving deprives us of something. And now we are starting to question it and withdraw our belief in it. So now when we watch a television news broadcast of the usual barrage of bad news, we may see it a bit differently. Perhaps we will not see the people involved as victims of seeming perpetrators. Instead we may view the victims as living unconsciously and creating their unfortunate reality as a consequence.

The ego-self may allow us to embrace this idea without resistance because its identity isn't immediately threatened. However, let us look at another scenario that may appear more challenging to it. Perhaps your partner or best friend storms in one day and ignores you, while clearly angry. You are puzzled, fearful, and/or resentful and ask, "What's wrong?" The response is, "Leave me alone. I don't want to talk!" By now your anxiety will be noticeable and your immediate thoughts would probably be fear-based: "What did I do?" "He/she doesn't love me." "Get me out of here!" "We need to communicate. Now!" In a dramatic scenario like this, we rarely notice our thoughts long enough to seek clarity; we usually engage in the old familiar fearful thoughts and then respond in a fearful way.

Our new thought system would respond by getting our attention and shifting our awareness to be the observer of our thoughts and reactions rather than the victim. It would remind us to:

a) Observe our reactive thoughts and feelings without responding to our partner.
b) Accept *what is*. The reality right now is that your partner is in conflict. If your thoughts are arguing with reality, then you add to the conflict.
c) Identify and accept whose business this is, which, in this case, is your partner's, not yours. So respect his or her wishes and mentally refrain from analyzing or otherwise getting involved in thoughts that are their business, not yours.

Then if dysfunctional thoughts are too demanding to resist, try Byron Katie's "The Work."[77] Using pen and paper, ask yourself the four questions and do "The Turnaround" exercise. (See Appendix I.)

During the first stage of undoing the ego, we are open to the idea of this new way of seeing the world but are often unprepared for its initial challenges. We may be able to mentally grasp the concept that we each project the reality we see and experience. However, when we're actually faced with personal problems that include any of our most valued relationships, material belongings, or beliefs, we tend to unconsciously exclude those from our new perception, because these challenges are too threatening and we are not yet ready to take responsibility for them. For example, when faced with a crisis in a relationship or on the job, the ego-self argues its usual point that the problem is "out there," while at the same time we are beginning to learn that the problem is *really* with our own thinking and beliefs. We are in conflict, then, because we are hearing the voices of two opposing, or conflicting, thought systems.

We begin to examine our mind's new idea that what we are seeing "out there" is only a reflection of thoughts and beliefs in our own mind. This means our job is to own up to the responsibility of healing our own mind, the sole cause all our problems. We begin to switch our focus from attempting to change the world and the troublesome people in it to changing how we think about the world.

Beliefs are the acceptance by the mind that something is true or real; they flourish because we never question them. The fact of the matter is that our uninvestigated beliefs are responsible for shaping our world and the way we relate to ourselves and the people in it. In his book *The Translucent Revolution*, Arjuna Ardagh tells us:

> We may believe in past lives, but we don't need to believe in yesterday. In other words, we hold beliefs about things that we don't know about from direct experience. Why? Because we are unwilling to stay in not knowing. We need belief because we feel cut off from a deep connection to what is real. Animals, small children, and translucent [awakened] people do not need to believe anything, because they are loyal to what is.[78]

At this point in our spiritual development, we have begun to grasp the idea that we *will* our thoughts and beliefs and project them outward only to have them reflected back to us. We recognize that it is our own mind that projects reality as we see it. That means we have the power to break the guilt-blame-fear cycle of projection. Now when we perceive someone offending us, we can choose to either see Truth (that another's behavior is a call for help) or we can respond with attack, which only reinforces our mistaken beliefs.

When we begin to adjust our worldview from believing that our problems are caused by external influences to understanding that we make our own reality, there is likely to be discomfort. All our life we mistakenly blamed the world outside us for all our problems, and this justified our belief in judgment, condemnation, attack, and defense. Whenever threatened, we would automatically see the cause as separate and apart from us, argue with reality, and blame others. Now we must reverse our way of operating in the world.

Another word of caution. Since we have begun to embrace the truth that there is no one "out there" to blame for our problems, that we are not the victim we thought we were, and that we create our own reality, we begin to see the role *we* play in our failed relationships. Now for the first time we have to take full responsibility for all our problems. That being the case, we tend to direct blame onto ourselves instead of others. The truth is that there is no guilt outside *or* inside us. That is why it is so important to understand the principle that *no one* is to blame, not even ourselves, and we must learn not to judge and condemn ourselves any more than we do others.

Another symptom of this initial phase when we are shifting thought systems is acute inner *conflict*. The mind needs unity, and it works fairly well as long as we are aligned to one particular consistent thought system, which for most of us, until now, has been the ego thought system. But now we have suddenly introduced a new thought system that is totally alien and opposed to that of the ego-self, sending our minds into turmoil. The ego recognizes the threat to its existence and it begins to put up a good fight. It reasons with us that, before the intrusion of this Higher thought system, it gave us occasional, temporary times of relief or escape, and it tempts us once again to return to the familiar good old days of blaming The Source, other people, or situations, such as our job, family, or our financial circumstances.

The ego-self also looks into the past and defends our lack of peace by insisting that someone or something in the past is responsible for our current unhappiness. All of its tactics are illusions. It can just as easily point to the future and entertain fantasy to distract us from the present moment. It will keep us juggling between hope for peace in the future and blame the past for lack of peace in order to prevent us from seeing that we can experience peace now, in every moment. Again from Ardagh's *The Translucent Revolution* (Adyashanti speaking):

> Are we divided inside? If we are divided inside, there's no way in hell or heaven that tomorrow we're not going to have a divided world. It doesn't matter if we've got the best intentions in the universe, what really matters is the state from which we act.[79]

Below is a set of criteria that may help us to determine when we are listening to the voice of the ego. By being forewarned about the main strategies that the ego-self employs to get us to resist growth, we can be better prepared and perhaps even alleviate much of the inner conflict that is characteristic of this initial phase. We can be sure we are listening to the wrong voice if we find ourselves thinking and believing any of the following:

- I would have peace and happiness if only...
  ...he/she loved me more.
  ...I could find a new love relationship.

...my financial situation would improve.

...I weren't so pre-occupied with work.

...I didn't have to work anymore.

...I could find my purpose in life.

...I had more friends.

...I could get in shape and lose weight.

...I could only get the approval, recognition, or validation I need.

In these cases, we believe our peace and happiness can be found only in the *future*, as we imagine it to be. This is *our business* (and therefore our responsibility).

- I'm unhappy and distressed because ...

  ...my childhood was dysfunctional.

  ...my partner left me and I'm angry and feel abandoned, unloved, and unlovable.

  ...I lost my job.

  ...I had an argument with my partner (friend, colleague, family member) last week, and he/she put me in a bad mood.

Here we believe our lack of peace and happiness is caused by events of the *past*. This, too, is *our business*.

- I'm upset because...

  ...my mother drives me nuts.

  ...my work associate is irritable and demanding and annoys me.

  ...my partner should love me more.

  ...the kids continually distract me.

  ...the neighbor is too talkative and noisy.

Here we perceive that the cause of our problem is "out there," in *someone else*. Others' thoughts and behavior are *their business*.

- I'm in bad shape because...
  ...my prayers are never answered.
  ...the world is so dysfunctional I cannot be myself.
  ...the Universe is so lacking that I cannot be financially secure.
  ...God made me like this, so I can't be more spiritually evolved.

Here we blame *The Source* or *the world* (our environment or circumstances) for all our problems. This is *The Source's business*.

- I'm unhappy because...
  ...I'm unlikable.
  ...I'm a misfit.
  ...I'm a reject.
  ...I can't seem to succeed in anything.
  ...I'm useless, a loser, not good at anything.
  ...I'm not attractive, thin enough (etc.).
  ...I'm getting too old to be worthwhile.

In these instances, we are our own worst critic and blame *ourselves* for what seems to befall us. This is the inner-guilt trip, and it is *our business*.

These arguments in reality are purely uninvestigated beliefs. Our ego-self slams us hard with an endless barrage of false accusations intended to reinforce its dysfunctional thought system. When any of these conflicting thoughts or beliefs arise, Katie's "The Work" exercises (Appendix I) might be helpful here as well. We can ask ourselves the four simple questions and do the turnaround exercise. If we wish to avoid long periods of discomfort, we must learn to recognize and address our conflict, because if we try to resist, evade, deny, or disguise it, we will be in trouble. The only way to Peace is to resolve all inner, or seemingly outer, conflict by courageously asking that Truth be revealed.

According to *A Course in Miracles*, the three premises on which the entire ego-self belief system is based are: "...that you have been attacked, that your attack is justified in return, and that you are in no way responsible for it."[80] The Universal Inspiration's response is in direct opposition, reminding us: "You cannot *be* attacked, attack *has* no justification, and you *are* responsible for what you believe."[81] In truth, only something that is unreal can possibly be destructible; anything real is absolutely indestructible.

Whatever our beliefs might be, we can be sure we teach those beliefs to others by demonstration, whether we are aware of it or not, and in turn others will either reinforce our beliefs or they will demonstrate another belief system. However, we ourselves cannot hope to attain Liberation in this lifetime until we overcome the illusion that we can be attacked. We might be able to understand this truth—that *anything real is absolutely indestructible* (and therefore requires no defense)—through the intellect, but we will never be able to *experience* it without practicing Quantum Forgiveness, which simply means recognizing that others' perceived attacks are *calls for Love* in disguise. When we fully embrace that truth, we will evolve toward Wholeness and experience Peace in ways we never thought possible.

The Poison of Projection

Earlier we talked about how our split mind was formed by the seeming separation and how the ego-self, consumed by the guilt over its belief that it split off from The Source, is intent on justifying its separate existence. It uses its trick of projection to get us to believe that everyone and everything is separate and different. Anything we deny, suppress, dissociate from, or disown is projected outwards onto people, situations, and things, and then we (unconsciously) see an aspect of ourselves (such as laziness or anger) appearing to be in someone else and immediately judge them for it. In other words, the despicable aspects we react to in others are really the unseen, unowned parts of our own psyche or personality. The degree to which we admonish others is the degree to which we secretly condemn ourselves, thereby withholding our own self-Truth, which is self-Love. The more ugliness we see in others, the more we secretly cling to ugliness within ourselves. This is no way to gain freedom! "What you project you disown, and therefore do not believe is yours."[82]

The incredible truth underlying all this projecting is that, while we *seem* to be judging others outside us, we are in fact always condemning ourselves. Every time we get angry, resentful, and frustrated, we unconsciously attack ourselves. That is why we feel so low, dispirited, and depleted of energy when we experience any conflict, for example, at work, or with our partner or family. We unknowingly drain our life-force each time we believe and justify negative judgment against others. Whatever sinister aspects of others we find distasteful are hidden aspects of ourselves; to attack these aspects in others is to continue to separate ourselves and keep us from healing. The only purpose of projecting guilt is to keep the illusion of separation and chaos alive.

When we judge others, we are telling ourselves we are guiltless, and we try to obscure the fact that we attacked ourselves first. Anger, whether directed against another or ourselves, is not possible without projection. This is the ego-self's way of destroying our pristine perception of another and ourselves all at once. When we take the time to think logically about projection, we can see clearly how insane it is. Firstly, it begins by denying and suppressing something we don't like about ourselves. Then, through judgment, it projects our disliked aspect onto another, thereby disowning it. The entire dynamic is geared so that we will experience separation and attack by another. And if we believe that projection of guilt is destructive most times, but in some cases our anger is justified, we are mistaken. Projection is *always* a destructive illusion and the fundamental cause of *all* our unhappiness. It is the root cause of all seeming chaos in this world. Every single time we believe we see disharmony outside ourselves, we are attacking ourselves and separating from others. There are absolutely no exceptions. Projection of any sort is always a lie, and the faster we learn to drop it, the more quickly we will experience Peace.

When we project guilt, we either direct it at others (more common) or we direct it at ourselves. Not blaming anyone or anything else anymore, the ego-self turns to accusing itself, and we criticize ourselves as being ignorant, slow, or bad. Either way, we attack with judgment, blame, and anger. To put it another way, projection of guilt is like injecting poison into ourselves every time we judge, whether we are judging ourselves or judging others. *Self*-condemnation is just as poisonous as blaming others. After a while, we would be so filled with poison we would shrivel up and die. Most of us are unconsciously saturated with this poison but continue to point our finger inside or outside and wonder why we're slowly dying, emotionally or physically. The body, being controlled by the mind, will inevitably suffer greatly through the projection of judgment. If we could grasp what we are doing, we would stop. Our bodies would surely heal and be healthier for much longer if the poison of projection were willingly surrendered. This insight is a miraculous tool for healing, both inner and outer.

Absence of Guilt

The journey through these early stages in the development of Trust seems to exaggerate guilt because we recognize all our problems are coming from our own mind and we are therefore beginning to take responsibility for the life we create. Any guilt that we ourselves feel is of the ego-self because it fosters fear and separation. We separate ourselves from Love and connection when we are in guilt. The Source created only Love, and we, with our split mind, made everything that is not Love, Peace and Joy. Because we, and not The Source, made suffering, we have the power to heal it, not sometime in the future, but right now—this very minute. How? By recognizing and accepting that we can decide each moment to abide by either the laws of the ego-self or those of our Unified Self. We might ask ourselves: What is the quality of our thoughts? If we have made harsh judgments on others or ourselves, simply release them to the Universal Inspiration. All that is required in this moment is our heartfelt desire to be rid of judgment and the consequent poison it consistently injects into us.

If we find that judgment is too difficult to relinquish, then perhaps we are addicted to being right. Our ego-self loves to be right; it loves to win at the exclusion of others. It wants to be seen as being the best, the cleverest. Entering the earlier stages of Trust means we must, above all else, make Peace a priority in each moment. This requires that we observe our thoughts and make a conscious, deliberate choice for Peace whenever we are challenged. For example, a work associate may behave arrogantly, wanting you to acknowledge him or her as being right and therefore superior. You have two options:

1) The ego-self, seeing hostility outside, would urge you to defend yourself, attempting to make the other person see *you* as right and superior and himself as wrong and inferior.

2) Your Unified Self would choose to overlook your work associate's apparent hostility and remind you that his/her arrogant behavior is, at its core, simply a disguised call for Love or healing.

If we respond to the other person's ego-insanity with

confrontation, we will be reinforcing attack within and separating as well. We will be injecting ourselves with more poison. However, if we decide to overlook our co-worker's error and attempt to see the truth behind illusion, we heal ourselves profoundly. We may not realize that, in this one act, not only have we reversed cause and effect, but we have also helped heal another mind. This may not be apparent immediately; our work associate may continue to appear irrational and arrogant for a while, but eventually Love always wins. If we persist, we will see miraculous transformations that mirror our own inner transformation. Try it. It works!

Next time you are confronted with the temptation to retaliate, ask yourself, "Do I want to be right (perpetuate illusion and suffer the poison), or do I really want Peace (liberation and true happiness)?"

If at times your ego-self is convinced that it always seems to be the one who has to do all the forgiving and overlooking of error in relationships, that it's the one who forgives and restrains itself from anger, or complains that, "This is not fair. Why do I always have to be the bigger-hearted person?," the reason is that you are the saner person. You are aware enough to choose to be right-minded. You are the decision maker and you know that there is a choice, and it is your responsibility to make the only sane choice, the choice for Love. It could be that many of the people around you are not yet aware that they have a choice between ego and Unified Self. If this is true, recognize it and accept it for now. For unless we have begun to undo the ego, we will believe our identity *is* the ego-self and from this perspective, there is no choice available. You can maybe see that you have a wonderful opportunity to teach by example now, by living these principles. Do not seek approval from outside. Learn how to give yourself your own approval; otherwise, you will mistakenly resent anyone who does not give you what you think you need. This is a common trap in these early stages. That's why, if we're feeling resentful or angry, it's important to get pen and paper and do Byron Katie's "The Work," including "The Turnaround" (see Appendix I). This easy set of steps brings us back to Peace and Optimal Reality.

At any given moment, we hear two inner voices: the first and loudest is our ego-self; the second and softest is our Unified Self, which is also the Universal Inspiration. Eventually, with practice we will automatically and effortlessly follow the Higher Voice of our Unified Self. Remember, the ego-self's voice projects and the Unified Self's Voice extends; one calls for fear and separation, and the other Peace.

The only way we can find true happiness in this world is to learn to give to others what we ourselves need to know: who we *really* are, deep down. What do we need to know about who we are? What we don't ever want to find out is that we are: flawed, imperfect, treacherous, mean, selfish, weak, insubordinate, useless, insufficient, unclean, perverted, homeless, undisciplined, insensitive, unhealthy, ignorant, deceitful, dishonest, uncaring, needy, unworthy, helpless, stupid, two-faced, self-centered, or a traitor. The truth is that none of these traits are who we are—neither others nor ourselves. Yet, we are so quick to see these aspects in our partners, family, friends, and colleagues. Even when reading newspapers or watching television, we love to pass judgment on people and situations that are none of our business. We see such ugliness in others and secretly or publicly persecute them for it. Can we see how utterly ridiculous and futile this pastime is? We say we want Love, acceptance, understanding, and forgiveness; yet, we get lost in seeking it outside. On top of it all, we accumulate more and more inner poison through compounding negativity by projecting it onto others. We refuse to openly and unquestioningly give to others what we ourselves yearn for: unconditional love, understanding, acceptance, and forgiveness.

The fastest way to learn what and who we are is to look for it in others. Unconditional Love, Joy, Peace, acceptance, under-standing and forgiveness—that is *who* and *what* we are! We will never know this until we realize that every single person is a part of us; they only appear to be separate, in time and space. We overcome this palpable illusion only when we overlook error and give to others all that we deeply seek for ourselves. This way, by practicing it literally, we begin to learn who we truly are and we experience profound Love and Joy. When we stop seeing ugliness out there, we will see the truth within all existence: Love. When we see guiltlessness in others, we will see guilt-lessness in ourselves.

Giving *Is* Receiving: Undoing the "Getting" Concept

In this beginning phase of the journey, we start to learn what is truly valuable in our life. Until now, we could not know because the ego-self prepared a list and then sought after and manifested all that we presently call valuable. Included under its label "valuable" are: relationships, people, the body, possessions and material goods, beliefs, image or identity, recognition, successful career, health, and financial wealth.

A Course in Miracles teaches a simple principle that, if practiced with a pure intent and consistent commitment, *will* lead us to manifest a life of utter Joy and Peace. It is: "To have, give all to all."[83] In evolutionary terms, practicing this maxim provides one of the quickest routes to enlightenment currently known in the space-time continuum. The idea is totally alien to ego-self—the very opposite of its "getting" concept—and therefore we tend to overlook it or pass it off as unimportant. Yet its significance is not to be underestimated, because undoing the "getting" concept depends on learning that, to put it yet another way, "...*having* rests on giving, and not on getting."[84] By practicing this principle, we learn to recognize that whatever we give we receive. Whenever we extend (give) Love, we receive Love. When we are kind, we receive kindness. And when we genuinely offer forgiveness, we in turn receive forgiveness.

The ego-self, knowing only "giving to get," has no way of understanding the principle taught in *A Course in Miracles*. It teaches that we sacrifice and *lose* what we give and bases its security on getting and trying to keep. It does not realize that anything exclusively coveted for oneself will eventually be lost because it is not real. Anything that is *real*, and therefore of real value (Oneness, Unity, Love, Joy, Peace), can only be increased by sharing (giving away). Anything in this world, be it an object, person, or money, is purely energy at its core. What makes it special to us is only our perception of it at the time. If we use the ego-self's "getting" concept to acquire something, we search out our prize, sacrifice for it, and threaten anyone or anything that may steal it from us. And to guard our prize from loss or theft, we invest heavily in its protection. We don't yet realize that, if something requires protecting, then it is not real and must also then be worthless.

The Universal Truth is that anything of *real* value in this world can only increase by being shared. If we give Love, compassion, forgiveness, understanding, and acceptance, these qualities multiply in ourselves, in our lives, and in the lives of the people around us. Whatever the giver gives, he or she receives. Even when the recipient doesn't seem to notice or acknowledge our gift of unconditional love, we still receive. The act of giving is an infinite one that does not depend on time in order to work its miracles. Never be disheartened if your heartfelt giving appears to be rejected or unnoticed. Always remember that the act of your giving immediately resonates beyond time and space and goes on to create and extend forever. You cannot know just how many people are affected by your one act of giving because it reverberates as Love throughout the Universe. In his book *Communion With God*, Neale Donald Walsh explains poignantly the miraculous transaction that occurs through practicing the principle that *having rests on giving, and not on getting*:

When you know that there is enough, you stop competing with others. You stop competing for love, or money, or sex, or power, or whatever it is you felt there was not enough of.

The competition is over.

This alters everything. Now, instead of competing with others to get what you want, you begin to give what you want away. Instead of fighting for more love, you begin giving more love away. Instead of struggling for success, you begin making sure that everyone else is successful. Instead of grasping for power, you begin empowering others.

Instead of seeking affection, attention, sexual satisfaction, and emotional security, you find yourself being the source of it. Indeed, everything that you have ever wanted, you are now supplying to others. And the wonder of it all is that, as you give, so do you receive. You suddenly have *more of* whatever you are giving away.

The reason for this is clear. It has nothing to do with the fact that what you have done is "morally right," or "spiritually enlightened," or the "Will of God." It has to do with a simple truth: *There is no one else in the room.* [italics ours]

There is only one of us.[85]

The eventual surrender of our ego-self depends on our living and learning the principle that *giving is receiving*. This is the solid foundation from which our liberation will gain its momentum. To the ego-self, the "getting" concept is one of its most difficult rules to relinquish. Most, if not all, of its survival depends on our personal investment in the "getting" concept. Once we begin to introduce the notion that "giving is receiving," be forewarned: the ego-self will express its outrage in many forms, from deceivingly subtle to blatant.

The purpose of undoing the ego is to remove the blocks to Optimal Reality, which is learning to know that we already are Love and already have what we need: an endless supply of Love,

Peace, Joy, and abundance of spirit. The best way for us to arrive at this understanding and experience it is to practice extension: sharing and giving, without giving for the sole purpose of getting in any way.

One very successful method of learning how to sort out the valueless from the valuable is through the use of *contrast* (as discussed early in Chapter 5). As we journey through the stages of Undoing, we gain many insights through looking back and contrasting what was previously seen as valueless with what we are now recognizing as truly valuable. In fact, we begin to see so many of our prior attachments as not just value*less* but downright destructive. Contrasting is one of the Universal Inspiration's ways of helping us find liberation.

Let us take a look at our culture's addiction to "getting" and "having." Have we ever really carefully examined what we believe about giving? At the center of the ego-self's belief is the concept that *having* can only be acquired through *getting*. To get something requires some degree of manipulation, and we see this most clearly in close relationships. When we are involved in a special relationship, it is easy to detect how the ego-self equates love with trade and metes out "love" according to what it views as tradable. For example, if our partner is late, with no phone call and no explanation, we judge this behavior as an attack and we respond by withholding love, or with coldness and aloofness, which is a form of counterattack. However, if our partner arrives home early and brings a surprise gift, we respond with "love" and happiness.

In other words, in the ego's world, we give "love" if our needs are met and we hate if they're threatened or unfulfilled. So what do we teach by the example of this routine? When we love one minute and are angry or hateful the next, we are teaching that love and hate can co-exist as opposite sides of the same coin, and that love is fickle and variable according to whether or not certain conditions are met. We are unconsciously hooked into getting, which always leads to disappointment and unhappiness. The ego-self constantly seeks to gain by plotting, contriving, and manipulating. So even love is conditional and is gained through purchase. To the ego, there is always a cost to getting what we believe we do not have.

Romantic relationships are unknowingly based on a belief in lack or scarcity. Believing ourselves to be incomplete and inadequate, we seek attention, approval, appreciation, validation, and love from outside ourselves and automatically get angry or frustrated when our perceived needs are not met satisfactorily. If we think that our partners are not meeting our needs, what do we do in response? We withdraw our attention, approval, appreciation, validation, and love for them. We firstly perceive attack and then we counterattack.

By way of another example, we may plot to please our partners. However, in order to do so, we feel that we have to play a role and not be authentic, true to ourselves. After all, we reason, a little sacrifice seems a small price to pay if we can get some approval in return. But our bargain backfires when our partner does not respond, and we become angry. Next, we withdraw love, and temporary separation occurs between us. How can this be?: Because we are raised to believe that love can be turned on or off, like a water faucet. The truth is that Love never falters, never dies, never recedes, never contracts; it consistently and eternally extends and is in and around us always. We cannot see Love because our ego-self is like a dark cloud that obscures the sunlight. The sun never disappears, but clouds block its rays, causing varying degrees of darkness. Like thick, heavy clouds, the ego-self blocks the bright expanse of Love's presence from our perception, darkening our lives and our world. Thus, special-relationship bargaining, which is based in our belief in lack and scarcity, effectively blocks Love from each other and from our lives.

The first steps in our journey to Wholeness are geared to

removing these blocks to the awareness of Love's presence. We must be prepared to have our delusions revealed and removed by learning to sort out the valueless and the valuable. Through this process, we recognize that our past method of "sorting out" was based on fear, not Love.

Relationship Reform

If at this early phase of developing Trust we are involved in special relationships, we will soon discover that they will inevitably undergo transformation. In fact, the symptoms of our shift of thought system are primarily felt in relationships because, after all, our ego-thought system is slowly being replaced with its opposite, a whole new way of relating to the world. Until now, our relationship was based on the rule "give and take" (bargaining). Now we are learning that we create the world we see and that giving is the *same* as receiving. Difficulties, such as frustration, confusion, and anger, can escalate in this early phase because the very foundation and direction of all our relationships is turned upside down, or, more accurately, right side up. *A Course in Miracles* explains that this early part in the transition of the relationship can "...seem disturbed, disjunctive and even quite distressing."[86]

Many of us may ask: "Why does the beginning of this journey seem so difficult?" According to *A Course in Miracles*, this initial difficulty is necessary for the following reason:

It would not be kinder to shift the goal more slowly, for the contrast would be obscured, and the ego given time to reinterpret each slow step according to its liking. Only a radical shift in purpose could induce a complete change of mind about what the whole relationship is for. As this change develops and is finally accomplished it grows increasingly beneficent and joyous. But at the beginning, the situation is experienced as very precarious.[87]

Never underestimate just how much the ego-self secretly deceives us. Just as we see only a fragment of an iceberg sitting above the waterline and don't see the mass of ice below the water, so too do we see only the tip of our ego and underestimate the enormity of the ego-mass that lies concealed below our consciousness, out of our view. In order to undo the ego-self's thought system, we must initially overturn not just the obvious fragments that we see but, more importantly, the gigantic mass that lies below our conscious knowledge. At this early stage, we will be presented with plenty of opportunities that show us the contrast between the two opposing thought systems—that of the ego-self and that of Unified Self—so that we can experience the difference between the two. The two contrasting experiences produce enormous conflict because we have not yet made a choice between the two. When this conflict becomes intolerable, and we see what we *don't* want in the relationship, we are usually motivated to make the choice for Truth and embrace positive change.

Perhaps the most difficult of all early-stage relationship challenges is that within an established romantic relationship, which is included in the category known as *special relationships* (see the section "What is a Special Relationship" in Chapter 4). Because our goal is so radical, our style of relating will also change and cause suspicion, fear, and confusion. Forgetting that we project our fears, we further exacerbate conflict by seeing it in our partner, and we react to a perceived attack.

Being forewarned that this period in our journey is quite likely to be fraught with turmoil, conflict, and confusion means we can make a conscious choice for Peace in advance. The instant conflict and chaos enter, we are now prepared to either be the observer of our emotions and thoughts or lose ourselves in ego and possibly risk our relationship as a consequence. Once we recognize that this initial chaos is inevitable, we remind ourselves that its only purpose is to reform our relationships.

"Many relationships have been broken off at this point, and the pursuit of the old goal [ego-self giving to get] re-established in another relationship."[88]

We can now recognize the enormous temptation to abandon a relationship that seems lost in chaos. However, we can just as easily see the situation as a learning opportunity, and if we look more closely, we will see past the illusion. If we step out of a relationship at this premature phase, we will more than likely seek to return to our familiar, dysfunctional thought system. This is a tempering time that we would do well to embrace rather than resist. Any discomfort we feel is always born from our resistance to *what is* at any given moment.

If we are distressed to find that our relationships are particularly challenging at this stage, we may be comforted with knowing that the vehicle of the relationship is probably the fastest way to attain liberation in this lifetime. *A Course in Miracles* points out that years of meditation and contemplation (as in the Eastern religions) as well as a primary focus on fighting against sin (as in the Western religions) are both time-consuming and future-focused. Both paths tend to suggest we need to go through a lengthy perfection process in order to reap our rewards.

This Course...does aim at saving time. You may be attempting to follow a very long road to the goal you have accepted. It is extremely difficult to reach Atonement by fighting against sin. Enormous effort is expended in the attempt to make holy what is hated and despised. Nor is a lifetime of contemplation and long periods of meditation aimed at detachment of the body necessary. All such attempts will ultimately succeed because of their purpose. Yet the means are tedious and very time consuming, for all of them look to the future for release from a state of present unworthiness and inadequacy.

Your way will be different, not in purpose but in means. A

holy relationship is a means of saving time.[89]

So, if we are determined to attain the state of Optimal Reality and achieve our goal of Love, Peace, and Joy in this lifetime, we would be wise to remind ourselves just how valuable our relationships are to us on our journey to freedom. Have faith in yourself and your partner at this first change in direction because, as mentioned previously, the beginning is the roughest patch to be experienced. Once over the initial confusion, we find our relationships grow deeply into a Love more secure, rich, and multifaceted than we could ever have imagined possible.

In the beginning of this chapter, we gave some examples of possible crises that might motivate us to find a better way of relating in the world. Again, the initial crisis could be, for example, a relationship break-up, identity crisis, career loss, personal tragedy, accident, or illness. This is the turning point at which our lives begin to change for the better.

The first stage is a period of undoing and, as such, we usually take a while to recover from it, frequently seeing only the negative aspects of the experience for a time. This could take months or even years. Yet, the light of awareness eventually dawns in our minds, and we begin to see that the changes we experienced in our relationships, though perhaps initially painful, were beneficial in the long run. We gradually embrace the truth that all that happens occurs for a Higher Reason, and when we finally realize this, we are ready to move on to the second stage, "Sorting Out."

Ego-release: Needs and Wants

When we embark on the journey to Trust, we will most likely find that what we want and what we need seem to be worlds apart—and in many ways they are (Figure 6.1). Needs include lessons that teach us the value of forgiveness, accepting, allowing, trust, and love. Wants, on the other hand, most often present themselves as ego attachments, i.e., our limited beliefs, opinions, and conditioning. Most of what we consciously value and desire is born from the ego's need to sustain control. Ego-release is a process of undoing and unlearning. The influence and guidance of the Unified Will seems to increase in our life as we release the ego's control.

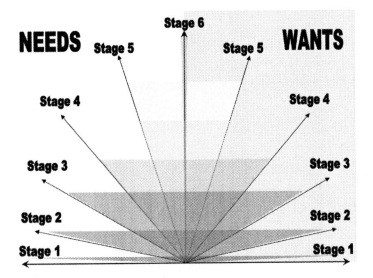

Needs include lessons that teach us the value of forgiveness, acceptance, allowing, trust and love.

Wants most often present themselves as ego attachments, being our limited beliefs, opinions and conditioning.

Stage 1: The angle of conflict between needs and wants is at its greatest
Stage 2: As we make progress we start to see similarities between needs and wants
Stage 3: We practice integrating needs and wants willingly
Stage 4: With the great peace experienced here, it is easy to see the congruity of needs and wants
Stage 5: Needs and wants are almost aligned as the last ego attachments are released
Stage 6: Here we know the Unified Will is our will and our needs and wants are one; there is no conflict.

Figure 6.1: Needs and Wants

During stages one to three, when there is likely to be change occurring in our outer circumstances, our lack of Trust can mistakenly cause the perception that our needs are not being met, despite our newfound allegiance to adopting this new thought system. This is not so. We do not know our own best interests; therefore, how can we possibly know what our needs are? Our ego will demand that its desires be met, and if they're not met, resistance surfaces as inner conflict—emotional, physical, and/or mental—and we find that we are resisting *what is*, arguing with reality *again*! When this occurs, as quickly as possible, acknowledge the conflict, or disappointment. Observe any thoughts or feelings of being a victim of *what is*. Remember that what you *want* right now may not be what you *need*, and there's a very good reason for this, although your ego wants things its way—right now. If you are not receiving what you think you need, ask the Universal Inspiration for help and guidance in surrendering to *what is*.

During this first stage, it is likely that what our ego desires and what is for our highest good seem almost diametrically opposed. For instance, a long-standing friendship that was previously based on *specialness* seems to be breaking down, or maybe a career that was steady but boring and dispiriting collapses. Our ego will still *want* to keep the friendship and it will *want* to keep the career because it has no idea about Truth. In the early stages, when we are presented with what we *need* (from the perspective of the Higher Wisdom), we may not yet see it as a blessing in disguise.

When we are feeling like a victim of our circumstance, we might remind ourselves of the following Truth, as stated by Jacquelyn Small (again from her book *The Sacred Purpose of Being Human*):

If we can remember that we came here as spiritual beings to learn how to be human (Principle One [of her twelve principles]), we will never confuse what's happening to us with who we are. Instead, we intensely involve ourselves in life, even in the painful times, with the questions: "What lesson is there here for me?" "What is my soul's intention in this situation?" This places us upon a higher rung of our evolutionary ladder. We can learn to see things from above the storm while passing right through them. This way of living works beautifully for passionate souls. It gives intense pleasure to work toward seeing the sacred meaning to otherwise rather mundane experiences. It makes us feel connected to our Source. We can fall in love with the journey itself when we stop letting our conditions define us.

No matter how chained to the rock you may feel yourself to be in any situation, the divine Spark in you is steadily moving you toward your full unfolding.[90]

Stage 2: Sorting Out

During this stage, we gradually learn that not just some changes are helpful, but that *all* changes are helpful. Here we get to look at things, people, situations, habits, and attitudes that we are perhaps challenged to either transform or relinquish altogether. Since the ego-self is still quite immersed in its belief that transformation will mean loss, we tend to resist change because we interpret it as sacrifice, even though this is not true in the real sense. We also generally realize that some of our present vices are definitely not in alignment with our new commitment to Truth and may decide to relinquish them, which can be experienced as painful if we view their relinquishment as sacrifice.

For instance, if we have overly identified with our career or our role as a parent and unknowingly intertwined our identity with our work or our parent role, we may face the crisis of a loss of identity if our career collapses or our children leave home. Once we have recovered from the initial crisis, we would recognize that this seeming loss has been helpful in many ways.

Perhaps the career was a mask for an overachiever or perfectionist who had been struggling to seek endless approval or praise from outside. Now the person finds that approval inside and is closer to family as a consequence. Maybe now without external distraction and stress, creativity is awakened and a far more personally fulfilling purpose begins to unfold. However, in order to pursue this new purpose, there are a number of adjustments yet to be made.

The reforms called for in this stage will most likely be seen as sacrifice. It is not until we actually begin to fulfill these changes and witness the benefits that we start to appreciate that *all* changes are helpful. Now we grow to be a little more trusting and begin to look at change in a new light.

Alongside this more empowering attitude that we are acquiring, a new resistance from the ego-self arises, and there may seem to be further challenges. The temptation at this point is to feel hopeless and helpless, blaming The Source for our dilemma. Resentment and feeling like a victim are signs that the ego-self is swaying us.

The objective of this stage is to truly grasp that we, through our mind, make all the reality we perceive. We are in charge and not a victim of others, circumstances, or things. If we are not happy, we must take responsibility and change our thinking, which may or may not call for a change in our outer situation.

I **am** responsible for what I see.
I choose the feelings I experience, and I decide upon the goal I would achieve.
And everything that seems to happen to me I ask for, and receive as I have asked.[91]

This is where the truth that only our own thoughts cause us pain begins to register in our mind. We need to consciously be one hundred percent personally responsible for our thoughts and resolve to give up all blame. Learning to see that we are making this reality—not just some of the time, but *all* the time—is a process, requiring time. And we will at first see this in some areas of our lives, but with most of our lives still seemingly dictated by outer influences for which we take no responsibility.

All of our inner conflict is caused by operating from within two opposing thought systems. In some areas of our life, we actively live from our Unified Self; yet, we still hold many of the ego-self's illusions as real. For example, we may have finally reached Peace with a longtime relationship, but in the same day we lose our temper at a lazy store clerk. We are learning that extending Peace gives us Peace, but we have not yet learned to apply this principle to all circumstances.

We must remember that we have only recently embraced the concept that "giving is receiving." Our ego-self is insistent and consistent in its firm argument that *having is the opposite of giving* and asks, "How can *giving* lead to *having* something?" We clearly have two opposing thought systems going on in our minds at once. Sometimes we understand, practice, and reap the rewards of "giving is receiving," and at other times our ego-self obliterates Truth by denouncing *It* as insanity! Here we are seemingly at the mercy of opposite beliefs and our conflicted mind sees conflicted outcomes. Rest assured that this dilemma is temporary, and Peace will be restored once we come to understand, accept, and *practice* solely the thought system of the Universal Inspiration. This does take time and discipline.

Any exterior disappointments and conflicts are surely an outer manifestation of our own inner confusion between thought systems. Just be honest and recognize and acknowledge those times where we seem to run off track. If inner or outer conflict is apparent, sit down with pen and paper and do Byron Katie's four questions in "The Work" (Appendix I) and get back to sanity and Peace. You can also use the "PIQ" (Presence-Inquiry-Quantum Forgiveness) formula. Simply asking the Universal Inspiration to return us to right-mindedness also works wonders. The Universal Inspiration always hears and answers our call.

May the Conditions That Cause My Fear Be Removed

We spoke earlier (in the section "Fear and Now" in Chapter 2) of the existence of two types of fear, one of which is called emergency fear. Emergency fear is a built-in physiological response, also called "fight or flight," that surfaces when we are confronted with sudden immediately life-threatening danger. Acknowledging that *all* fear (even the life-threatening variety) originates in the mind, the type of fear we are more familiar with is the daily barrage of psychological fear based on concerns about the past or the future. The ego invests in these worries and preoccupations so that it can keep our minds out of the now moment, where there is freedom from fear. This way, the ego can maintain control, without becoming exposed.

Nearly all the worry, concern, conflict, and fear we experience emerges from the insecurity, or sense of vulnerability, of the ego-self. Being nothing but illusion, it has no real core, and therefore it must consistently defend itself by maintaining vigilant control over all that it perceives as threatening to its existence. The ego will avoid, deny, defend, suppress, attack, manipulate, or disguise anything that may threaten its specialness—its attachments, beliefs, values. The enormity of its task to control and avoid exposure is massive. It thinks it is in control of every second, minute, and hour, twenty-four hours a day, seven days a week, our entire life. The only moments the ego is given a break is when we are actively observing and correcting our own thoughts and reactions and when we suspend all thought and enter into mindful awareness of the now moment. Once our trust is developed sufficiently, we are then able to accept that our freedom lies in relinquishing the ego's control.

If the ego causes all our psychological fear (worry, concern, need to control, and resistance to *what is*), then it must also be the cause of *all* our fears and conflicts. The Source and the Universal Inspiration cannot see or acknowledge illusion, and fear is the ultimate illusion. Because we are so accustomed to believing that fear is real and caused by something "out there," we usually ask for the fear itself to be taken away or for whatever we perceive to be the external cause of our fear to be removed. For instance, we may have a friend who is ill, and we ask for the illness to be healed. Or we may be challenged with a frightening task, and we ask for the task itself to be removed or made easier. In both cases, our request is a denial of our fear. Asking for what seems to cause the fear (the symptoms of an illness, a loss, a challenge) to be removed cannot be fulfilled because neither the fear itself nor our projections of it are real. Illusions cannot be healed or eradicated by making them real. If we wholeheartedly want release from fear, then we need to first identify the cause, which *always* lies in our minds, not outside us in any way. Any person, thing, or situation that elicits fear in us is purely a symptom of the under-lying cause of fear. Once we acknowledge that we want freedom from the conditions that caused the fear (our *choice* for separation), then we may surrender the symptoms to the Universal Inspiration, Who will take care of them.

When we feel fear, it is a sure sign that we have allowed the ego's thoughts to dominate us. As soon as fear arises, the remedy to remove it is to consciously ask that our thoughts be returned to right-mindedness, and Peace will return to our mind. This allows our Unified Self to take over and dissipate the real cause of the fear.

When you are fearful, you have chosen wrongly. That is why you feel responsible for it. You must change your mind, not your behavior, and this *is* a matter of willingness. You do not need guidance except at the mind level. Correction belongs only at the level where change is possible. Change does not mean anything at the symptom level, where it cannot work.

The correction of fear *is* your responsibility. When you ask for release from fear, you are implying that it is not. You should *ask instead, for help in the conditions* [wrong-mindedness] *that have brought the fear about.*[92] [italics ours]

When we want release from fear, then, we must ask for the conditions causing the fear to be brought to Light and therefore removed, returning us to right-mindedness. Conflict in all its forms emerges when the ego desires one thing or outcome, while our Unified Self knows exactly what we need. These two thought systems are diametrically opposed (one is false, the other our natural state), and this is the source of *all* conflict, which in turn causes fear. Quite simply, we can never be happy and fulfilled when we're not in alignment with the Unified Will, our natural state.

Conflict occurs in a split mind in either of two ways: (1) we choose to do two or more conflicting things simultaneously or successively; or (2) we do what we think we *should* do but not what we really *want* to do. Both these situations produce great strain, because we are acting in a manner contrary to our Truth. We are not being authentic, true to our real nature. This produces conflicted thought and behavior, which in turn produces fear. In any case, whenever we feel conflict, it is a sign that we have chosen to listen to the voice of the ego, and the remedy is to ask for our thoughts to be returned to right-mindedness.

Time, Thought, and Emotion

Here is a reference-point "reality check" that we can use any time fear or conflict arise as we progress through these initial stages. This process can be done very quickly, and it enables us to do the following:

- Become aware of and recognize loss of Peace and perceived conflict, either inner or outer.

- Honestly acknowledge this loss of Peace. Ask immediately, "Please remove the conditions that caused my fear." This returns us to right-mindedness.
- Decide which action restores Peace/Love and is therefore Truth, versus which action requires attack/defense and is therefore insanity and protection of the ego.
- Implement the required action.

In his compelling book *Embracing Heaven and Earth*, Andrew Cohen explains:

> ...the three fundamental yet most confusing aspects of the human experience: the movement of time, the arising of thought and the presence of feeling.
>
> It is our always conditioned and deeply compulsive relationship to these three fundamental components of our experience that creates the painful prison of illusion that is ego.[93]

If at any point we feel lost, angry or sad, it is always because we are experiencing a dysfunctional relationship with time, thought, or feeling.

(a) *Time*

If it is *time* that we are caught up in, then we will experience thoughts and feelings of anticipation, waiting for the future to arrive. We invest in the future by believing that it will be an improvement on the now moment. Meanwhile, we are avoiding being here and now and are therefore removed from everything occurring in this instant. Because we are absent from the now, we are absent from ourselves, others, our surroundings, and Higher Guidance. We are absent from Life itself.

Thus, if we are feeling anxiety or fear, we tend to bypass the system and jump into waiting for the future when we will feel better, not realizing that Optimal Reality is available *now*, not later. There is nothing to escape from and there is nowhere to escape to. The challenge we face is to realize that, whatever the now presents for us, it will always be an opportunity to embrace. Our rewards arrive only in the now, by being consciously present right here, right now. All answers are available in this one precious moment. We are always equipped with everything we need right now, for every now moment. It's only our ego-self that sees lack or fear and tells us that now is not right, that later will be better.

(b) *Thought*

We are not our thoughts. We give our thoughts all the meaning they have for us, and we exist independently of thought. To be free from conflict, we must observe ourselves thinking and not mistake our thoughts as being what we are. Again from Cohen (*Embracing Heaven and Earth*):

> Like pictures in a photo album, when seen objectively, thoughts in and of themselves are recognized as being nothing more than abstract representations of historical events. Ceasing to make the pivotal error of believing thought to be inherently real instantly reveals the truth that who we are always has been free from and prior to the awareness of thought....Lost in and helplessly distracted by thought and the arising of thought, most of us spend our entire lives alienated from our own depths and, as a result, often experience a puzzling sense of separation from the world in which we live.[94]

When we allow ourselves to be lost in compulsive thought, the ego-self is demanding control. It uses thought in an attempt to immobilize our Unified Self. Nearly all our thoughts are a *judgment* of some kind. Almost all of our thinking is in evaluation-and-analyze mode, sifting through perceived data to make assumptions that are almost always geared to feed or defend the ego-self's preset beliefs. Just watch, or better still, write down your thoughts over the next three minutes. How many thoughts contained any of these words or their meanings: should, shouldn't, want, need, must, more, less, better, worse? How many self-limiting beliefs did you acquire from these illusory thoughts?

And how many of our thoughts were based on evaluations of ourselves, others, circumstances, or things? Our thoughts are making millions of mini-judgments every day; yet nearly all of them are untrue. Nearly all are based on the past or future. We think; then we project our thoughts outward, and ego-reality flashes back to us a mirror image of our assumptions, seemingly proving our projections to be fact. None of it is true. The only truth is Love. To experience Love, simply surrender *all* judgment and evaluation to our Unified Self! Remind yourself: "I do not perceive my own best interests"[95] and ask for a return to right-mindedness. Our Unified Self will always give us an answer that leads us to Peace, never conflict, inner or outer. The mechanism of thought controlled by ego-self has never solved, and never will solve, any problem because it itself is the source of the problem.

(c) *Emotion*

To attain a reasonable degree of impersonal perception, we must firstly look at emotion for what it really is. Our emotions are like the weather, totally unpredictable, changing without warning, at a whim. For example, if we wake up feeling miserable, we will perceive our day through a distorted lens of depression; and if we are angered by someone, we will see through the distorted lens of anger. We are indoctrinated to follow our emotional responses and don't realize that emotions, like thought, are independent from who we are. If we are truly committed to liberation in this lifetime, we must learn to become fully aware of, and alert to, our emotions. We are not our emotions, no matter how real and intense they may be.

If we allow our emotions to dictate our responses, then we lose our power. To be free means to be wholly committed to healing our split mind. This is our first priority—Peace. If our emotions disturb that Peace, we can remedy the situation by stopping, being the observer of *what is*, and inviting the Universal Inspiration to coach us through the experience. It takes great discipline to work with and through emotions. So, be patient! Implementing Byron Katie's "The Work" (Appendix I) is a great way to help us heal beliefs that cause painful emotions. The Enneagram and the "PIQ" formula are also powerful tools that can help you with this process.

If we find that we are trapped in, and feel a victim of, emotions seemingly caused by the past or fears of the future, it is imperative to our healing that the Light of Truth be cast on them. Bring all your fears to the Light of the Universal Inspiration! At this stage, anything that seems to have disempowered us will require unearthing and reevaluation so that we can see clearly that we were never the victim we thought we were. This process (best achieved with pen and paper through Katie's "The Work") allows us to see the uninvestigated beliefs that caused us so much pain, without blame or guilt.

We can gauge the degree of our Trust by observing how we have improved in the areas of perception and taking things personally. As we progress, we will find we become more loving and impersonal and less selfish and judgmental. Increased Peace and Joy will always be the result of this fundamental change.

An Impersonal View

What do we think of when we mention the word "impersonal"? Most of us would probably equate the word with terms such as detached, cold, aloof, and heartless. Yet, the true meaning of the word "impersonal" is quite the opposite.

Today, people are obsessed with being special, unique, famous, the best, young, and so on. This sense of specialness we seek is a trap to lure us into separation, into believing that we are all different and therefore special. It is a ploy to segregate ego-reality into classes of superiority, mediocrity, and inferiority and everything in between, and it is another reason why the ego-self always judges wrongly. We judge ourselves, others, situations, the past, and the future, keeping ourselves trapped in limitation and separation, the confines of time and space.

The ego-self desires to be special and to be the author of reality. Its fuel is its belief and devotion to the personal. It administers dictatorial control by manipulating our lives and our reactions to reality. The meaning of the word "personal" in ego-self terms includes separate, different, unique, inferior, superior, exclusive, mine, and yours. If we perceive someone's behavior as being offensive and we take it personally (as an attack on us) instead of seeing it as a call for love, we immediately judge the person, dislike (condemn) them for it, and become defensive (counterattack) as a way of punishing them. To take anything personally places us in a small and dark world where the endless cycle of separation, judgment, and retribution follows us like a fearsome shadow.

The *true* meaning of "impersonal" is inclusive, whole, undivided, loving, without judgment, accepting, allowing, expansive, and extending. When we learn to accept life without judgment, without taking things personally, we become more objective and less critical. Embracing the impersonal allows us to step back and observe the overall plan of the Universal Order unfold. In this space, we release our self-centered impulses and maintain our equilibrium, even amidst chaos and confusion. We uphold an unyielding stability that is self-supporting and thoroughly dependable for others who may need our help.

Temptation to Deny and Avoid

Probably one of our greatest temptations during the first and second stages is to deny and avoid. Because this new thought system is one of opening up and uniting, our ego-self feels imminently threatened when we choose to face everything and avoid nothing.

The ego-self strives for separation, while the Unified Self longs for Oneness and Wholeness. When we begin to embrace Wholeness (Liberation) and reveal the ego-self's deceptions, we most likely will experience a backlash of fear. That is because the ego-self feels threatened by this initial investigation and so resists it by using fear against us. The last thing the ego-self wants us to discover when we look into our own minds is guiltlessness (sinlessness), because that would signal its demise.

An inevitable part of this whole process is arriving at a point where we begin to see just how much we have projected and denied. We squirm when we discover the extent of our ego-self's addiction to projecting our own unconscious guilt onto others. This we wish to obscure from our awareness. However, our real and pressing challenge is to do the exact opposite, to offer all of it to the Universal Inspiration for reinterpretation. By turning over all our mistakes to the Universal Inspiration, we learn Trust, and we grow to realize that *sin never did exist* except within the ego-self's delusional belief system with its attraction to guilt.

It is here where we are tested once again to make a decision to either cling to our separated state, giving renewed life to our ego-self, or courageously surrender our darkest fears to the brilliant illumination of Truth. Liberation comes when we dare to investigate what motivates us to make the choices we make. Often we are appalled at what we find and want to avoid or deny our ownership of it. True freedom lies in our disciplined decision to expose the layers of concealed deception that have previously been responsible for causing all the chaos in our life.

One of the most important things to remember when tempted

to deny or avoid is the depth of commitment we have made to fully and wholeheartedly embrace Truth. If our passionate intention is for ultimate freedom, which is Peace, then we owe it to ourselves to be consciously alert to any impulse to delay our progress with avoidance or denial tactics. Only then can we constructively observe our inner reactions and uncover the deceitful urge behind them. None of this is meant to shame or blame us. The usual response on discovering our own projections and fears is one of self-blame. It doesn't occur to us that we are just shifting the blame from outside to inside, which is just as destructive.

Taking full responsibility for ourselves, our perception, and our reality is a giant leap away from the ego-self's compulsive blame but unfortunately entails a period of an increased sense of *self*-guilt. This is really all the guilt that we have unconsciously projected outside onto others for so long. This new shift in consciousness helps us withdraw our blame from externals so that we stop seeing others as guilty. But as we begin to withdraw judgment from outside, we suddenly become aware of it in ourselves. The purpose of exposing it is so that we can finally heal it. This part of the process, then, is geared to exposing and eliminating the destructive aspects of our split mind. Remember, the thought and emotions of guilt can only have the meaning we give it. *Any guilt we may feel is not real.* To summarize: Sin is not real. Guilt is not real. Fear is not real.

Moving Out of Stage 2: "You Will See It When You Believe It"

The secret to moving onwards from the second stage is faith and willingness. We will be faced with situations that seemingly justify defense. However, our commitment calls for us still to offer the gift of Peace. This period in our journey calls for us to practice Quantum Forgiveness, overlooking error, despite the fact that people and circumstances may seem threatening. We will never gain Trust until we put *A Course in Miracles* principles into play. So, at this stage, we will be practicing forgiveness, even though much of the time we will not feel very forgiving. We get to practice the extension dynamic without the ego's investment in an outcome. This will be challenging at first because this concept is alien to the ego and in direct opposition to its values. Faith and willingness are the key qualities that we learn to apply, and through the actual practice of this dynamic, we will see its evidence in our daily lives. We learn now that, by consistently applying the forgiveness principle, "...the miracle will justify your faith in it,..."[96] as *A Course in Miracles* promises. Increasing inner Peace, Joy, and relief become more regular experiences for us as we develop our Trust through willingness.

As we demonstrate Love, Peace, forgiveness, and giving, we encounter these gifts from others in return, even in what previously may have seemed like hopelessly irreversible situations. At this stage, we have embraced the idea of Optimal Reality and prefer it to the confines of ego-reality. Now when we act, we choose more and more to act from the place of our Unified Self. We have made a decision to be free of the inner conflict between two opposing thought systems by largely adopting the one for Truth.

Contemplation and Meditation

Right-mindedness becomes easier as we naturally spend more time in the present moment. The ego-release process is one by which we undo the dysfunctional layering that we gathered throughout our life. Cultivating mindful now-moment awareness helps us to detach ourselves from the ego's compulsive thought and emotion cycles. Thinking comes from a sense of lack, and its purpose is to *gain*, but because our Unified Self is Whole and cannot perceive lack, there are no questions, answers, or needs that are not fulfilled by this One Self.

One of the most beneficial practices for stilling the mind is meditation. Through it, we free our mind, developing awareness and acceptance of *what is*. As we practice this exercise, we let go of fear, guilt, judgment, and the incessant need to control and to know. Time, thought, emotion, having, getting, and becoming all recede rapidly as we embrace the peace of meditation. In this spacious silence, we know we are safe. Only in the present moment can we hear and feel the call or instruction of the Unified Self.

During meditation, we learn to discipline the mind and allow our attention to become quietly aware and perfectly alert. Contemplation, on the other hand, can be accessed at any moment and does not require us to be still, or seated, or have our eyes closed. It is simply being present and observing our thoughts and the circumstances that surround us at that time. Being the mindful watcher, we are acutely present, yet not absorbed in thought. Contemplation is the act of being consciously present in whatever we are doing, wherever we may be. Here is what Dr. David Hawkins has to say about contemplation in his book *The Eye of the I*:

> Contemplation: This is the most fruitful and meaningful activity of spiritual work. With every little practice, one can acquire the capacity to function in the world with only minor interruption of reflection and contemplation. Meditation as it is usually practiced, however, is limited in time and place and often involves seclusion and cessation of activity. Although contemplation and reflection seem less intense, actually, by their constant influence, they wear away the obstacles. Contemplation is therefore a mode of meditation that is not lesser or inferior to sit-down, cross-legged meditation.[97]

Generally speaking, our minds act in two parts: one is "thinking" and the other is "awareness." The thinking part uses logic, thought, language, and reason, and it works in a linear manner, forming its own conclusions by which it defines itself and the world. It can only know *about* something or someone; it can never intrinsically *know*. The part of our mind that is "awareness" (the Unified Self) is peripherally aware of *all*, all at once, all the time. It operates beyond time and space. This awareness is limitless and inclusive. It has no need to learn or to know about anything because it inherently *knows*. This is that quiet and alert mind we learn to access more readily as we travel through the stages in the development of Trust. Consistent meditation and/or contemplation are useful practices for us to experience once again our original knowledge of absolute Wholeness and inter-connectedness.

Stage 3: A Period of Relinquishment

During the first two stages, we experience the most difficult of all adjustments: abruptly shifting to an entirely different thought system. This initial phase seems to escalate our inner conflict instead of soothing it. But in moving to the third stage, we begin to travel away from conflict and steadily towards Peace. Now we establish that we prefer to act from our Unified Self, but we are not totally convinced because we still see and act from the ego-self in some cases. There is still a significant portion of our unconscious self invested in ego-reality, and this stage presents us with opportunities to both recognize and say "no" to ego perception.

A Course in Miracles, Manual for Teachers speaks of this stage as follows:

> If this is interpreted as giving up the desirable, it will engender enormous conflict. Few teachers of God escape this distress entirely. There is, however, no point in sorting out the valuable from the valueless unless the next obvious step is taken. Therefore, the period of overlap is apt to be one in

which the teacher of God feels called upon to sacrifice his own best interests on behalf of Truth. He has not realized as yet how wholly impossible such a demand would be. He can learn this only as he actually does give up the valueless. Through this, he learns that where he anticipated grief, he finds a happy lightheartedness instead; where he thought something was asked of him, he finds a gift bestowed on him.[98]

The Tree of Judgment

Nearly all our judgments come from the ego-self. Every decision we make in each moment, ranging all the way from what to watch on television to whom we will marry, emerges from the original seed of ego. And the first shoot to appear quickly spreads the inherently destructive fronds of belief in guilt and fear that come from the seed of separation.

All the ego wants, at its deepest core, is guilt and fear. This is what it desires for us and what it searches for while we are oblivious to its unconscious intent on our destruction. We wonder why there is so much chaos in our lives! So much disappointment and inconsistent bouts of happiness interspersed with sadness and despair! The reason is because we are unknowingly being directed by the dysfunctional ego whose very existence depends upon the regular sustenance of both guilt and fear. For most of us old enough to read this book, the first delicate young shoot of guilt and fear has by now developed into a great, monstrous tree with thousands of branches and a mammoth hulk of a trunk. When we look at it this way, we can imagine the size of the ego's root system!

The ego's foundational belief that sin is real and justifies punishment is the basis for its heavy investment in fear, guilt, and judgment. If we were to embrace the truth that *there is no sin*—that every mistake is always caused by one error, which is purely "a call for love"—then we would have no guilt! And having no guilt to project onto others would mean that we would have no fear.

Fear follows guilt and judgment. This is a fact. And because the ego's livelihood depends on judgment to reinforce its guilt, the last thing the ego ever relinquishes is its addiction to judgment. If there is no guilt and no judgment, there is no fear, and this *is* the end of the dysfunctional ego. It is important for us to realize that the ego casts judgment for the express purpose of reinforcing our own unconscious guilt. We think that by seeing others as guilty, we ourselves will be less guilty. This is the upside-down thinking of the ego, always deluding us into believing in separation.

When we believe that we rejected The Source (which we think we did at the time of the separation), our mind wants to "...deny itself, and escape the penalty of denial."[99] By punishing someone else, it then assumes that it will escape retribution. This is the very foundation of the reason we think we need to judge. Judging is the fuel, and our sense of separateness is the fire.

We unconsciously accept judgment as an everyday necessity when, in fact, it is a deleterious preoccupation. Just imagine if we did not judge, if we willingly relinquished judgment. What would we be giving up? We would be releasing all our grievances, anger, frustration, and despair. All our guilt, conflict, anxiety, loneliness, and emptiness would vanish.

The bottom line is that our urge to judge comes from an insane source. The ego-self does not know...

...who it is;

...why it is;

...where it is;

...how it is; or

...what its purpose is.

How can it possibly judge anything or anyone sanely? Obviously not just some but all our beliefs, assumptions, and values will require transformation if we are to find Liberation. Right here and now, we have every manner of assistance possible to help us disentangle our erroneous beliefs. It's called Reality. Whatever and whoever is present in our lives now, no matter how seemingly irritating or fearsome, is the perfect catalyst for us to begin and continue to learn to love *what is* (accept reality). If it is love, understanding, and acceptance we want, we must first encourage acceptance within and without. In fact, anyone or anything that causes us anxiety or distress provides a perfect opportunity for us to investigate the thinking behind our judgment or belief.

We judge in order to separate ourselves. The ego creates grievances in order to reinforce fragmentation. What the ego does not realize is that in truth, we are not separate. We are all one, dreaming an illusory experience of separation. Realizing this, it becomes evident that when we judge or attack another, we attack ourselves. If we judge another, it is always the projection of our self-judgment. What we abhor in another is really a projected image of our own guilt. When we do the questions in Katie's "The Work," we come to the final turnaround, where we often see clearly that our misery was caused solely by our faulty beliefs. There is no blame, no guilt, only crystal-clear clarity and a sense of real liberation.

The ego separation cycle (Figure 6.2) emanates from fear, control, and guilt. Most of our desires, including the desire to *become*, are born from the ego's original dysfunctional perception of fear, control, and guilt. The consequences of this are disempowering thoughts and emotions, the desire to judge or attack, and giving to get. These lead to conflict, dependency, addictions, and special relationships. This cycle will continue until we willingly recognize, acknowledge, and release the ego's control and embrace the Unified Self.

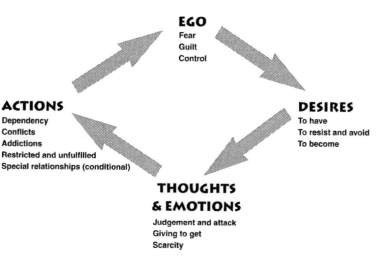

Figure 6.2: The Ego Cycle

Relinquish Judgment

During this stage, we slowly learn that the two opposing thought systems, that of the ego-self and that of the Unified Self, cannot co-exist in our minds. We have to make a clear choice for one over the other, and that means really understanding and practicing that, "...attack [judgment] cannot *be* justified."[100] We are, at this stage, likely to refrain from judgment/attack if the seeming confrontation is not too personal. However, we may occasionally "lose it" when we are greatly challenged. If this happens, as soon as possible, call for right-mindedness and realize that we are learning to relinquish attack one hundred percent across the board, not just most of the time.

The most thorough way to grasp this lesson is to physically, mentally, and emotionally practice it. "To have peace, teach peace to learn it."[101] To be convinced of this, we must practice it. As we demonstrate Peace we in fact teach it, and in teaching this way, we learn this truth congruently.

Quantum Forgiveness and Responsibility

Relinquishing judgment means practicing forgiveness. Remember to implement the PIQ formula (Presence–Inquiry–Quantum Forgiveness). Some ways to do this are to:

(1) *See past the ego of the other person.* If you see conflict, see it only as *a mistake caused by an ego* (not real). If you see this mistake as real, you yourself have momentarily lost your sanity and you have then validated the illusion. The truth here, in this dream, is that this other person is really you and is giving you the opportunity to heal your unconscious guilt.

> You're not really there. If I think you are guilty or the cause of the problem, and if I made you up, then the imagined guilt and fear must be in me. Since the separation from God never occurred, I forgive 'both' of us for what we haven't really done. Now there is only innocence and I join with the Holy Spirit [Universal Inspiration] in peace.[102]

(2) *Remember that any attack is purely misguided and a call for love.* This is a plea to you for right-mindedness and the offering of Peace. It is a gift of an opportunity for you to choose Love and Peace instead of chaos and illusion.

(3) *Accept reality just is as it is.* Realize that everything in your life, no matter how external it seems, is as it is. The only real control you have is to realize that, "I am responsible for what I see," and "I choose the feelings I experience, and I decide upon the goal I would achieve."[103]

We are learning that our thinking and beliefs are the cause and the world is the effect, not the other way around. This means we are realizing the vital importance of our thinking. We remember to regularly watch our thoughts and our physical and emotional reactions. If we experience a loss of Peace, we quickly remind ourselves that nothing outside us can hurt us.

The Unified Self

We make thousands of decisions every day, some so tiny that we are not even aware of them. A large part of this liberation process involves learning exactly which of our two inner voices is the one to trust. As discussed in Chapter 3 ("Intellect versus Intuition"), the ego speaks first and loudly. The Voice of our Unified Self speaks in a subtle whisper that quietly but steadfastly beckons us to consider its message. We are very conditioned to respond to the ego-voice, or feeling. Becoming skilled at hearing the Unified Self at first requires patience and a lot of practice. We unlearn to respond to internal and external stimuli by consciously tuning in to the quiet voice, urge, or feeling within. Say, for instance, you get a phone call on your day off from work and a close friend spontaneously asks you to accompany her on an afternoon excursion. Inner conflict flares because you had visualized this day as one where you would do what you really love to do. What happens next? Which of the possible choices should you make? Wouldn't it be best to choose the outcome that feels most peaceful? Take a few moments to mentally visualize yourself in each of the scenarios. In each one, ask yourself, does this feel right? Does this feel peaceful? Usually through this simple exercise you will hear and heed the Voice of your Unified Self.

Complications occur, however, when there is hidden guilt or an agenda underlying the making of a decision. If you find yourself reasoning that your friend owes you a favor or you owe your friend in some way, the ego is speaking. Any signs of bargaining, guilt, frustration, anger, or upset are definite indicators that some inner work is required.

Making Headway

Since our initial turning point and decision to find "a better way," and the difficult journey through the first and second stages, we have come a long way. Although we are still in the preliminary phase, our consciousness has shifted significantly. Before, we may have felt "punch-drunk" from all the movement and changes, mostly internal, that we needed to accommodate. The difference now is that we are far more conscious of our inner choices and prefer to respond to our Unified Self rather than the ego-self. We are beginning to really value the Universal Inspiration in us more than before. Trust is developing. By the time we hit the point where we truly prefer to consistently hear and respond to the Unified Self, then we approach the halfway mark and our commitment to our goal becomes more harmonious.

Around this time, we will begin to experience a deepening understanding of how the ego thought system works and its purpose. The goal of this stage is to reveal hidden aspects of ego and to seek out the core of its beliefs. This is where the fundamental change in our allegiance will occur.

What generally occurs during this phase is the gradual discovery of our own unique layers of ego dysfunction. First we will begin to see many of our unquestioned beliefs being raised and undone, while new insights will replace them. However, as we journey toward the center of the ego's thought system, our entire value system will be exhumed, and this can be quite uncomfortable. We will be astonished at just how devious and elusive the ego can be, and the process will evoke all kinds of emotional reactions, especially when we get closer to the ego's core.

All thoughts of anger, fear, rage, and frustration are now products of an assortment of various problems. The ego bamboozles us with its insane confusing complexity. We learn through facing our own ego-illusions that our myriad problems gradually undergo a distilling process whereby we eventually recognize that there is, and always was, only one dilemma, and it is the sole obstacle to the presence of Peace and Love in our life:

the separation, or, more accurately, our *belief* in the separation. Over time, we see that we would do well not to deny or avoid whatever seems to press our ego's buttons. As a matter of fact, we would do well to welcome those moments! For if we experience that familiar loss of Peace, we can look to it as an immediate sign that we still have work to do in undoing the ego's belief in separation. Discomfort then becomes an opportunity and freedom one step closer.

Every time we become aware of loss of Peace, simply ask for right-minded thought to return to our mind. The Universal Inspiration never fails to respond to a heartfelt request for Oneness, Peace, and sanity.

What We Truly Want

We have come to the point in our journey where we might ask ourselves: Do we fully appreciate, accept, and understand that The Source's Will and our will are the same? If at this stage we are not sure, perhaps we don't know our own will and do not yet know what we really want.

We began this journey by learning that we did not want the ego and its endless attack, guilt, and confusion, and that we did want Peace, Love, and Wholeness. We are learning to appreciate, accept, and understand Love and the security it brings. Although this means exposing the ugliness of our ego's workings, we now value its undoing.

At this point we are quickly embracing the idea that the Unified Self with its endless Peace is not just what we want, but that it is the very reason for our existence! Here we reevaluate what we have been accustomed to choosing instead of Peace (to be right? to get? to win? to distract? to defend? to judge?). We make the conscious decision for Peace first. We give Peace and receive it, and as we share it, we experience it. Although our Peace is not consistent yet, we desire to live more fully in that state of serenity. Here, we desire Peace more often, but there are instances where we still perceive that judgment or anger are justified. We will find that there seem to be things that the ego wants more than Peace. And it won't be until we associate suffering with *every* instance of non-peace that we will make a wholehearted commitment to ensure that Peace is *all* we want.

As we travel along this path, we are faced with the realization that what we always thought we wanted is not really true. We come to see with increasing clarity that the only thing we want and the solution to every seeming problem is Truth, which is Peace. Here we receive first-hand insights revealing that there is One Perfect Will and that our purpose and joy are increased in each moment as we recognize that Will as our own.

At the same time that we are gathering momentum in learning to Trust, we may also be discovering more previously hidden aspects of the ego than we realized existed. This can be disturbing until we willingly join in the search to weed out the ego's specialness in ourselves. As we see the benefits of doing this work, we are able to lessen our resistance. This is a powerful time where our new-found strength of Self enables us to relax our responses to the ego when its ugliness is exposed. The ego gains strength when we react to it as a real threat. This makes it feel significant and invincible. As we gain inner strength, we can look upon the ego's outbursts with increasing humor. We often see through its meager attempts to gain ascendancy and see the funny side of its ridiculous antics. We are learning not to give the ego the satisfaction of making any fear, anger, or judgment real for us.

If we make Liberation, Peace, Love, and Joy our foremost goal, we dethrone our ego. The ego's needs are not our priority any more because our attention and focus are wholeheartedly on keeping a state of right-mindedness. When we shift to that space of right-mindedness and now-moment awareness, without recrimination or judgment, we become acutely aware that all things, people, and circumstances are in right relationship with each other. There is no "good" or "bad." It just is. We become increasingly conscious that a Higher Intelligence is directing everything, including ourselves. When our focus is withdrawn from feeding and defending the ego every minute of each day, we receive the gift of Trust. Our Trust develops as we learn there is only One Will and that we will always be unhappy until we share and recognize that Will as our own Unified Will.

The Decision

We have come to the point in our journey that *A Course in Miracles* refers to as "The Branching of The Road."[104] Up until this point, we have journeyed toward Peace, while encountering some serious inner conflict along the way. Our conflict, of course, was generated by still entertaining some ego illusions while being chiefly focused on attaining Wholeness. However, the two goals, that of Wholeness and Oneness and that of the ego's state of separation, are mutually incompatible. Therefore, this is the point at which we must make a renewed, wholehearted commitment to Truth as the Unified Self, through the Universal Inspiration's guidance. Here we are faced with a decision in light of all that we have learned. In truth, the decision has already been made, but sometimes we choose to stagger or hold up the process by searching for a bypass (see Figure 6.3). This will often manifest as the ego's last stand in its search for specialness, which is separation. It knows its existence is at stake and will pull out all stops to ensure its survival. At this point in its game, it could play an ace, a core deep-seated issue or belief that will rock our new confidence. These are the ego's last tricks to keep us trapped in the ego-separation cycle (Figure 6.2) and avoiding the present and ultimate decision, which is to commit fully and unequivocally to Truth. We cannot, at this point, go back; all we can do is go forward, fully pledged to Truth, or decide to stall a while and endure more of the ego's conflicting turmoil. If we do opt for the cycling, we can be sure we will experience some very uncomfortable and painful lessons, all of which are geared to contrast ego-self and Unified Self. We will, due to the intensity of discomfort, eventually seek refuge and visit once again the branching of the road, where, this time, our sanity makes the single choice for Liberation without further delay.

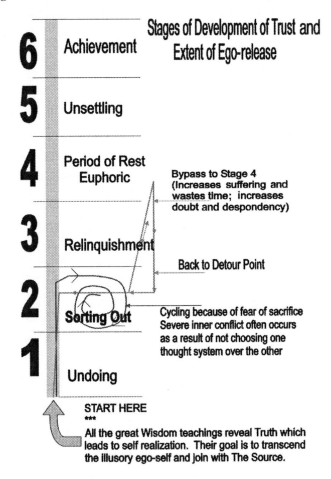

Figure 6.3: Temptation to Cycle and Bypass

Liberation comes from integrating our spirituality into our lives through the choices we make. It comes when we can no longer live in conflict, with one spiritual code of ethics for one aspect of our lives and the everyday rules of ego for another. For example, the competitive business person who is at the same time a loving family person becomes a recipe for inner and eventually outer conflict and ill health.

True and lasting Peace emerges from making a wholehearted commitment to living every area of our life from the mind-set of the one sane choice, that is, Truth. Ego-release demolishes the ego's obsession with compartmentalizing ideas as worthy or not worthy, valuable and not valuable. We hear again from Adyashanti (*Emptiness Dancing*):

> Throw your life into Truth. Don't try to stuff Truth into your life.[105]

About arriving at the fork in the road, *A Course in Miracles* states,

> When you come to the place where the branch in the road is quite apparent, you cannot go ahead [as previously, with *both* ego and Unified Self, in conflict]. You must go either one way or the other. For now if you go straight ahead, the way you went before you reached the branch, you will go nowhere [except re-enter painful lessons]. The whole purpose of coming this far was to decide which branch you will take now.[106]

We will recognize this point in the road when we reach it. And upon making the only valuable choice to be made, we are then ready to enter the last half of our journey Home.

Without the inner conflict of two opposing thought systems, our decision to seek our Unified Goal brings great peace and gratitude. Because we are now wholeheartedly committed to Peace and rebuking conflict, we find the way becoming gentler and easier. It is here where we clearly see the stark emptiness of the ego's happiness that we once believed we needed, a type of happiness that was always under threat of loss or change and seemed to come from outside of us. And with this new appreciation of unchanging happiness comes a sense of security and safety that we have never previously encountered. A profound sense of interconnectedness and Higher Order permeates our resplendent happiness. Again, from *A Course in Miracles*:

> The escape from darkness involves two stages: First, the recognition that darkness cannot hide. This step usually entails fear [the first three stages]. Second, the recognition that there is nothing you want to hide even if you could. This step brings escape from fear. When you have become willing to hide nothing, you will not only be willing to enter into communion but will also understand peace and joy [giving peace, extending Love by giving].[107]

Stage 4: Settling Down

Of the six stages in the development of Trust, only two are defined mostly as peaceful and joyful. They are the fourth and sixth stages, where we quite literally join with Love, Peace, and Joy, and our lives are fully transformed. We take a well-deserved rest on arrival at the fourth stage. One of the greatest blessings we now recognize is that previously valued relationships, possessions, and beliefs, which have now undergone change or loss, are not perceived as having been sacrificed. Quite the opposite is true: We look back, and we not only see that what we previously valued before has no value at all—therefore, nothing was lost!—but we also see that all changes were necessary and helpful learning opportunities, and the legacy they left behind for us is an ever-increasing bounty of happiness. As we review the past, we come to realize that the difficult challenges we faced and changes that have occurred so far have helped us dis-identify with ego, and we are greatly relieved and deeply grateful for the new insights that are leading us to Truth. Our Trust in the unfailing presence and guidance of the Universal Inspiration is strengthened, and we are confident that our future progress, too, will be testament to the faith we have developed.

We have now entered a period characterized by a state of sheer Joy in many respects because we have made a united decision for Truth, and we recognize that only we have the power to make it happen. We will see things now so clearly that fear and doubt appear to be words from the distant past. Being able to grasp and appreciate the enormous leap that we have made, we see the world anew, with pristine vision devoid of the veil of ego. Our newfound Peace gives way to many valuable insights, and perhaps a welcome flood of creative inspiration flows through us. We endured the suffering caused by the first three stages of unlearning and thus disempowering our ego: undoing; sorting out; and relinquishing. After all that upheaval, we can certainly be forgiven if we have the slightest hope that we have now arrived at our final destination of awakened consciousness without further opposition.

The goal of the first half of this journey was to reveal and remove the blocks to the awareness of Love's presence, which is Truth. This second half, without the intense inner conflict, reveals the face of Love we so yearned to see in ourselves and others. The Source emanates in all that we do, all whom we meet, and all that we experience.

A Course in Miracles explains that the fourth stage is really a rest station—the last one—and there is still a long way to go:

> ...he sees in it his whole way out. "Give up what you do not want, and keep what you do."...He has not yet come as far as he thinks.[108]

Gathering Mighty Companions

Thus, as we progress through the fourth stage, we realize there is still much more to do, but we recommence now with a mind at peace within itself. We are encouraged and comforted with these words from *A Course in Miracles*:

> Yet when he is ready to go on, he goes with *mighty companions* beside him. Now he rests a while, and gathers them before going on. He will not go on from here alone.[109] [italics ours]

It seems that at this stage, we enter into the Unified (Holy) Relationship and we travel on from here, together, hand in hand, mutually committed to one goal, the Unified Goal. We will develop relationships—"mighty companions"—with others committed to the truth. Mutual support and the shared Unified Goal will create a life-long foundation from which we will manifest all manner of abundance. Another correct interpretation of our "mighty companions" would be that they are the Universal Inspiration and Quantum Forgiveness. As far as the authors are concerned, each of us will recognize our mighty companions emerging in the perfect form for us at the time.

As mentioned earlier, at this stage in evolution our fastest and surest route to awakening fully to Love's presence is through the Unified Relationship. This is the answer to global awakening and the literal realization of the Infinite State (Heaven) on earth. Again from Adyashanti:

> When you liberate yourself, it's not just your self, it is *the* Self that is liberated. You're remembering everybody's Self because it's the same Self. When this is realized, it enables the total transformation of human interaction.[110]

Spiritual Seeking and Truth

Is there a difference between spiritual seeking and surrendering to Truth? When we actively set about to seek spirituality, our primary goal is the experience of a spiritual "high" that will some day grow from being an occasional "high" to a consistent one. This is what many think enlightenment is—an experience that we search for and hopefully, one day, we find and keep. We think we can *acquire* it with practice, discipline, and accumulated knowledge on the subject. The problem with this perception of spiritual seeking is:

- *Who* is doing the seeking? The ego or the Unified Self? The Unified Self is Whole and Infinitely interconnected; it needs no result, knowledge, training, or seeking. On the other hand, the ego thrives on seeking, especially for enlightened or spiritual "highs," anything *but* the truth, which will reveal and demolish the ego.
- The idea of seeking often carries with it an expectation of achieving something that is outside oneself, is in the future, and is an experience with spiritual value, rather than revealing the truth of *what is*.

We can get hooked on spiritual experiences, or spiritual "highs"; then we fall flat again once they recede. Getting addicted to achieving spiritual experiences is not liberation and will rarely take us to Truth. Occasionally, the euphoric experiences often felt in the fourth stage in the development-of-Trust process can be addictive. That is why it is important to stay forever focused on asking for Truth rather than seeking an experience. It, too, is an illusion.

We do not yet know who we are or what our true purpose is. Looking for an experience called enlightenment is not really going to take us there. What we really need to ask for and look at is Truth. Truth is beyond any *experience* because it reveals the Infinite Love that we already are. Seeking spiritual experiences implies that we need to *acquire* something in order to *become* more spiritually advanced. "Acquiring" is a nice way of saying *getting*, and to *become* is a soft way of saying you're not there yet (not now, but perhaps in the future). Both meanings come from ego perception and therefore are not real. The ego cleverly attempts to mask itself as the Universal Inspiration and with its navigational skill steers us everywhere but to the ego's hiding place. All this is executed in the name of spiritual seeking.

When we think of the word "enlightenment," we tend to associate it with a process that involves persistent seeking, improving, and learning. Many present-day teachings paint a rather future-oriented view of Self-realization that focuses on achieving spiritual experiences, deeper meditation, blissful states, and more spiritual knowledge. Often included in spiritual workshops are techniques to enrich our lives, along with information on how to "know" ourselves more deeply, how to fix what is mere illusion, and how to live fearlessly without getting at the cause of the fear. While all this information is positively geared toward helping us connect with our higher nature and purpose and to make us happy, it will not, of itself, bring enlightenment. Nor will it bring abiding happiness.

If we are intent on Self-realization, or enlightenment, it is important to ask ourselves consistently: Just "who" is the one that thinks it needs more knowledge and improvement? It must be our mistaken identity, the ego.

"Enlightenment is a demolition project."[111] [italics ours] We cannot uncover it without dismantling everything we think we know. It is about unlearning everything that keeps us tied into believing we must maintain control. Ego-release requires the removal of *every* block to the awareness of Love's presence that inhibits us from experiencing and knowing Love, Peace, Joy, and abundance. This is our identity and our purpose.

There is only here and now. *The Unified Self is already enlightened; everyone is.* This is not a state or experience to accomplish through external searching or internal improvement. There is nothing to search for or improve upon. The most difficult challenge we can possibly face is the act of surrender, the unconditional acceptance of *what is*. This is releasing control. This is the ultimate humility born from the truthful acknowledgment of not-knowing.

Truth reveals itself when we surrender the obstacles that obscure its presence. Truth is Love. The one obstacle to our knowing Love, and therefore Truth, is our accepted identity, or rather *mis*-identity, the ego. The way to remembering *who* we are is through the truth behind our having forgotten when we fell asleep and began to dream. In other words, the journey Home is one of surrendering, undoing, and unlearning through ego-release.

Stage 5: Absolute Certainty via a Period of Unsettling

The fifth stage in the journey is likely to be a time of confusion and fatigue. The confusion generally comes from reexperiencing some of our earlier challenges, but this time with full awareness. It can be a type of *déjà vu* experience. This time around, however, we see things more clearly, with a new interpretation, and receive another opportunity to recognize, acknowledge, and act on Truth without the previous emotional attachments and upheavals that are characteristic of the first three stages. Unlike the fourth stage, where we felt totally connected, the fifth stage can be a lonely place in terms of our connection with The Source. We have learned so much; yet we still yearn for the elusive connectedness that we experienced in the fourth stage. We remember how real and strong our connection to the Infinite State was, but for some strange reason, we just cannot capture it now.

This can be a period where a sense of both passion and direction ebb, leaving us in a quandary, not knowing anything except for what we do not want. We arrive at a state where the old ways are gone, but the new level of consciousness has not yet fully manifested. This period might be experienced as feeling as though you are in suspended animation.

The first three stages were spent cleansing our perception in order to *see* reality, and we peeled away the remnants of illusion. Then in stage four, we got to *be* that Reality. So, most of the unsettling we experience in this stage is in learning to surrender the *doing* to finally embrace *being*, because our final surrender will be to the Infinite Knowledge within, that we *are* and *have* everything, always.

Lessons that may accompany this transition period, where we still move from *seeing* to *being* the Unified Self, revolve around our external circumstances. Having come through the first four stages, we may be left with some worldly hangovers, as in the legacy of loss or transition in areas such as finances, career, relationships, and health. For example, the collapse of a career that may have occurred in stage one, perhaps leading us to find our true vocation and creativity, may temporarily cause financial hardship all the way through to stage five. Sometimes our everyday practical life will reflect bare simplicity at this stage. However, there is no resentment because we have truly learned the value of simplicity. In fact, we openly choose simplicity over complexity. After all, the ego is all about complexity.

If upon entering the fifth stage we find that our living circumstances are out of synch with the level of our spiritual awareness, this is never to be misunderstood as scarcity. There is no scarcity, only endless abundance. However, we may be tempted once again to fall back into the ego's version of lack or scarcity within the dream. Thoughts of lack will cause fear; fear makes us compromise, and compromise leads to sacrifice. For example, fear may present as financial insecurity. Feeling the fear of lack as real, our ego will strike a bargain and tell us that we can work in adverse conditions in order to regain financial security. This is how the ego maintains its cycle of fear, by seeing lack where in reality there is an abundance of what is real.

At this stage we may find that we have for the most part

reached an inner state of Optimal Reality, but our outer worldly reality has not yet caught up. Remember, to love *what is* means you know that nothing is wrong. *What is* is perfect. Often it is simply that yet another *contrast* is occurring to teach us and reinforce what we have already learned. We are being presented with wonderful opportunities to overlook seeming scarcity, and with Absolute Certainty see the only Truth there can be, which is that our outer reality will soon reflect our inner abundance. Be patient, because now we need to internally implement the principles we learned through stages one through four. This is where we learn to have Absolute Certainty in the Universal Order of things. Everything occurs in perfect timing; timing is The Source's business, not ours. Our business is perfect faith — Absolute Certainty.

The fifth stage usually takes a long time. There are still many lessons to learn and much consolidation to be done. Whereas the first four stages required reform and action on our part, here we are challenged to act *only* when the Universal Inspiration instructs us. We may find our initiatives not yielding any results. The purpose of this is to teach us how to let go of control and allow Higher Guidance to lead us.

Any resistance on the part of our ego will thwart our ability to access this wonderful perception and state of Love. Resistance comes in the form of temptation to judge and control independently (with the ego) without consulting the Universal Inspiration. This period gives us the opportunity to become a specialist at reviewing our thoughts and decisions. We train ourselves to prioritize in our decision-making, maintaining Peace as our number one goal, especially in times when we perceive attack or when we are tempted to indulge in the special relationship's bargaining cycle, giving to get. We question the deep intent behind all our decisions, even minor ones that may seem inconsequential. As we have learned by now that no thought is without consequences, we make sure to monitor our minds and protect our thoughts from any misinterpretations by calling on the Universal Inspiration for help.

Here we listen intently and we feel intuitively. Should any unexpected emergency arise, we are now prepared to quickly quiet both our own ego's panic and the panic of others by emanating a sense of Peace, calm, and certainty. We immediately counsel ourselves that *reality is* and we accept the fact that what is happening is as it is, allowing us to elicit Peace by not arguing with reality. In the event of an upsetting incident, we can offer much calm and insight because we will more than likely be the only person present (in the now moment) at the time. By the word "present," we mean not in the ego's fear-based past or future and not mentally dwelling in any one else's business but your own. When we are present, fully aware, conscious, and devoid of ego, we are in our Optimal State of Reality. From this state we can:

- access clear guidance from the Unified Self;
- maintain our Peace;
- help others effortlessly; and
- be instrumental in resolving any problematic situation most efficiently.

During this stage, we truly learn that there are no decisions we would want to make without first consulting our Inner Guide. And if pressured to make a decision that is not yet ready to be made, we quietly recognize and accept that the answer will come at the perfect time.

When interacting with others who still mistake their ego as themselves, we are exceptionally patient and clearly congruent as we share Truth. Truth is delivered without attack, judgment, or accusation. And, even if the receiver's ego interprets Truth as attack (which often happens), we offer no defense.

During this stage, we have grown accustomed to abdicating

most of our ego's control, and we are far more comfortable with the state of not-knowing than previously. However, there is still more relinquishing to be done if we are to truly embrace Liberation. We are called to surrender all ego control, and this brings up fear. The last vestige of ego is the concept of control, and the ego usually guards this piece of its identity through vehement denial.

Not-knowing brings up our worst fear, which is related to the idea of not-existing, and this equates to the fear of death. To the ego, loss of control, i.e., not-knowing, feels like death because if we were to abdicate control to the Universal Inspiration, the ego-self would no longer exist. Relinquishing the will to control means that the dysfunctional ego-self no longer exists. The ego resists not-knowing because that means death to itself. It is a type of death, even though nothing real dies.

We may ask, then, whether or not this ego "surrender," or letting go, happens when the body dies. The answer is "no." Adyashanti tells us that we could incarnate repeatedly over ten thousand lifetimes; yet, the ego would still maintain its will to control.[112]

What this signifies is that the ego's will to control survives even physical death; that is how persistently it wants to maintain control. We're not even free from it after death. If our earthly life goal is to find ultimate Liberation in Truth, then it seems logical to form the conclusion that our fundamental goal is *ego-release*. In a nutshell, undoing the ego is a basic prerequisite for elimination of the concept of a physical death. With the full release of this deluded thought system, we relinquish every fragment of the original guilt caused by the separation. This shockingly massive unconscious guilt is what caused our desire to hide from Truth, Love, and The Source in the first place. It is the fundamental driver that keeps us all locked in to the birth-and-death cycle. It is an absolute illusion. Why go through another thousand "lifetimes" of births, survival, suffering, and deaths when we could just as easily, at any moment, get this one ego-release over and done with?

To allow the Universal Inspiration to direct our lives and to unite with the Unified Will means to *live free from the will to control*. This is ego-relinquishment at its core and also the last issue of fear we will ever have because the root of fear is the will to control. The ego's great fear is of not existing, of death, of nothingness. That is why physical death poses such a threat, particularly to those who are not certain of an afterlife. The idea of not existing as "me as I know myself" is the absolute relinquishment of all control. If "me as I know myself" does not exist, then the ego no longer has anything to control. By the time we reach this stage, we grow to realize that the ego-will is full of holes and always lets us down when we identify with it. We have experienced enough of the Unified Will to trust that this is the only Will that consistently reveals Truth and the Infinite Love behind all seeming reality.

From Preference to Total Trust

During the first four stages, the predominant characteristics were reform and action. In the fifth stage, our most important characteristics are learning to lay all judgment aside (relinquishing the ego's need to control) and *being*. The unsettling we feel at this stage often comes from being accustomed to reform and action, but here we learn to exchange them for *being, allowing* (the now present), *accepting*, and *vigilance*. Here we learn to be so present as to hear or feel minute-to-minute guidance. Every choice we attempt to make on our own (the ego) must be relinquished to our Unified Self. This requires a focus on being in the now moment, no matter what we are doing or where we are. Vigilance is present-moment awareness, and through this practice we move from the reforming-and-action phase (the first four stages), to being a conduit through which we effortlessly express the Unified Will. The enormous energy that was required to sustain the illusory ego is now freed up to extend itself limitlessly and effortlessly through our Unified Self.

In the previous stages, we were accustomed to action and reform. Now we need to let go each instant to the instruction of the Universal Inspiration. We need not act from our own space any longer; we learn now that the Unified Will *is* our Will. The following is a description of the fifth stage from *A Course in Miracles*:

> The next stage is indeed a "period of unsettling." Now must the teacher of God understand that he did not really know what was valuable and what was valueless. All that he really learned so far was that he did not want the valueless, and that he did want the valuable. Yet his own sorting out was meaningless in teaching him the difference. The idea of sacrifice, so central to his own thought system, had made it impossible for him to judge. He thought he learned willingness, but now he sees that he does not know what the willingness is for. And now he must attain a state that may remain impossible to reach for a long, long time. He must learn to lay all judgment aside, and ask only what he really wants in every circumstance. Were not each step in this direction so heavily reinforced, it would be hard indeed![113]

The problem facing us now is that we still perceive sacrifice in withholding *all* judgment, control, and decision making and turning the entire process completely over to the Universal Inspiration. It is obvious that there are still some judgments and decisions that still remain to be relinquished—ones, however, that the ego prefers to keep. We still have lessons to learn about our way of sorting out the valuable and valueless.

To repeat from the quote above, "He thought he learned willingness, but now he sees that he does not know what the willingness is for." Yes, we did learn willingness: during the first four stages, we learned a great deal about increasing our willingness to prefer the new thought system. Again (as cited above), "And now he must attain a state that may remain impossible to reach for a long, long time." What will seem to take a long, long time can be shortened greatly by just *one* adjustment. Would you want to experience an unsettling state for any longer than is absolutely necessary? The one undeniable correction beckoning us on to Liberation is our single-minded commitment to surrender ourselves completely to, and have unwavering faith in, the Universal Inspiration. By going a step beyond conscious preference into a state of total surrender and Absolute Trust, we achieve complete right-mindedness. It means *absolute* right-mindedness with no preferences.

Once this decision is wholly made, it will be the final decision we ever make because from here on, our Unified Self is, indeed, without ego-limitations. The Universal Inspiration, expressing Itself through us, *is* our decision maker, and we struggle and control no more. Making this one commitment totally removes the last existing block to the awareness of Love's presence, and we literally become a conscious Co-creator, unrestricted by any previous thoughts or seeming reality.

We may take an exceedingly long period of time to learn to distinguish between the Voice of Truth and the voice of ego. Ultimately, however, we come to realize there is only one decision to make, and that is the choice for Truth, once and for all.

Put very simply, there is no hierarchy of illusion. At this stage, we realize that there is not one illusion left to which we assign greater value than the others just because it appears more true to our ego. We see that all illusions are the same: untrue.

> It is impossible that one illusion be less amenable to truth than are the rest. But it is possible that some are given greater value, and less willingly offered to truth for healing and for help. No illusion has any truth in it. Yet it appears some are

more true than others, although this clearly makes no sense at all. All that a hierarchy of illusions can show is preference, not reality. What relevance has preference to the truth? Illusions are illusions and are false.[114]

Vigilance

During the first two stages, we were faced with enormous conflict between thought systems, and the third stage still involved some conflict. However, during the fifth stage, our greatest challenge is to maintain conscious guard against any possible conflict or judgment that may threaten our inner Peace. At any point where we feel a loss of Peace, we immediately acknowledge it as a warning sign and implement right-mindedness accordingly. This is not difficult, nor does it require effort; it is simply a moment when we aim to go from consistent vigilance with our thoughts to a point where our auto-pilot takes over. Once on auto-pilot, we have no need to be wary of conflict or judgment because these will not be part of our consciousness anymore.

This stage involves healing, which is accomplished through our extension of Love and Quantum Forgiveness. Healing in this context means the correction of the fundamental error of our belief in separation and the recognition that all guilt, pain, illness, and depression come from this wrong-minded state. And so having come this far, we learn that our only function in this world is to help heal the minds of others. We will never be happy or feel complete unless we extend this Love to others. We become a welcomed mirror in which people see beautiful and innocent reflections of themselves instead of guilt, fear, and judgment.

We recognize that many others are still heavily sedated by living in the ego-dream, but we do not share their nightmare; instead we offer a Light of Truth by which to see a way to awakening. At this stage, we find that we not only desire meaning and connection in our lives, but that we *need* these attributes. We are embracing the principle that "giving is receiving," and we are familiar with the Joy and Trust that this dynamic instills in us. No longer are we content to separate; we actively seek to engage in extension with others through Love and forgiveness. We realize that, by nature of our newfound Peace, we become a healing impetus for all we involve ourselves with. And now we witness miracles that healing others heals us. There is no greater Joy to be had than this.

Possible Changes

When we are living mostly in Optimal Reality, a few natural adjustments may occur, all of which are highly beneficial. We usually find ourselves spending many moments in the now, because we no longer rely on the ego's preoccupation with time and thoughts of the past or future. We do not worry about what has just happened or what might be about to occur. We do not need to concern ourselves with what we need, what to buy, and how to get it. Every day in every way we meet each moment with complete responsibility and awareness, making sure we act on all instructions from our Unified Self. We know now that taking care of business means first listening and responding to the Unified Will (or intuitive feeling), and then any other practical issues that require attention will take care of themselves, effortlessly.

If we are faced with a disappointment, for example, if we had in mind a preferred outcome that did not happen, we immediately recognize the truth that there are no unsuccessful outcomes. We recognize that everyone we encounter is a blessing, even if in disguise. We fully know that everything that happens occurs for a reason, and we never argue with reality. We always appreciate any changes that come along. They all contain important lessons to be learned.

Our bodies, too, fall into alignment with right-mindedness. Gone is the ego's need for willpower and resistance in order to overcome bad habits like smoking, drinking, over-eating, poor nutrition, and lack of exercise. The natural progression is that our bad habits give us up, not the other way around. This process requires no effort or sacrifice, as right-mindedness calls the body to health. Our bodies become cleaner, clearer, lighter, and more refined, and tell us what we can and cannot tolerate. For example:

- If alcohol was never a problem, even in small proportions, it may nonetheless suddenly cause insomnia or heart palpitations, urging us to relinquish it altogether.
- We may find we can no longer tolerate some of the common foods that were not good for our bodies but which we nonetheless ate all our lives. Examples are wheat products, greasy foods, and dairy products.
- A lifetime of smoking can stop without notice and without causing uncomfortable symptoms of withdrawal.
- An addiction to meaningless distractions, such as television or video games, can disappear overnight.

We cultivate an exceptional appreciation of nature at this time. We find exquisite beauty and gratitude in the simplest of things in nature. The beauty we see in others and our surroundings often sends us into rapture. We are continually aware of any signs or opportunities being presented to us, and we act on them. We now know without a doubt that *all* our needs are fulfilled, and great Peace washes over us. Our lives are filled with simplicity and beauty, while complexity in any form is not a part of our reality.

We joyfully recognize that our Will always was, is, and ever shall be at one with the Universal Inspiration. Now that pristine perception is restored, our majestic vision beholds only Truth, Love, and beauty everywhere and in everyone, always.

Stage 6: A Period of Achievement

Once we have fully aligned with the Unified Will, the pathway becomes straight and effortless. From *A Course in Miracles:*

> Once you accept His plan as the one function that you would fulfill,...He will go before you making straight your path, and leaving in your way no stones to trip on, and no obstacles to bar your way. Nothing you need will be denied you. Not one seeming difficulty but will melt away before you reach it. You need take thought for nothing, careless of everything except the only purpose that you would fulfill.[115]

Our Unified Relationships are living instruments through which we bring healing to the entire world. At this stage, we are actively engaged in living the Truth as a limitless extension of Love, Peace, and Joy. We have joined in mind with others to share the only Purpose we were born to fulfill. This is a miraculous manifestation of the Joyful State that our ego had denied us for so long.

At this level of consciousness, the sense of "I," "me," "myself," and "mine" are overcome. There is no ego-self left to hold fixed and rigid positions on perception. Immense liberation is a by-product of relinquishing the finite self who perceives everything as separated. The ego, because of its fixation on duality, sets up a rigidity of perception that cannot avoid judging, controlling, and analyzing. It takes one aspect of seeming reality and selectively chooses to either favor or abhor it, refusing to see that to perceive from only one perspective is to deny that any other perspective exists. It would be like seeing a cup on a table with its handle and pattern out of view. From one perspective we see a plain cup with no handle, and the ego says, "This cup is plain and has no handle." On the other side of the table someone else views the cup from a different angle and says, "This cup has a handle and a pattern." The truth of the cup can never be appreciated through perceiving it from only one perspective, or even from many different perspectives. It is not until we accept that the cup is simply *what is*, *without* our own limited perception of it, that we can begin to appreciate it. In truth, the cup is 99.9% empty space masquerading as solid matter, and in the highest interpretation we do not even know what the cup is *for*. Likewise, every single person, place, object, and circumstance that we see with our eyes is not known by our limited self.

The ego views our identity as completely separate and has an addictive habit of seeing things from this extremely narrow, one-pointed fixed perspective. The "I" is seen as separate from everyone, everything and anything, and every circumstance. It evaluates from the perspective that it is separate: I like, I don't like, I see, I feel. The "I" sees itself as apart from all that it perceives.

What occurs in this final stage is that the "I" no longer perceives separation or lack or inequality. Perception has become inclusive, seeing everything as a part of everything else, without the slightest differentiation. Resistance in every form is over.

When the ego-self has been released, a profoundly expansive and integrated "witness" is fully revealed. This witness sees things multi-dimensionally without restrictions like judgment or resistance. This witness is our Unified Self. In this state, the unrivaled truth that the illusion of individuality causes all suffering dawns on us. Here we see that we are everything and everyone and they are us. The Universe is us and we are the Universe. What we look upon we are; what we are we look upon.

We see others as us and find our love for them is indiscriminate. We overlook the ego and are magnetized by the immense beauty of each soul we behold. We recognize that while most people are asleep in ego, their Unified Self is pure and unwavering Love, and we acknowledge that everyone will eventually awaken from the dream of limitation and separation.

Here is an insight of personal awakening (*Power vs. Force*, by Dr. David Hawkins):

> Everything and everyone in the world was luminous and exquisitely beautiful. All living things became radiant, and expressed this radiance in stillness and splendor. It was apparent that all of mankind is actually motivated by inner love, but has simply become unaware; most people live their lives as though they're sleepers unawakened to the perception of who they really are. Everyone looked as if they were asleep, but they were incredibly beautiful – I was in love with everyone.[116]

At this final stage, we do not encounter the ups and downs associated with spiritual "highs." Here we are no longer the experiencer; we are the experience.

Extreme gratitude sometimes overcomes us as we remember our original state of Oneness, and, as a result, an infinite urge to extend Love becomes a common occurrence. We know everything is alive, pulsing with radiant energy. We no longer delineate between ugly or beautiful, dead or alive. All is beauty. All is serene. Time seems to slow down and all needs to plan, control, or manipulate have disappeared. There is no desire to hope or strive to gain. The Universal Inspiration is now our Sacred Autopilot that directs our life moment to moment. Expanded synchronicity envelopes our existence; nothing is random. All seeking comes to an end as our existence continually unfolds.

At this stage, we find that we have left our familiar sense of self behind, and we see that who we thought we were was just a mish-mash of acquired beliefs and ancient emotional attachments. When we try to draw on the memory of this self, we are astounded because it really does not exist anymore. The memory is blurry or non-existent. Because we have learned now to perceive without the muddied lens of ego, we see things and people as they are, not as the distorted ego projects them. No projection means that we have no need for distorted memory. It is here that we leave behind the meaningless memory of who we were. We marvel that our previous self is gone, but what is left defies any self-definition. We are more alive, more present, more joyful, and more loving than we could have ever imagined. With no "self" to speak of, we are everyone, everywhere, all at once, and still living on earth in this body.

At this final stage, we are no longer the manufactured "I" of ego—this has been released to reveal the Self behind and beyond the illusory concept of "I." We still retain a thread of ego so that we can maintain the body; however, this thread has been surrendered entirely to the Universal Inspiration. This state is absolutely remarkable. It is free from the burden of our previous responsibilities. Every need to control has left us. We are amazed at how there is nothing to "need," nothing to resist, nothing to strive for, nothing to fear, and, of course, nothing to protect and defend. The notion that we experienced sacrifice to reach this point is ludicrous. On this side of the fence, we just cannot believe how much we once resisted relinquishing our personal identities that we once cherished and defended.

At this stage, we still have emotions. However, they are not fixed; they cannot adhere to us anymore because there is no remaining identity on which to stick them. Instead, we let emotions gently pass through us without giving them any reality. And when we need to access a particular emotion or behavior, we can thumb through our impartial filing system, selecting the folder with the appropriate response.

There are no stories left in our psyche to feed any separating beliefs or feelings. The separation file is not only empty at this stage; it has been deleted from memory.

While still living in this world, our passion is directed toward the enlightenment of others. Our inexhaustible extension of Love helps heal the minds of all people we come in contact with and even the minds of many we have not yet met or ever will. We see and participate in the waking of sleeping minds, knowing that this is our ultimate earthly purpose.

By now we have eclipsed the "I" or "me" and view our personality as being more of an "it," having no fixed position from which to elicit resistance and opposition. We still have preferences, likes, dislikes, styles, and certain habits, but they are not fixed or important. Therefore, we do not suffer from pleasure-seeking or pain avoidance. All is as it is. There are no attachments and no dependencies.

A greater part of this stage concerns learning to adopt a purer way of communicating, especially through language. As we advance through the final two stages, we are confronted with the recognition of the extent of meaningless, irrelevant communication through which most egos interact. Love and authenticity call for us to reinterpret the underlying truth behind each superfluous conversation. When asked questions, we take our time to let the Universal Inspiration answer through us. Every word is energy, and we note that the only energy we unite with is Truth; our conversations all hold the essence of Truth and Love. Humor increases in its ability to be a healing catalyst for many conversations. We can't help but see the funny side of life, and we infect others with this humorous outlook on what would normally be seen as a problematic existence.

There is a profound sense of consistent Peace interspersed with great surges of pure Joy at this final stage. No fear is possible here. We know that finally we have arrived at our real and only Home. The world seems to change its appearance and behavior as it is reflecting its divine and pristine nucleus. Everything and everyone is luminous with Loving energy. All is infinitely interconnected, and even seemingly sequential events reveal their immaculate synchronicity. Our right-mindedness interprets through true perception that everything is whole and complete. Now we understand the implicit meaning of perfection, and our mission leads us to assist others to rediscover their Identity and Purpose in this miraculous Oneness of which we are all part and to which we will eventually return.

CHAPTER 7

GUIDANCE ON THE PATH

This chapter considers support that is available for those who are going through the process of undoing the ego. This is not a journey that we have to take alone. As we surrender the ego to the now moment, we realize that we are part of the Whole, that we have a specific Purpose in life, and that we are able to attain Joy, Love, and Peace in this lifetime, now.

We Each Have a Specific Purpose

All of us have a specific purpose that we will eventually fulfill; *A Course in Miracles* refers to this Purpose as our "special function."[117] We get closer to recognizing our unique function as we progress further through the stages in the process of developing Trust. What we will all realize as we release the ego is that we are not alone. Perhaps in the early stages our focus was primarily on our own journey, but as we proceed we realize that our sense of caring and compassion continues to extend further and deeper to more people.

We begin to see each other not as different, but as more connected than we could have possibly imagined. We see each others' similarities with incredible clarity. We see that judging, comparing, and analyzing others is a waste of precious life force. We arrive at a point where, in order to feel fully alive each day, we must have meaning in our daily lives. As we deepen our trust in Truth, we may recognize that we have subtly been led to a particular point where our destiny begins to materialize, or manifest. We may see the pieces to the puzzle of our life finally making sense and coming together to form a coherent mosaic. Synchronicity seems to weave all the seemingly separate threads of our life together, and we start to see an intricately woven piece of fabric appearing—one of Truth.

We each have particular talents and abilities that will be utilized for our specific purpose. And as we progress, we are often amazed at how the unfolding of our lives reveals a rich integration of our strengths in areas that we did not know we had. We acquire certain abilities as we undo the ego. All the hidden potential within us, previously obscured by the ego, is awakened and unleashed. This is quite an awesome experience. We find that old limitations dissolve, and in their place we are delighted to discover a new and powerful dynamism working through us, with a momentum that carries us effortlessly to our Higher Purpose.

Our special function will always lead us to participate in the awakening of minds, although the form it takes may appear quite different for each individual. Each of us has recognized and unrecognized talents and abilities that will emerge as we live and extend Truth.

Carrying out our special function does not mean that we are free from error. The ego still confuses us at times. However, we are wholeheartedly committed to Truth, and serving our function now gives us an immense sense of meaning and purpose in our life. It is here that we may remember our former self who was possibly lost in its identity with illusion. Maybe it was restless, lost, unhappy, unsatisfied, and empty because it was searching for Love in all the wrong places. Finally, in coming to Truth, we not only find Love, Peace, and Joy, but our life now mirrors a clear, luminous sense of Oneness with All That Is, which once was eclipsed by the dark shadow of our small limited ego-self.

The Unified Will

The one Unified Purpose of our lives here in this world is to rediscover our ancient Unified State—our one Unified Self—and to learn how to experience our daily lives from that Self. Our aim, then, is to discover both that Purpose and our true Identity. The ego-release process and the deepening of Trust that it generates profoundly realigns us so that we may receive the unmistakable direct guidance of Higher Intelligence. This is the Unified Will of The Source, from which all manifestations of Love emanate.

Now we may conclude that we can trust ourselves to distinguish between what Love *is* and what it *is not*. However, more than likely we still live, think, and act largely from our ego-self, and this precludes us from truly knowing much at all in the earlier stages of ego-release. Again: we do not perceive our own best interests—there is great freedom in this acknowledgment. We live in a separated state, a dream that is playing out, while in Reality our indestructible Unified Self is quite unharmed by the events in the dream. All suffering, pain, hardship, and injustice are features of the dream and are interpreted as bad from inside this state. We could look around and say the world is falling to pieces, crime is on the rise, the economy is collapsing, ecological sustainability is rapidly declining, and governments are becoming increasingly more corrupt. On a more personal scale, we may see adversity in our financial situation, dis-ease in our bodies, injustice in the work environment, tragedy in our families, and crisis within relationships. However, these are all distracting symptoms of the *one* problem, which is our separated state of mind. They are all projections made by our split mind.

The ego-self cannot distinguish between the beneficial and the harmful. Its judgment is absurd and based on fear, separation, and scarcity. It has no ability to see any truth in any situation, whether it is loving or a call for love. The Unified Self, however, views all with stately detachment, knowing full well that absolutely nothing occurs in this reality that is not in accord with the Goal we all signed up for at the beginning of time. Every thing, every person, and every event we experience is a fragment of the mission we sought to accomplish. There is no good or bad about it. Nothing is random. As we said earlier in the book, *all* is either Love or it is an illusion. It cannot be partially Love and partially hate, some good and some bad. The Source *is* Love. We created our own dream here in this Universe, from which we are collectively trying to awaken. Any fear, hatred, or tragedy, however shocking or painful, is never to be judged by our ego-self as bad. We may feel the pain, anger, or grief but remain conscious at all times and know that no seeming adversity is ever an attack on us personally, others, or anything that is real.

Remember, in this ego-reality, we heal by recognizing that either something manifests as *an expression of Love* or it manifests as *a call for Love*. There is a Higher Intelligence that is Love—Infinite Love—and it cannot acknowledge any part of our reality that is not Love. Thus, it interprets any negativity as a call for Love, no matter what form it takes.

Many of us have been raised to believe in and cherish our own free will, believing that it is different from the Will of The Source. We unconsciously think that the Unified Will is in opposition to our own. We do not trust it and prefer to invest in our ego's thoughts, beliefs, mass conditioning, and past experience for our guidance in our minute-to-minute decision making. We trust this shabby little ego-self and its will, whose undivided mantra is *seek and do not find*, to take us to the Love and abundance we have always desired. But how can it? How can an entity whose agenda is literally to separate and terminate us as living beings be a trusted guide? Its will for us is permeated by a poisonous perception that projects and manifests hatred, war, death, illness, suffering, scarcity, inequality, corruption, loss, and sacrifice. If this sounds depressing, then good! The faster we learn to devalue the ego and its trappings, the more quickly we see and embrace Unified Reality here and now on earth.

As we are all expressions of The Source, we belong to an earthly reality that is born from Love and Unity, not fear and separation. The essence of *who we are* wants and deserves unlimited Love, Joy, Peace, creativity, and abundance. The Source is all these and more, never able to see or judge any form of sin or negativity. How can illusion enter or affect Truth? It cannot— ever! We created our illusion of this reality to be special and apart from The Source, making our ego the principal foundation for guidance with which we navigated our lifetimes. Any perceived sin or negativity is fabricated by the illusory ego-self. All justifications for judgment and persecution are also fabricated by this little self in order to deflect guilt and attract recrimination.

What Do We Fear in Ego-Release?

Fear of the Will of God [The Source] is one of the strangest beliefs the human mind has ever made. It could not possibly have occurred unless the mind were already profoundly split, making it possible for it to be afraid of what it really is. Reality cannot 'threaten' anything except illusions, since reality can only uphold truth. The very fact that the Will of God, which is what you are, is perceived as fearful, demonstrates that you *are* afraid of what you are. It is not, then, the Will of God of which you are afraid, but yours.[118]

What do we fear most in our release from ego? We avoid its release because we associate *loss* with its relinquishment. We believe that to undo egoic perception means we may lose what we value. The human ego is convinced that all its thoughts, agendas, beliefs, relationships, and possessions are worthy of coveting and defending. The reason we rely so heavily on its advice and directives is because we mistakenly invest in the delusional value system it upholds.

Everything it values is an illusion. All its attachments, including our reactions to their loss or transformation, are also an illusion. We do not yet know who we are or what our purpose is. How can we, then, possibly contrast and sort out what is valuable and what is not? We are addicted to valuing illusion and fearful and untrusting of anything that attempts to liberate us from the severely limited existence we presently endure. The ego's greatest fear, of course, is the threat of losing its identity. Without any identity, its will to control dies, and this is its final demise. Having no ego-identity means that we would face our greatest revelation: *we are The Source!* Without ego, we are the Almighty Grace and Power of the Infinite, and this is literally a terrorizing thought for the ego. It would rather endure a death of the body than face its own demise, relinquishing Absolute Liberation in exchange for limitation and suffering.

The six-stage process of learning to develop Trust is an invaluable guide for helping us to discover and enjoy the magnitude of our true Identity and Purpose. However, it first requires that we wholeheartedly commit ourselves to the Goal of Liberation. This means being willing to relinquish our ego's agenda and ask for our true Purpose to be revealed and fulfilled. Giving our life over to the full guidance of the Universal Inspiration through the Unified Self is not sacrifice. It is, rather, absolute freedom.

Once we relinquish our ego, what is it that we are really giving up? With ego-release, we give up guilt, judging, sacrifice, suffering, shame, insecurity, fear, and the feeling of always being alone, to name but a few. When we relinquish the ego, we really give up only the myriad dark feelings and beliefs that block our view of the Light of Love's presence. From *A Course in Miracles* we read:

> I have emphasized many times that the Holy Spirit [Universal Inspiration] will never call upon you to sacrifice anything....There is no difference between your will and God's. If you did not have a split mind, you would recognize that willing is salvation [Liberation] because it is communication.[119]

Our great fear of the unknown equates to a fear of loss of the known. The truth is, however, that if we were to willingly ask for Higher Guidance and follow it, the unknown would reveal itself as what we always yearned for in the first place, but could never find. And when we finally embrace what we actually exist for, we know it can never be substituted or lost, and the security of that knowing imparts an endless sense of limitless Peace, Love, and utter Joy.

We do not ask for what we really want, in the Highest sense, because we are terrified we might receive it, and we would! As *A Course in Miracles* explains:

> No right mind can believe that its will is stronger than God's. If, then, a mind believes that its will is different from His, it can only decide either that there is no God or that God's Will is fearful. The former accounts for the atheist and the latter for the martyr, who believes that God demands sacrifices. Either of these insane decisions will induce panic, because the atheist believes he is alone, and the martyr believes that God is crucifying him. Yet no one really wants either abandonment or retaliation, even though many may seek both....Fear cannot be real without a cause, and God is the only cause.[120]

Yet The Source is Love, not fear. So our Unified Will at its core is the same as The Source. When we wish from our ego, then we are requesting an illusion, something that will eventually harm us in this reality. A great many of our requests are unknowingly adverse to our own potential; yet we blindly seek to fulfill them. To make things worse, if our desires are not fulfilled we feel let down and lose faith. If we request an ego-desire to be met, we must realize we ask for nothing but pure illusion. So when a desire lies unmet or an agenda goes awry, we can cultivate appreciation for the protection we are given from the manifestation of our illusory desires. We are then given yet another chance to ask for what it is we truly need and not for what our ego desires.

Prayer

Every prayer that is aimed at the removal of fear or illusion is always answered, in the form that is most appropriate for that individual's higher needs. To the same degree that desire and willingness are expressed, fear or illusion can be removed or transformed. We may, however, choose not to hear the response and mistakenly conclude that our request was not answered, especially when it is not in the form our ego expects.

Any prayers requesting specialness will go unacknowledged because specialness is a form of illusion and the Universal Inspiration cannot deliver illusion. Its function is to help us undo fear and illusion, not reinforce or confirm it. In fact, if we were to sincerely ask that any mistakes or illusions be dissolved, the Universal Inspiration would respond positively; It always does. When we realize a mistake, in thought, belief, or action, we can and should ask for the Higher Intelligence to repair it and/or heal it. The Universal Inspiration will always work toward our best interest. Our own ego problem solving really creates more problems (because we don't know our own best interests), while appearing to be of assistance; deceit, of course, is its nature.

What would make us happy is what the Universal Inspiration wants for us. The problem is that the ego has no idea what would make us happy, and that most of our requests are born from ego perception. So, if we ask for something from a place of wrong-mindedness (ego), it is really a denial (of our Oneness) in the form of a request (to reinforce separation). To correct that error, we must acknowledge our ignorance about what would make us happy—we recognize that we do not know our own best interests—and surrender to *what is*. The outcome—usually one that our ego could never have imagined—will never disappoint us.

There is great Peace, power, and freedom in accepting not-knowing and overwhelming relief in the relinquishment of control.

Developing Trust usually takes time because of the level of fear we associate with the act of surrender. Again, to the ego, surrender means loss. Yet, in truth it brings nothing but gain. This learning process involves many levels of contrast, enabling us to learn to reevaluate the meaningful and distinguish it from the meaningless. A *Course in Miracles* tells us:

> The fact that God is Love does not require belief, but it does require acceptance. It is indeed possible for you to deny facts, although it is impossible for you to change them. If you hold your hands over your eyes, you will not see because you are interfering with the laws of seeing. If you deny love, you will not know it because your cooperation is the law of its being. You cannot change laws you did not make, and the laws of happiness were created for you, not by you.[121]

One of the fastest ways to surrender the ego-state is to accept reality as it presents itself—not to deny or resist it, because if we do, we are in conflict with ourselves and the Unified Will. We waste so much energy in defending, denying, and resisting *what is*! Instead, we could soften our resistance and invite the situation to teach us and lead us to what we really want. Any challenge we perceive serves purely as a vehicle to learn more about who we are and about our Purpose.

When Prayers Seem to Go Unanswered

According to *A Course in Miracles*:

> An individual may ask for physical healing because he is fearful of bodily harm. At the same time, if he were healed physically, the threat to his thought system might be considerably more fearful to him than its physical expression. In this

case he is not really asking for release from fear, but for the removal of a symptom that he himself selected. This request is, therefore, not for healing at all.[122]

So, if we ask for something like healing of the body, we may truly desire this healing, but unconsciously we are still afraid of it. The Universal Inspiration will never give us something that will increase fear in us. Hence this prayer seems unanswered. Again from *A Course in Miracles*:

> The very fact that the Holy Spirit has been asked for anything will ensure a response. Yet it is equally certain that no response given by Him will ever be one that would increase fear. It is possible that His answer will not be heard. It is impossible, however, that it will be lost. There are many answers you have already received but have not yet heard. I assure you that they are waiting for you.[123]

The power of prayer cannot be denied. However, our ego's wishes can and must be questioned. We have no idea what would be truly beneficial to us, whereas our Unified Self does know. The most valuable prayer for us or anyone is to ask for right-mindedness, for our minds to be healed. Once healing takes place, our Unified Will is free to synchronize unlimited miracles while releasing us from fear, control, and illusory need. There is truly nothing more valuable than this prayer, because it is the nucleus from which our own Heaven on Earth will flourish. To return to right-mindedness is the greatest gift we could ever give to mankind, for in our healed state, everyone around us will benefit greatly (because we are all one) while we attract and maintain a state of consistent Peace, Love, and Joy.

The Now Moment

As we journey through the stages in the development of Trust, we realize that waiting for anything is futile because we know with increasing clarity and confidence that all we ever need is with us and within us—now and always. That intimate instant of quiet surrender to the now moment, the security of Peace, reminds us that this is the only safe place to be. As we align with the Unified Will, it becomes obvious that being absent from ourselves in psychological time (past and future) robs us of our most precious commodity: the Peace, Love, and gratitude for our eternal Unity and Oneness with The Source.

We are so accustomed to incessant *thinking* that many of us are probably not familiar with being in a state of no-thought. The cessation of thought is the most powerful portal to linking immediately with our Unified Self. It is a vehicle through which we can spontaneously receive Higher Wisdom. There are absolutely no requirements for reaching the state of Unity, except the willingness to suspend thought.

If we use the mind constructively, it acts as a wonderful device to assist us in carrying out the Higher Directives that we are freely given on a minute-to-minute basis. We cannot know those Directives, however, if the mind is operating unguarded. Nearly all of us suffer from the rantings of our mind in the form of compulsive thought. We allow our minds to run rampant in a very destructive manner. It is not that we use our minds wrongly; the truth is that our thoughts control us. The problem exists because we mistake our thoughts for who we are, and our minds have taken us over. As Eckhart Tolle sums it up in his profoundly inspiring book *The Power of Now*: "Thinking has become a disease."[124]

We can begin to release compulsive thoughts by training ourselves to be the observer of each thought as it arises. We can thereby learn to watch and direct our thinking. This practice develops the recognition that we are *not* our thoughts. As we impartially look at each thought without judging it, we begin to relax and open up. Eventually we will identify ourselves as the observer and our thoughts merely the independent mind traffic passing by. When we truly accept that we are the observer (and not the thought), we get an immediate sense of liberation because we finally recognize that we are much more than just our mind. We are the "I" or the non judgmental awareness behind the mind. The mind is just the device we employ to navigate this life of ours. We recognize that the mind is not who we are.

We spoke earlier about how, when we meet new people or encounter new situations, we can rarely view them as they really are. When we approach anything new, we hardly ever see its present value because our own thoughts and beliefs, accumulated from past conditioning and experience, are subconsciously superimposed on the subject we see in the now. What this means is that we are really meeting the present with a distorted perception. And then we attempt to evaluate people, objects, and circumstance from this warped interpretation. No wonder so much of our past seems to repeat itself—we unknowingly *recreate* it by judging the new through the veil of past projections!

Without realizing it, any discontent we experience originates from our thoughts, which, in turn, create our beliefs. All the mass conditioning we received through childhood, school, the media, and life experience has solidified to produce a thick and sticky filter through which we attempt to view reality. Our main antagonizers are our unquestioned thoughts, and the voice in our head that is perpetually critiquing and evaluating is the ego-self voice.

The ego-self cannot remain in control without this endless stream of thought. It uses thought to harness our attention by causing us to be distracted from the now. As long as we are constantly preoccupied, the ego is safe from being discovered and then discarded. Keeping us occupied with thoughts of control, such as time, emotion, having, and becoming, is a sure way of trapping us in its web of limitation and suffering.

Freedom Is Learning to Suspend Thought

The idea of suspending thought may be frightening because "no-thought" means losing our identity, and losing our identity means emptiness. The truth is that being in a moment without thought actually expands our awareness. Because we have temporarily removed that thick sticky lens of thought, we get to experience the full extent of our senses. Our awareness peaks not just through our five senses, but, more importantly, we begin to experience a state of Oneness that expands far beyond anything that our thoughts alone could possibly deliver. We become increasingly aware that the "I" we thought we were is but a mere fragment of this expansive Self Who is joyfully connected to All That Is!

In suspending thought and becoming intensely aware of our breath, sounds, and physical sensations, we are free to just *be*. Being in this space encourages an acute sense of awareness where we enter the now reality. We can practice this anywhere, anytime. It does not necessarily require that our eyes be closed as in meditation. Try accessing the now moment while doing mundane daily chores, such as brushing your teeth. Be acutely aware of every sense, the sound of water, the sound of the brush against your teeth, the sensation of bristles zigzagging along your gums. Be right there and sense every single feeling and sound. This is present-moment awareness. Be there, in your action, whatever it may be, focusing attention on presence and not allowing yourself to be absent from the experience through the usual stream of thoughts. Practice by focusing attention on the everyday practice of present-moment awareness. See how often we can access this precious moment of full attention.

We gain a deepening sense of Peace, connectedness, and freedom as we accumulate more experiences of now-moment presence. Anxiety, worry, fear, and resistance lessen considerably, and our perception clears to make way for genuine moments of pure realization. It is here that we may see our culture's acceptance of compulsive thought as a largely undiagnosed and unremedied disease. We must commit to freeing ourselves from its destructive influence as a matter of urgency.

Ideally, once we establish a central core of Peace within, we will no longer be plagued by the persistent sense of threat that the ego uses to attract allegiance to it. This sense of threat merges with the illusion that we are separate, alone, and unsupported, fueling the need to have, to defend, and to become.

As we develop that core of Peace within, we realize that true creativity and insight are born from this expanded Self and not derived from the limited mechanical process of thought. True inspiration always comes from beyond the finite, leading us toward Liberation.

So many of us experience what seems to be random illness, depression, or accidents. However, much of our suffering is caused unconsciously by unexpressed emotions trapped in our bodies. Any negative feelings can be destructive blocks that build up physically in our bodies and cause disease. That is why it is important to develop awareness of our body's reactions because it is primarily through the body that emotion will express itself.

It is important to cultivate awareness of feeling and note where anxiety, fear, and anger are located in the body. Our health depends on this mind-body awareness so that we can effectively work with emotion and thought in a mindful manner. When we allow rampant and random thought and emotion to control us and then claim we are victims of our circumstances, disease of the body or mind will be an inevitable outcome.

The ego, being expressed through compulsive thought, is always trying to fix things. One of its major roles is to remove, repress, or resist emotional pain. This is a fulltime job that it works at without ceasing; hence the incessant string of thoughts that it generates. The ego drives hard to eliminate pain; yet, all it does is further intensify it. The harder the mind works to stop the pain, the greater the suffering. This is a never-ending battle, with the mind never arriving at a solution. Why? Because the ego *is* the problem.[125]

Love, Joy, and Peace

Love, Joy, and Peace are not emotions. Real Love, Joy, and Peace do not emerge from any source outside of us. But happiness, sadness, guilt, anger, and grief are all born from our emotions, and it is our thoughts and beliefs that cause our emotional responses—not any seeming outer person, thing, or circumstance. All our emotions are the product of our own perception and thus are subject to their opposite emotional expression. For example, something or someone makes us "happy" but also has the capacity to make us "sad," through loss or change. We are "content" with a situation or person, but when they do not meet our needs, we become "frustrated." And love, as most of us know it, is the special variety (see Chapter 4, "Love Relationships"), which is unfortunately not real Love at all, but rather "giving to get" in disguise. Special love has an agenda, and, because of this, it is susceptible to change and termination when its agenda is threatened.

Conscious Love, as we have said, has no opposite, is constant, cannot be destroyed, and extends itself infinitely without conditions of any kind. It seeks absolutely nothing because it knows it is everything in all ways at all times.

Love is a pure state that is absolutely interconnected with Joy and Peace. To experience one of these states is to *be* within this all-inclusive trilogy. Love, Joy, and Peace arise from beyond our limited senses. Defying explanation, Love-Joy-Peace comes from our central contact with a source—The Source. This Love-Joy-Peace induces in us a state of Grace, which we recognize as a Unified Expression of interconnectedness emerging from within.

Love, Joy, and Peace are states of being and therefore cannot be experienced through the ego-self. The ego depends on duality to make its existence real and does this through using emotion to contrast feelings. With Love-Joy-Peace, no contrast is possible. They are the conditions of our natural State of Being, only accessible when thought is suspended and we and the experience become inexplicably merged in Oneness. These moments of Grace are doorways to reclaiming our inheritance of Infinite Joy within the realm of time and space.

At one time or another, we may remember this instant of immense Peace, Love, or Joy. These moments cannot be defined by words, their magnitude defying description—for example, the birth of a baby, an awe-inspiring sunset, an overwhelming connection with nature, or a tender moment of oneness shared with a loved one. The present moment holds such power that we hardly recognize the magnificent opportunity we have in each second to start our lives over again. In just one wholly conscious moment, we can initiate great healing within ourselves and the Universe.

The essence of who we are, without the illusion of ego, is Love, Peace, and Joy. So in reality, every one of us is a sacred shard of the One Being: The Source. In this earthly reality, we imagine time as being real and limited, and we think everyone and everything is separate. The truth beyond the illusion is that time can only exist when we are under its spell, existing in the remembered past or imagined future. This is what Eckhart Tolle calls "psychological time."[126]

We said earlier that time was purely the succession of a string of now moments, but that we were not there for them. We were preoccupied with thought and missed the now in its full expression as it was occurring. Therefore, we were not there, not present. In order for us to begin to recognize who we and everyone else is and why we're here, we need to access this portal to right-mindedness. It is in the now moment, shining clean without past or future, that our true nature is revealed. In this instant, there is no guilt, no past, and no future fear—just the pristine Self we always have been and shall be forevermore. This Unified Self has been completely untouched by any mistakes or seeming injustices caused by ego, and it will continue to be magnificent and glorious perfection, no matter what.

In the now moment, there is no fear. Fear can only appear in thoughts of the past or future. Being wholly present in this moment obliterates fear. Our perfect Unified Self waits for us to awaken to Its unchanged perfection and reclaim our rightful inheritance as Co-creators.

Each now instant is clean and extends forever. This is where Infinite Peace-Love-Joy resides without change. Every time we pause, consciously leave our thoughts behind, and enter a now moment, we realize it takes no time to be *who* we are, without ego restrictions. Although our thoughts are preoccupied with the past or future, nothing really exists outside the now!

If the now is eternal and time does not exist, how can we understand time in the context of our daily lives? Every single thing we have ever done occurred in a now moment. The fact remains that we never went anywhere or did anything outside the now moment. Even "future" events (fantasy) occur in the now moment. In other words, the "future" is really a projected now, and when it "arrives" we receive it *now*.[127] And when we think of the "past," all we are doing is presently recalling memories that are stored in the mind. However, these, too, "happened" in the "former" now. In other words, when we're remembering the past, we're remembering it in the now moment. If our life is purely a string of now moments with the past and future being imagined, maybe we can ask ourselves, "How many now moments in my string of life was I truly present for?"

We can make a conscious decision to practice observing our thoughts by becoming the watcher of our mind's thoughts, emotions, and reactions. In a situation that elicits an uncomfortable reaction in us, try to maintain awareness without judgment of ourselves, the situation, or another. Let it all be neutral and watch how often we delve into thoughts of the past or future. With practice, we will identify ourselves as the observer rather than being ruled by our thoughts. Finally, we gain a secure foothold in the State of Being. We are the impartial observer, able to access the enormous Peace and clarity available at any moment we choose.

Powerful Keys to Freedom

Learning how to relinquish judgment and guilt are two of the most powerful keys to unlocking the doorway to Liberation. We get unconsciously stuck in the mire of accumulated psychological time. This prevents us from entering the present because we deny it, often through feelings of resentment, regret, grievances, guilt, or sadness. What we don't realize is that these negative feelings are caused by the stories or life situations that we create. They do not exist independently of our own interpretation of the experiences. In other words, how we perceive our past determines whether we label our stories negative or positive and ensures that our emotional state matches that of our particular perception. For example, if we had a long-term relationship and our partner left us for another, we could interpret this story in a number of ways according to the ego, all of which would lead us into a more separated state. Feelings of resentment and bitterness over our perceived abandonment would taint our story and become impediments to our willingness to enter the healing power of the now moment. That is why it is so important to question any story of ours that portrays us as a victim of any kind.

The people and situations we are most likely to recoil from usually are the very ones that hold the most potential for healing through exposing our shadow fears, the blocks to present Love and freedom. We don't need to go back and analyze our past to heal; we are always given in the now the perfect people and situations with which we can work through the same long-standing blocks. This is the absolute beauty and perfection of the now. Any one of us at any time can, with heartfelt willingness, heal past pain through present relationships. This is welcome news to those of us whose significant others are no longer physically present. Any resentment we carry withholds Love from us and serves to drive us to seek distractions elsewhere to quell our present discomfort. Our ego will never acknowledge our recognition that the source of our discomfort is a sense of disagreement with reality. Denial of reality sets us up for a long and often difficult course in life. Freedom comes from our willingness to take complete responsibility for the reality we create. The reality we live in is a projection from behind our lens of perception, and if that lens is distorted, our reality will mirror that distortion.

The situation that grants us the most potential for entering the now in order to heal our perception is a personal, close relationship (see Chapter 4, "Love Relationships"). While these usually give us what we want, they also challenge us by causing conflict at times. In the event of disunity with a loved one, such as an argument or heated disagreement, we can choose to use the powerful tool of now-moment awareness. By deciding to be the observer of our reactions rather than the emotional participant, we empower ourselves with that miraculous healing tool: the now. Tremendous recovery from past immobility is attained in every moment we choose to be consciously present without judgment or attack. Here from *A Course in Miracles* is a brief thought that you can say to yourself to quickly find release from any form of pain that may arise:

I *am* responsible for what I see.

I *choose the feelings I experience, and I decide upon the goal I would achieve.*

And everything that seems to happen to me I ask for, and receive as I have asked.[128]...

And to continue the text:

All that is asked of you is to make room for truth. You are not asked to make or do what lies beyond your understanding. All you are asked to do is *let it in*; only to stop your interference with what will happen of itself; simply to recognize again the presence of what you thought you gave away....Be willing, for an instant, to leave your altars free of what you placed upon them, and what is really there you cannot fail to see. The holy instant [now moment] is not an instant of creation, but of recognition. For recognition comes of vision and suspended judgment. Then only it is possible to look within and see what must be there, plainly in sight, and wholly independent of interference and judgment. Undoing is not your task, but it *is* up to you to welcome it or not. Faith and desire go hand in hand, for everyone believes in what he wants.[129]

Problems and Now

When we are consumed by our imagined problems, we are not present because we are preoccupied in psychological time, the past or future. We try to endure the unhappy moment by hoping that the future will be better. But the present is consumed by worry. So, we evade the very condition where the answer and freedom lie: the peaceful now moment. The ego is obsessed with control and problem solving. Its strategy for distracting us is derived from its fear of our surrender and ability to let go and move into present-moment awareness, because if we were to dare to take an "ego-break," all our problems would fade and we would find ourselves catapulted into a safe and secure State of Being. Here we are genuinely happy because unhappiness cannot exist in this place.

We all tend to think that there are some things in the past that did not go well or according to plan. When thoughts of such past events arise in our mind, we experience a wide range of feelings, from disappointment right through to devastation. Our ego is still resisting what seemed to happen in the past. Why? Because it views what happened as wrong and without value. It paints a picture that we were a victim of circumstances, and, through this belief, it feeds our need to control the future. When the now— *what is*—"arrives," the first thing the ego does is to resist it. Then it creates a thought of the "future" ("hope") to keep us going, making sure we avoid the now by becoming focused on such hopes of the future.[130] You can see just how deviously the ego maneuvers our attention to be anywhere else but in the now. Our unhappiness comes from avoidance of the now, and that is exactly what the ego wants. This way, we remain trapped in the ego's delusional method of problem solving.

The truth is that right at this very moment, problems or not, we are all right. If we keep our focus acutely in the present moment, undefiled by ego thoughts of tomorrow or last week, we realize that we are *not* our problems or our life stories. They just go on regardless. In fact, we have no problems or needs at all in the now. There is great Peace to be had in this place of Grace.

One of the greatest benefits of accessing the now is that it allows so-called problems to be solved without egoic influence. The ego could not survive without problems because its very identity thrives on them. Separation, inequality, and injustice are living food for the ego, sustaining its existence. Ideally, the path to our Unified Self requires us to abdicate the ego's problem solving and to surrender to the Universal Inspiration's *Knowing*. Therefore, when accessing the now, we need to ask for Higher Guidance and be consciously aware that we are the *observer* of our thoughts, feelings, and actions—we are not the thoughts themselves. The now holds all the answers that the limited and judgmental ego could never offer us.

Our Unified Will

Our ego-will is purely a defense against Reality. Beneath that defense are Truth and Love. The ego's constant preoccupation with control is evident every time it resists reality—*what is*—and tries to redirect it according to its value system. It has no clue as to what is in our best interests at any given moment; yet we, along with our culture, still afford it our undivided attention and allegiance. If reality presents as disagreeable to the ego, our reaction will reflect that incompatibility and a rejection takes place. We think we are rejecting an external structure, but in essence any rejection of reality is a rejection of ourselves and The Source. Its underlying message is that something is wrong. This causes us to contract and lose faith and become defiant, negative, or depressed. When our reality presents as incongruent with our limited ego's perception, fear overshadows our thoughts and we succumb to believing that we are besieged by a persistent sense of threat which we must apprehend. We are accustomed to translating reality into a negative context unless it is in line with our "free will" (ego). We judge what is good and bad, who is good or bad, while finding a way to justify the mental or physical administration of our verdict of the person or situation.

If only we knew without any doubt that reality as it presents itself is not our concern! Our concern is to recognize and trust that reality is a means through which we can awaken. Reality, when seen correctly, is a here-and-now gift through which we will undo all blocks to the awareness of Love's presence. The one stipulation here is that we willingly commit to renouncing any former interpretations we had of it and surrender reality to the Universal Inspiration for Truth to be revealed.

All our needs to control people, time, situations, and outcomes are all defenses against Reality. All plans (unless directed by the Universal Inspiration) are also defenses against Reality. Disappointment, guilt, anger, and frustration are all indicators calling us to seek Truth. Any anguish, anxiety, or despair is an immediate cue indicating a need for reinterpretation. There is no such thing as a bad situation, but only one that calls to be re-interpreted.

As we evolve spiritually, we learn to appreciate that Reality is like a mirror, reflecting the thoughts we project onto it, be they right-minded or misaligned. When we relinquish resistance to *what is* and see it as a friend and not an enemy, fear subsides and clarity dawns; now Higher Guidance is activated and we are shown questions and answers to which we were previously blind. The Source works Its way through all illusion because It is Love, being Truth. While we still perceive and believe our illusory world, Truth itself is always there, lying peacefully beneath our many delusions. Our freedom is gained through our sincere request for right-mindedness and recognition that our perception of *what is* is not necessarily Truth.

While the world seems random and chaotic, the Universal Inspiration, transmuting illusion always with One Goal, infiltrates all of it to urge us to recognize Truth—not pain, grief, and separation. From *A Course in Miracles*:

> All you need to do is but to wish that Heaven be given you, instead of hell, and every bolt and barrier that seems to hold the door securely barred and locked will merely fall away and disappear.[131]

The Futility of Planning

We quite innocently believe that planning is a constructive and necessary component that most of our goals depend upon. However, developing Trust asks us to surrender our plans by realizing that our ego-self's plans always emerge from the seed of separation. *A Course in Miracles'* Workbook Lesson 135 teaches:

> It is, perhaps, not easy to perceive that self-initiated plans are but defenses, with the purpose all of them were made to realize. They are the means by which a frightened mind would undertake its own protection, at the cost of truth. This

is not difficult to realize in some forms which these self-deceptions take, where the denial of reality is very obvious. Yet planning is not often recognized as a defense.[132]

The underlying and often unconscious intent behind all of the ego-self's plans is to lead us away from healing and into chaos, no matter how enticing its presentations may be. Our Unified Self, on the other hand, derives its momentum and direction from *one* intent, and that intent is Love. Direct communication with the Universal Inspiration leads us to people and situations that best assist us in our own particular undoing process; it knows which decisions and directions are most likely to benefit us.

Without undoing our illusions, we cannot be liberated. Conscious Love, Peace, and Joy are increasingly revealed as we face each instant with present-moment awareness rather than resistance. We learn that any time we feel resistance is an opportunity to recognize and acknowledge the resistance without guilt or judgment and surrender to the truth that "I do not perceive my own best interests."[133] There is so much freedom gained in openly recognizing that we just don't know anything that is interpreted by our ego. We really do not know who people are, what things and situations are for, why we are here, or how to correct things. Truly a great gift is the humility to say and mean, "I wish to be comfortable with not-knowing." The moment we surrender our limited experience of knowing, we are instantly relieved of our burden. In this instant we are joined with the Unified Will, whether we recognize it or not. Workbook Lesson 135 in *A Course in Miracles* teaches:

A healed mind does not plan. It carries out the plans that it receives through listening to wisdom that is not its own. It waits until it has been taught what should be done, and then proceeds to do it. It does not depend upon itself for anything except its adequacy to fulfill the plans assigned to it....A healed mind is relieved of the belief that it must plan, although it cannot know the outcome which is best, the means by which it is achieved, nor how to recognize the problem that the plan is made to solve.[134]

Owning up to not-knowing releases our fear and resistance because both are products of the ego's need to know. In admitting we don't know, we are asking the Unified Will to illuminate us and the situation.

Suppose we feel fearful, guilty, disconnected, or angry; simply observing these feelings without judgment and surrendering them to not-knowing invites the Unified Will to take over. At the seat of the ego lies a massive mound of guilt that equates with our need to judge and condemn, which is an attempt to offset this guilty burden. That persistent sense of threat we feel comes directly from the ego's insistence that we are guilty at our core, hence the ego's obsession with control through its will.

Opening up to the Unified Will means we acknowledge that guilt drives our ego, our fears, and our desires, which translates to "free will" being born from fear and destined to separate us in many ways. With this realization, it seems logical to want to relinquish our need to control, judge, and plan and to willingly embrace the process of developing Trust, which is aligning with our true Identity and Purpose. Workbook Lesson 135 teaches:

> If there are plans to make, you will be told of them. They may not be the plans you thought were needed, nor indeed the answers to the problems which you thought confronted you. But they are answers to another kind of question, which remains unanswered yet in need of answering until the Answer comes to you at last.[135]

One of the most popular misperceptions we have is the notion that aligning with Unified Will means that we would lose something valuable. The word "valuable" is the one misperception here because, in truth, we *would* lose something, but by no stretch of the imagination can guilt, fear, and suffering be classified as valuable.

Wrong perception is the wish that things be as they are not. The reality of everything is totally harmless, because total harmlessness is the condition of its reality....You do not have to seek reality. It will seek you and find you when you meet its conditions....Wholeness heals because it is of the mind. All forms of sickness, even unto death, are physical expressions of the fear of awakening. They are attempts to reinforce sleeping out of fear of waking....Healing is release from the fear of waking and the substitution of the decision to wake. The decision to wake is the reflection of the will to love, since all healing involves replacing fear with love.[136]

We are Love. Once we wholeheartedly decide to adopt Unified Perception, we will learn to relinquish the ego's thought system. Then we will see everyday reality as the perfect vehicle through which our transformation takes place. As our resistance to *what is* softens, our Trust in the Unified Will increases. Along the journey, we gain confidence as we look back to see not disaster, but simply the unfolding of our pathway, its only value being that it eventually led us to awakening. We see then the futility of our needless resistance to reality, gratefully accepting that its only purpose was to help us undo the illusory perception that kept us from Love for so long. Again from *A Course in Miracles*:

Remember, then, that God's Will is already possible, and nothing else will ever be. This is the simple acceptance of reality, because only that is real. You cannot distort reality and know what it is. And if you do distort reality you will experience anxiety, depression and ultimately panic, because you are trying to make yourself unreal. When you feel these things, do not try to look beyond yourself for truth, for truth can only be within you.[137]

We belong to The Source; we are living parts of Love Itself. In each of us, the Universal Inspiration waits for our recognition of our Unified Self.

CHAPTER 8

TRUTH

To be free, liberated, or awakened is to embrace Truth. Truth is greatly feared by the ego because to stop resisting reality reveals Truth and results in the demise of ego. Embracing Trust means to consciously end our argument with reality as it presents itself through ourselves, others, situations, circumstances, and material objects. It means abdicating our need to control all these things, because ultimately any need to control equates to resisting or denying Truth. As we grow in our understanding, we begin to grasp the notion that reality (everyday life) cannot be changed. It is as it is. The reality of our everyday life, as we perceive it, is but a dream, created by ego. Yet, The Source has never left us (and in Reality we have never left The Source) and is always present, emanating from every perceived particle in our Universe. Our job is not to resist this reality; it is to embrace it. It is not to transcend or overcome it; it is to *enter into* it, consciously. Truth is revealed as we develop Trust by surrendering the ego-self and letting go of the desire to control.

We are not our thoughts, bodies, beliefs, values, or achievements. This life of ours is precious, no matter how ugly it gets. Why? Because in all its twists and turns, it always offers us an opportunity to reframe it, by not taking it personally, not judging it, not manipulating it, but just allowing it. Each moment, we are given the opportunity to see either illusion or to see Truth. It's entirely up to us to choose our perception. Facing this reality as it is, and all our relationships within it, is the most *perfect* learning situation any of us could ever need, want, or hope for. Any confusion, pain, or suffering arises from resistance—mental, emotional, or physical.

We know nothing Real through the ego. When we can own this fact totally, we realize we are safe to relinquish our need to know. We think we know and need to know because the ego sees knowledge as an opportunity to control, direct, and manipulate. It sets up a fixed point of view and adds this to its list of things to defend, manifesting doubt, distrust, and separation. This entire process of developing Trust (awakening) and ego-release is one of undoing, unlearning, and dismantling.

When adversity seems to appear in our life, remember that it is always an opportunity in disguise. Its purpose is never to punish or mislead us. No matter how unpleasant it gets, it is awaiting our recognition as a catalyst by which we undo our illusory past perception of it. Where formerly we perceived adversity as disaster, a pain, bad luck, we now recognize it as an opportunity to ask for the truth beneath its appearance—to ask for reinterpretation.

Entering the passage to Truth asks us to relinquish our sense of helplessness. The lessons to embrace here are twofold: "I do not perceive my own best interests"[138]; and "I am not the victim of the world I see."[139] Truth and Trust cannot coexist with doubt and victim consciousness. To gain Truth, we must drop our perception of the notion of victimhood. We resist Truth, and therefore Trust, to the same degree that we consciously or unconsciously believe we are helpless victims. The purpose of ego-release is to help us release our resistance to Truth, thereby increasing our Trust.

Allow Truth every instant. Don't get sidetracked by spiritual "highs" or ego "lows." They are all distractions. Truth cannot be sought after or strived for, minute by minute. It can only unfold as our humility opens our hearts to it. Our resistance is the only thing that can block it.

No matter where we are or what our life circumstances may be, we *always* have within us the means to access Truth. All that is required is:

- absolute commitment to Truth;
- willingness to relinquish control and extend Quantum Forgiveness;
- vigilance and consistent discipline for right-mindedness;
- diligent awareness, being fully present, and questioning everything, including all our beliefs, with radical self-honesty; and
- surrender of perception, thoughts, and emotions to the Universal Inspiration to allow the underlying Truth to shine through.

Because we are so programmed to perceive lack within ourselves and our lives, it may be difficult to recognize that we *are* and *have* everything we need to complete this journey. The truth, however, is that we have, right now, all we will ever need in order to awaken. If we desire with all our heart and soul to return to Love, to be living consciously in the Optimal Reality here on earth, then we *will* rediscover our identity along with the purpose we were born to fulfill.

Humility, heartfelt intent, and radical self-honesty are all available to us in every moment. There are no situations, circumstances, or people to hold us back. Any apprehension, excuse, or need to control can be recognized as the ego resisting transformational change. Suffering, addictions to having and becoming, special relationships, victim consciousness, giving to get, judging, or attacking are all products of wrong-mindedness.

While neither right nor wrong, good nor bad, we still exist inside this dream, and while we're asleep we continue to experience nightmares. If we were to hear the *call* to awaken, why would we want to doze back off to rejoin our nightmares? Wouldn't it be better to be free of the nightmares? Wouldn't we jump at the opportunity for liberation, not just for ourselves, but for everyone?

A Guide to Decision Making

We all need to make decisions in our daily lives, but sometimes we are in a quandary about how to go about making a decision, and it is not clear to us whether or not we are listening to the voice of the ego (which is usually the case) or that of the Unified Self. Here is an inner question-and-decision-making screening process that can help you make your choice. If practiced regularly, this guide will become automatic and save you time and, possibly, needless suffering. Before making a choice, check your options according to the guidelines below.

An option or choice from *ego*:

It feels: exciting, attached, hooked into a result. Deep down it feels *wrong*.

It desires: specialness (being separate and exclusive); not to extend, give, or share; safety, control, protection and/or defense of emotions, physical body, and/or mind.

Clues: distraction, competitiveness, judgment, blame, lack, scarcity, fear, guilt, anger, exclusiveness, separation, giving to get, manipulation, suppression.

An option or choice from *Unified Self*:

It feels: challenging or frustrating to the ego's desires. Deep down it feels *right*.

It desires: Unity, Wholeness, and interconnectedness; extending, unconditional giving and sharing. It has no need to be seen as special. Because it is *already* safe, it has no need for defense or protection.

Clues: forgiving, sharing, giving, inclusiveness, trust, appreciation, awareness, opening up, unconditional nature, attentiveness, compassion, abundance.

The Beginning

We may know that we want Love and Liberation, but are we prepared to release the thought system responsible for closing us off from it? We say we want Peace, Love, and Joy, but are we prepared to release our own perceptions of judgment and attack? And we want to experience abundance, but are we ready to release our perceptions of scarcity and embrace the truth that *giving is receiving*?

Truth is all-powerful. If we were to contemplate this one symbol—the word "truth"—with all the reverence and loving intent we could muster, the mystery behind the word would become known to us. The way to Truth lies in our defenselessness. It is in the acceptance and recognition that *what is* is. It's the desire to surrender all control and suffering to The Source and to awaken to the Reality that there is only One Will and that we are all expressions of that One Will. We are all One! There is no seeking to be done, no effort to be made, nothing to be accomplished.

There is, however, a dream from which we are being *called* to awaken, a dream of limitation and separation. Each one of us can awaken now by simply choosing Peace. Peace is Truth is Love.

Throughout this book, we have briefly outlined a means by which we can all awaken to Truth. Your freedom lies within; so do Truth, Peace, Joy and Love, because that is Who You Are.

When you hear the unmistakable *Call to Truth*, you will summon the courage, commitment, and willingness to release the dream and reclaim your inheritance as a magnificent Co-creator. This *is* the end of suffering because all suffering is merely the fear of awakening.

You will remember everything the instant you desire it wholly, for if to desire wholly is to create, you will have willed away the separation, returning your mind simultaneously to your Creator and your creations. Knowing Them you will have no wish to sleep, but only the desire to waken and be glad. Dreams will be impossible because you will want only truth, and being at last your will, it will be yours.[140]

APPENDIX I

"THE WORK" WORKSHEET

THE JUDGE-YOUR-NEIGHBOR WORKSHEET

• JUDGE YOUR NEIGHBOR • WRITE IT DOWN •
• ASK FOUR QUESTIONS • TURN IT AROUND •

Fill in the blanks below, writing about someone (dead or alive) you haven't yet forgiven one hundred percent. Use short, simple sentences. Don't censor yourself—try to fully experience the anger or pain as if the situation were occurring right now. Take this opportunity to express your judgments on paper.

1.   Who angers, frustrates, or confuses you, and why?

I am _____ *at* _____ *because*

_____

Example: *I am **angry** at **Paul** because **he doesn't listen to me, he doesn't appreciate me, he argues with everything I say.***

2.   How do you want them to change? What do you want them to do?

I want _____ *to* _____

_____

263

Example: *I want **Paul** to see that **he is wrong**. I want **him** to apologize.*

3. What is it that they should or shouldn't do, be, think, or feel? What advice could you offer?

_____ *should/shouldn't* _____

_____

Example: ***Paul** should take better care of **himself**. **He** shouldn't argue with me.*

4. What do they need to do in order for you to be happy?

I need _____ *to* _____

_____

Example: *I need **Paul** to **hear me and respect me**.*

5. What do you think of them? Make a list.

_____ *is* _____

_____

Example: ***Paul** is **unfair, arrogant, loud, dishonest, way out of line, and unconscious**.*

6. What is it that you don't want to experience with that person again?

I don't ever want to _____

Example: *I don't ever want to feel unappreciated by Paul again. I don't ever want to see him smoking and ruining his health again.*

The Four Questions

Investigate each of your statements from the Judge-Your-Neighbor Worksheet using the **four questions** and the **turnaround** below. The Work is meditation. It's about awareness, not about trying to change your thoughts. Ask the questions, then take your time, go inside, and wait for the deeper answers to surface.

In its most basic form, The Work consists of **four questions and a turnaround**. For example, the first thought that you might questions on the above Worksheet is "Paul doesn't listen to me." Find someone in your life about whom you have had that thought, and let's do The Work. "[Name] doesn't listen to me":

1. Is it true?
2. Can you absolutely know that it's true?
3. How do you react, what happens, when you believe that thought?
4. Who would you be without the thought?

Then turn it around (the concept you are questioning), and don't forget to find three genuine examples of each turnaround.

Turn it Around

After you've investigated your statement with the four questions, you're ready to **turn it around (the concept you are questioning)**.

Each turnaround is an opportunity to experience the opposite of your original statement and see what you and the other person have in common.

A statement can be turned around to the **opposite**, to the **other**, and to the **self** (and sometimes to "my thinking," wherever that applies). Find a minimum of three genuine examples in your life where each turnaround is true.

For example, "**Paul doesn't understand me**" can be turned around to: "Paul *does* understand me." Another turnaround is "I don't understand Paul." A third is "I don't understand myself."

Be creative with the turnarounds. They are revelations, showing you previously unseen aspects of yourself reflected back through others. Once you've found a turnaround, go inside and let yourself feel it. Find a minimum of three genuine examples where the turnaround is true in your life.

As I began living my turnarounds. I noticed that **I was everything I called you**. You were merely my projection. Now, instead of trying to change the world around me (this didn't work, but only for 43 years), I can put the thoughts on paper, investigate them, turn them around, and find that I am the very thing I thought you were. In the moment I see you as selfish, I am selfish (deciding how you should be). In the moment I see you as unkind, I am unkind. If I believe you should stop waging war, I am waging war on you in my mind.

The turnarounds are your prescription for happiness. Live the medicine you have been prescribing for others. The world is waiting for just one person to live it. You're the one.

APPENDIX II

RECOMMENDED READING RESOURCES AND THEIR WEBSITES

Undoing the ego is an exceptional life purpose. This false-self image called "ego" has plagued us for millennia, and it will not surrender without summoning every bit of resistance possible. Knowing this, preparation can make our transition much less uncomfortable.

If we are committed to Truth and wish to positively transform our lives, then we need both the means by which to attain it and the support and guidance to help see us through. We, the authors, have lived much of the ego-release process ourselves. We wish to alleviate, for others, what was for us a long and confusing time that entailed an unnecessary level of suffering. We are dedicated to facilitating the process of ego-relinquishment through offering our support via group presentations and "Undoing the Ego" workshops; visit www.TakeMeToTruth.com.

A Course in Miracles (ACIM) offers a powerful means to Truth through its Text, Workbook of 365 daily lessons, and Manual for Teachers. The lessons are daily resources to help us awaken from the ego-dream. Ego-release and developing Trust will require a wholehearted and honest commitment to undoing illusion, and we may find we each need various tools and resources for assistance on this path. While ACIM offers perhaps the quickest and most brilliantly lit pathway to awakening, below is a list of other resources we have also found helpful on our journeys.

A Course in Miracles, Foundation for Inner Peace.
　　Website (Foundation for Inner Peace): http://www.acim.org

A New Earth, Eckhart Tolle.
    Website: http://www.eckharttolle.com
Absence from Felicity: The Story of Helen Schucman and Her
    Scribing of A Course in Miracles, Kenneth Wapnick, Ph.D.
    (more books listed in bibliography).
    Website (Foundation for A Course In Miracles):
    http://www.facim.org
Awaken from the Dream, Kenneth and Gloria Wapnick.
    Website (Foundation for A Course In Miracles):
    http://www.facim.org
Awakening the Buddha Within, Lama Surya Das.
    Website: http://www.dzogchen.org
Communion With God, Neale Donald Walsch.
    Website: http://www.nealedonaldwalsch.com
Emptiness Dancing, Adyashanti.
    Website: http://www.adyashanti.org
Excuse Me: Your life Is Waiting, Lynn Grabhorn.
    Website: lynngrabhorn.com
Healing the Cause: A Path of Forgiveness, Michael Dawson.
    Website (Australian Centre for Inner Peace):
    http://www.acfip.org
Living Enlightenment, Embracing Heaven and Earth, Andrew
    Cohen.
    Website: http://www.andrewcohen.org
Love Has Forgotten No One: The Answer to Life. Gary R. Renard (to
    be published in 2009).
    Website: http://www.garyrenard.com
Loving What Is, I Need Your Love—Is That True?, Byron Katie.
    Website: http://www.thework.com
Matthew Andrae
    Website: http://www.matthewandrae.com
Pathways of Light, a non-profit organization providing spiritually
    focused courses with *A Course in Miracles* orientation.
    Website: http://www.pathwaysoflight.org

Power vs. Force, David Hawkins, M.D.
Website:
http://www.beyondtheordinary.net/drhawkins.shtml
Radical Forgiveness, Colin T. Tipping.
Website: http://www.radicalforgiveness.com
Reality and Illusion , Robert Perry.
Website (Circle of Atonement):
http://www.circlepublishing.com/
Spiritual Enlightenment: The Damnedest Thing, Jed McKenna.
Website: www.WisefoolPress.com
The Disappearance of the Universe, Gary R. Renard.
Website: http://www.garyrenard.com
The End of Your World, Adyashanti.
Website: http://www.adyashanti.org or http://www.sound-strue.com
The Eye of the I, David Hawkins, M.D.
Website:
http://www.beyondtheordinary.net/drhawkins.shtml
The Findhorn Book of Forgiveness, Michael Dawson.
Website (Australian Centre for Inner Peace):
http://www.acfip.org
The Journey Home, Allen Watson.
Website (Circle of Atonement):
http://www.circlepublishing.com/
The Power of Intention, Dr. Wayne W. Dyer.
Website: http://www.drwaynedyer.com
The Power of Now, Eckhart Tolle.
Website: http://www.eckharttolle.com
The Road Less Traveled, M. Scott Peck, M.D.
Website: http://www.mscottpeck.com
The Sacred Purpose of Being Human, Jacquelyn Small.
Website: http://www.eupsychiainc.com
The Translucent Revolution, Arjuna Ardagh.
Website: http://www.translucents.org

The Wisdom of the Enneagram, Don Richard Riso and Russ Hudson.
   Website: http://www.enneagraminstitute.com
Undefended Love, Jett Psaris and Marlena S. Lyons.
   Website: http://www.undefendedlove.com
Your Immortal Reality, Gary R. Renard.
   Website: http://www.garyrenard.com

BIBLIOGRAPHY

Adyashanti. *The Impact of Awakening: Excerpts from the Teachings of Adyashanti.* Los Gatos, Calif.: Open Gate, 2000.

—. *My Secret Is Silence: Poetry and Sayings of Adyashanti.* Los Gatos, Calif.: Open Gate, 2003.

—. *Emptiness Dancing: Selected Dharma Talks of Adyashanti.* Los Gatos, Calif.: Open Gate, 2004.

—. *The End of Your World: Straight Talk on the Nature of Enlightenment.* Boulder, Colo.: Sounds True, 2008.

Ardagh, Arjuna. *The Translucent Revolution: How People Just Like You Are Waking Up and Changing the World.* Novato, Calif.: New World Library, 2005.

Blanton, Dr. Brad. *The Truthtellers: Stories of Success by Radically Honest People.* Stanley, Va.: Sparrowhawk Publications, 2004.

—. *Beyond Good and Evil: The Eternal Split-Second Sound-Light Being.* Stanley, Va.: Sparrowhawk Publications, 2005.

—. *Radical Honesty: How to Transform Your Life by Telling the Truth,* rev. ed. Stanley, Va.: Sparrowhawk Publications, 2005.

Bodian, Stephan. *Meditation for Dummies.* Hoboken, NJ: Wiley Publishing, Inc., 1999.

Bodian, Stephan, and Jon Landaw. *Buddhism for Dummies.* New York, NY: Wiley Publishing, Inc., 2003.

Bodian, Stephan, and Georg Feuerstein, eds. *Living Yoga: A Comprehensive Guide for Daily Life.* Los Angeles, Calif.: Tarcher/Putnam, 1992.

Cohen, Andrew. *Enlightenment Is a Secret: Teachings of Liberation.* Larkspur, Calif.: Moksha Foundation, Inc., 1991.

—. *Embracing Heaven & Earth: The Liberation Teachings of Andrew Cohen.* Lenox, Mass.: Moksha Press, 2000.

—. *Living Enlightenment: A Call for Evolution Beyond Ego.* Lenox, Mass.: Moksha Press, 2002.

Das, Lama Surya. *Awakening the Buddha Within: Eight Steps to*

Enlightenment: Tibetan Wisdom for the Western World. New York: Broadway Books (a division of Bantam Doubleday Dell Publishing Group, Inc.), 1997.

Dawson, Michael. *Healing the Cause: A Path of Forgiveness.* Findhorn, Scotland: Findhorn Press Ltd., 1993.

—. *The Findhorn Book of Forgiveness (The Findhorn Book Of Series).* Findhorn, Scotland: Findhorn Press, 2003.

Foundation for Inner Peace. *A Course in Miracles,* rev. ed. New York: Viking, 1996.

Hawkins, David R., M.D., Ph.D., *Power vs. Force: The Hidden Determinants of Human Behavior.* Sedona, Ariz.: Veritas Publishing, 1995.

—. *The Eye of the I: From Which Nothing Is Hidden.* W. Sedona, Ariz.: Veritas Publishing, 2001.

Katie, Byron, with Michael Katz. *I Need Your Love—Is That True?: How to Stop Seeking Love, Approval, and Appreciation and Start Finding Them Instead.* New York, NY: Harmony Books, 2005.

Katie, Byron, with Stephen Mitchell. *Loving What Is: Four Questions That Can Change Your Life.* New York, NY: Harmony Books (a division of Random House, Inc.), 2002.

McKenna, Jed. *Spiritual Enlightenment: The Damnedest Thing.* USA: Wisefool Press, 2002.

Peck, Morgan Scott, M.D.. *The Road Less Traveled: A New Psychology of Love, Traditional Values and Spiritual Growth.* New York, NY: Touchstone (a division of Simon and Schuster Inc.), 1978.

Psaris, Jett, and Marlena S. Lyons. *Undefended Love.* Oakland, Calif.: New Harbinger Publications, 2000.

Perry, Robert. *Reality & Illusion: An Overview of Course Metaphysics.* West Sedona, Ariz.: The Circle of Atonement, 1993.

—. *Relationships as a Spiritual Journey: From Specialness to Holiness.* West Sedona, Ariz.: The Circle of Atonement, 1997.

Rabbin, Robert. *The Sacred Hub: Living in Your Real Self.* Carlsbad,

Calif.: Inner Directions Foundation, 1996.

—. *Echoes of Silence: Awakening the Meditative Spirit.* Carlsbad, Calif.: Inner Directions Foundation, 2000.

Renard, Gary R. *The Disappearance of the Universe: Straight Talk About Illusions, Past Lives, Religion, Sex, Politics, and the Miracles of Forgiveness.* Carlsbad, Calif.: Hay House, 2004.

—. *Your Immortal Reality: How to Break the Cycle of Birth and Death.* Carlsbad, Calif.: Hay House, 2006.

—. *Love Has Forgotten No One: The Answer to Life* (to be published by Hay House in 2009).

Riso, Don Richard and Russ Hudson. *The Wisdom of the Enneagram: The Complete Guide to Psychological and Spiritual Growth for the Nine Personality Types.* New York, NY: Bantam Books (a division of Random House), 1999.

Small, Jacquelyn. *Awakening in Time: The Journey from Codependence to Co-creation.* Austin, TX: Eupsychian Press (formerly Bantam Books, New York, NY), 1991-2000.

—. *The Sacred Purpose of Being Human: A Healing Journey Through the 12 Principles of Wholeness.* Deerfield Beach, Fl.: Health Communications, Inc., 2005.

Tolle, Eckhart. *The Power of Now: A Guide to Spiritual Enlightenment.* Novato, Calif.: New World Library, 1999.

—. *Practicing the Power of Now: Essential Teachings, Meditations, and Exercises from The Power of Now.* Novato, Calif.: New World Library, 1999.

—. *Stillness Speaks.* Novato, Calif.: New World Library, 2003.

—. *A New Earth: Awakening to Your Life's Purpose.* New York, NY: Penguin Group (USA) Inc., 2005.

Walsch, Neale Donald. *Conversations with God,* Books 1-3. Charlottesville, Va.: Hampton Roads Publishing Company, Inc., 1996-1998.

—. *Communion with God.* New York, NY: The Berkley Publishing Group (a division of Penguin Putnam Inc.), 2000.

—. *Tomorrow's God: Our Greatest Spiritual Challenge.* New York,

NY: Atria Books, 2004.

—. *What God Wants: A Compelling Answer to Humanity's Biggest Question.* New York, NY: Atria Books, 2005.

Wapnick, Kenneth, Ph.D. *A Vast Illusion: Time According to A Course in Miracles,* second edition. Temecula, Calif.: Foundation for A Course in Miracles, 1991.

—. *Ending Our Resistance to Love: The Practice of A Course in Miracles.* Temecula, Calif.: Foundation for A Course in Miracles, 2004.

—. *The Healing Power of Kindness, Vol. 1: Releasing Judgment.* Temecula, Calif.: Foundation for A Course in Miracles, 2004.

—. *The Message of A Course in Miracles: All Are Called, Few Choose to Listen.* Temecula, Calif.: Foundation for A Course in Miracles, 1997.

—. *Forgiveness and Jesus: The Meeting Place of A Course in Miracles and Christianity,* sixth edition. Temecula, Calif.: Foundation for A Course in Miracles, 1998.

—. *Absence from Felicity : The Story of Helen Schucman and Her Scribing of A Course in Miracles.* Temecula, Calif.: Foundation for A Course in Miracles, 1991.

—. *The Journey Home: "The Obstacles to Peace" in A Course in Miracles.* Temecula, Calif.: Foundation for A Course in Miracles, 2000.

—. *Glossary-Index for A Course in Miracles,* fifth edition. Temecula, Calif.: Foundation for A Course in Miracles, 1993.

—. *The Fifty Miracle Principles of A Course in Miracles,* fifth edition. Temecula, Calif.: Foundation for A Course in Miracles, 1992.

Wapnick, Kenneth, Ph.D., and Gloria Wapnick. *Awaken from the Dream: A Presentation of A Course in Miracles,* second edition. Temecula, Calif.: Foundation for A Course in Miracles, 1995.

Wapnick, Gloria, and Kenneth Wapnick, Ph.D. *The Most Commonly Asked Questions About A Course in Miracles.* Temecula, Calif.: Foundation for A Course in Miracles, 1995.

Watson, Alan A. *The Journey Home,* Book #10 in a Series of

Commentaries on *A Course in Miracles*, West Sedona, Ariz.: The Circle of Atonement: Teaching and Healing Center, 1994.

What is Enlightenment? magazine. Lenox, Mass.: What is Enlightenment? Press, 1992-2005.

Wolf, Fred Alan. *Mind into Matter*. Needham, MA: Moment Point Press, 2001.

—. *Matter into Feeling: A New Alchemy of Science and Spirit*. Portsmouth, NH: Moment Point Press, Inc., 2002.

From the Acknowledgments page:

---

[1] www.word-fix.com.au/

[2] www.mindwire.com.au

[3] www.worxbyruss.net.au

KEEPING IN TOUCH

We are pleased to offer workshops and presentations, based on our book *Take Me to Truth: Undoing the Ego,* for groups around the world. Please contact us if you would like to help host a workshop in your city. For more information on our "Undoing the Ego" workshops, including scheduling and other valuable ego-release resources, visit our website,

www.TakeMeToTruth.com

If you would like to share your own experience of ego-release, or if you would like to offer feedback on our book, workshops, or presentations, we would be very happy to hear from you. You may email us at:

info@takemetotruth.com

ABOUT THE AUTHORS

Nouk Sanchez and Tomas Vieira

Initially inspired by the study and practice of the teachings in *A Course in Miracles* (ACIM, or "the Course"), the seventeen-year spiritual-awakening journey of the authors, Nouk Sanchez and Tomas Vieira, led to the almost total deconstruction of their lives and belief systems before emerging from the process together. Their uniquely dynamic family experience of learning and practicing the Course, as a couple, with their daughter Rikki Vieira, and their close spiritual family, is unprecedented. No amount of theory or other substitute can hold a candle to the *experience* of Truth. Amidst much lightness and laughter, these authors share a profound dedication to learning and living the Course, without one iota of compromise to its principles.

Nouk and Tomas joined in a divine commitment in 1984. The call they heard beckoned them to discover the indestructible nature of love. And the precious insights gained from their life-transforming experience are shared in both the book *Take Me to Truth* and their "Undoing the Ego" workshops. The result is this profound, yet practical guide that clearly defines the blocks and the stages that lead to spiritual awakening.

Respected for their practical expansion of the Course's section on the "Development of Trust" in the *Manual for Teachers*, Nouk and Tomas have been invited to deliver dynamic workshops around the world. They are keynote speakers at the prestigious Omega Institute in Rhinebeck, New York; the International A Course in Miracles Conference, San Francisco, California; and The Miracles Network in London.

Visit their website for articles, interviews and workshops:

www.takemetotruth.com

ENDNOTES

Preface
1   *A Course in Miracles* (hereafter cited as ACIM), second ed.; Mill Valley, CA: Foundation for Inner Peace (1992).

Acknowledgments
2   ACIM, M-4.I.A, pp. 10-11.

Chapter 1
3   Small, Jacqueline, *The Sacred Purpose of Being Human: A Healing Journey Through the 12 Principles of Wholeness*; Deerfield Beach, FL: Health Communications, Inc. (2005); Australia: HarperCollins; Introduction, pp. xxvi-xxvii.

4   ACIM, T-in.1:7, p. 1.

5   We define "Christ Consciousness" as the living, unreserved, and total awareness of our Wholeness and Oneness with all our brothers, united in the Sonship, in total dependence on The Source (God, our Creator).

6   Small, pp. 45-46.

7   ACIM, T-26.V.3:5, p. 550.

8   ACIM, T-19.IV.C.5:6, p. 418.

9   ACIM, T-2.I.3:6-7, p. 18.

10 ACIM, W-pI.49.4:3, p. 78.

11 ACIM, T-18.V, pp. 382-384.

12 ACIM, M-13.1:2, p. 33.

Chapter 2
13 ACIM, T-12.V.7:1, p. 226.

14 ACIM, W-pI.54.1:2, p. 88.

15 ACIM, T-21.in.1:1, p. 445.

16 ACIM, T-7.II.3:1,3, p. 114.

17 ACIM, T-8.III.4:2, p. 142.

18 Wolf, Fred Alan, *Matter into Feeling: A New Alchemy of Science and Spirit*; Portsmouth, NH: Moment Point Press, Inc. (2001); p. 148.
19 ACIM, W-pI.126.7:5, p. 228.
20 ACIM, T-11.V.5:3, p. 203.
21 ACIM, W-pI.135.18:1, p. 255.
22 ACIM, T-13.V, pp. 247-250.
23 ACIM, T-15, pp. 301-329.
24 ACIM, W-pII.340.13.1:3, p. 472.
25 ACIM, W-pI.24, pp. 36-37.
26 Adyashanti, *Emptiness Dancing: Selected Dharma Talks of Adyashanti*; Boulder, CO: Sounds True (2004); pp. 18, 20.
27 ACIM, T-in.2:2, p. 1.
28 Tolle, Eckhart. *A New Earth: Awakening to Your Life's Purpose*; New York, NY: Penguin Group (USA) Inc. (2005); p. 68.

Chapter 3
29 ACIM, T-5.II.3:7-10 pp. 75-76.
30 ACIM, W-pI.24, pp. 36-37.
31 Katie, Byron, with Stephen Mitchell, *Loving What Is: Four Questions That Can Change Your Life*; New York, NY: Three Rivers Press (2002).
32 Katie, pp. 3-4.
33 ACIM, W-pI.135.18:1, p. 255.
34 ACIM, T-27.VIII.6:2, p. 586.
35 ACIM, C-4.1:1-3, p. 85.
36 ACIM, W-pI.152.3:1, p. 281.
37 Katie, p. 249.
38 Katie, back cover.
39 ACIM, W-pII.127.1:1-7, p. 230.
40 Riso, Don Richard, and Russ Hudson, *The Wisdom of the Enneagram: The Complete Guide to Psychological and Spiritual Growth for Nine Personalities Types*; New York, NY: Bantam Books, a division of Random House, Inc. (1999).

41 Riso, p. 10.

42 Riso, p. 28.

43 Riso, pp. 10-12.

Chapter 4

44 Vigil, Sparo Arika (see "Acknowledgments" in this book), Sept. 2005.

45 Cohen, Andrew, "What Is Enlightenment," feature article in *The New Enlightenment* magazine, Issue #25.

46 Ibid.

47 Katie, Byron, *I Need Your Love—Is That True?: How To Stop Seeking Love, Approval, and Appreciation and Start Finding Them Instead*, New York, NY: Harmony Books (Random House, Inc.) (2006).

48 Katie, *I Need Your Love*, p. 76.

49 ACIM, T-12.IV.1:1-5, p. 223.

50 ACIM, T-15.VII.8:5-6, p. 318.

51 ACIM, T-8.IV.7:11, 8:1-5, p. 146.

52 Peck, M. Scott, M.D., *The Road Less Traveled: A New Psychology of Love, Traditional Values and Spiritual Growth*; New York, NY: Touchtone (Simon and Schuster, Inc.) (1978); p. 87.

53 Peck, pp. 88-89.

54 ACIM, T-17.III.1:4, p. 354.

55 Peck, pp. 81-82.

56 Vigil, Aug. 2005.

57 ACIM, T-13.VI.2:3; 5:1-3, pp. 250-251.

58 ACIM, T-18.VI.13:6, p. 388.

59 Psaris, Jett and Marlena S. Lyons, *Undefended Love*; Oakland, CA: New Harbinger Publications, Inc. (2000); pp. 11-12.

60 Renard, Gary, *The Art of Advanced Forgiveness* (DVD), Pathways of Light, http//www.pathwaysoflight.org.

61 ACIM, T-18.III.8:5-6; T-18.VII.5:2-3; and T-18.VII.6:3, pp. 380 and 389.

Chapter 5

62   ACIM, T-11.VIII.13:1-3; 14:4-5, p. 214.

63   ACIM, M-4.I.A, pp. 10-11.

64   ACIM, M-4.I.A.3, p. 10.

65   ACIM, M-4.I.A.4, p. 10.

66   ACIM, M-4.I.A.5, p. 10.

67   ACIM, M-4.I.A.5:5, p. 10.

68   ACIM, M-4.I.A.6, pp. 10-11.

69   ACIM, M-4.I.A.7, p. 11.

70   ACIM, M-4.I.A.8, p. 11.

71   ACIM, W-pI.138.4:6, p. 264.

72   ACIM, W-pI.24 and W-pI.25, pp. 36 and 38.

73   ACIM, T-in.2:2, p. 1.

74   ACIM, T-4.II.6:8-9; 8:4,8-9, p. 58.

75   Cohen, Andrew, *Living Enlightenment: A Call for Evolution Beyond Ego*; Lenox, MA: Moksha Press (2002); p. 24.

Chapter 6

76   ACIM, M-4.I.A, pp. 10-11.

77   Katie, *Loving What Is*.

78   Ardagh, Arjuna, *The Translucent Revolution: How People Just Like You are Waking Up and Changing the World*; Novato, CA: New World Library (2005); pp. 94, 95.

79   Ardagh, p. 99.

80   ACIM, T-6.in.1:3, p. 91.

81   ACIM, T-6.in.1:7, p. 91.

82   ACIM, T-6.II.2:1, p. 96.

83   ACIM, T-6.V.A, pp. 104-106.

84   ACIM, T-6.V.C.6:1, p. 110.

85   Walsch, Neale Donald, *Communion with God*; New York, NY: The Berkley Publishing Group (a division of Penguin Putnam Inc.) (2000); pp. 75-76.

86   ACIM, T-17.V.3:3, p. 362.

87   ACIM, T-17.V.5:1-4, p. 363.

88 ACIM, T-17.V.3:8, p. 362.
89 ACIM, T-18.VII.4:5-11, 5:1, p. 389.
90 Small, p. 59.
91 ACIM, T-21.II.2:3-5, p. 448.
92 ACIM, T-2.VI.3:2-7; 4:1-3, p. 29.
93 Cohen, Andrew, *Embracing Heaven and Earth: The Liberation Teachings of Andrew Cohen*; Lenox, MA: Moksha Press (2000), p. 61.
94 Cohen, *Embracing Heaven and Earth*, p. 65.
95 ACIM, W-pI.24, pp. 36-37.
96 ACIM, W-pII.13.4:3, p. 473.
97 Hawkins, David R., M.D., Ph.D., *The Eye of the I, From Which Nothing is Hidden*; W. Sedona, AZ: Veritas Publishing (2001); p. 133.
98 ACIM, M-4.I.A.5:2-8, p. 10.
99 ACIM, T-13.in.1:5, p. 236.
100 ACIM, T-25.III.1:2, p. 523.
101 ACIM, T-6.V.B.7:5, p. 108.
102 Renard, Gary R., *The Disappearance of the Universe: Straight Talk About Illusions, Past Lives, Religion, Sex, Politics, and the Miracles of Forgiveness*; Carlsbad, CA: Hay House, Inc. (2002); p. 256.
103 ACIM, T-21.II.2:3 and 4, p. 448.
104 ACIM, T-22.IV, pp. 477-478.
105 Adyashanti, p. 118.
106 ACIM, T-22.IV.1:1-4, p. 477.
107 ACIM, T-1.IV.1, p. 11.
108 ACIM, M-4.I.A.6:5-6, 10, p. 11.
109 ACIM, M-4.I.A.6:11-13, p. 11.
110 Adyashanti, p. 23.
111 Adyashanti, p. 195-196.
112 Adyashanti, p. 156.
113 ACIM, M-4.I.A.7, p. 11.
114 ACIM, T-26.VII.6:1-7, pp. 554-555.

[115]   ACIM, T-20.IV.8:4-8, pp. 433-434.

[116]   Hawkins, David R., M.D., Ph.D., *Power vs. Force: The Hidden Determinants of Human Behavior*; Carlsbad, CA: Hay House, Inc. (1995), p. 14.

Chapter 7
[117]   ACIM, T-25.VI, pp. 529-530.
[118]   ACIM, T-9.I.1, p. 160.
[119]   ACIM, T-9.I.5:1,3-4, p. 161.
[120]   ACIM, T-9.I.8:1-5, 9:6, pp. 161-162.
[121]   ACIM, T-9.I.11:5-9, p. 162.
[122]   ACIM, T-9.II.2:4-7, p. 164.
[123]   ACIM, T-9.II.3:2-7, p. 164.
[124]   Tolle, Eckhart, *The Power of Now: A Guide to Spiritual Enlightenment*; Novato, CA: New World Library (1999); p. 13.
[125]   See Tolle, *The Power of Now*, p. 23.
[126]   See Tolle, *The Power of Now*, p. 46.
[127]   See Tolle, *The Power of Now*, p. 41.
[128]   ACIM, T-21.II.2:3-5, p. 448.
[129]   See ACIM, T-21.II.7:6-8, 8, pp. 448-450.
[130]   Tolle, *The Power of Now*, pp. 51-52.
[131]   ACIM, T-26.II.8:5, p. 546.
[132]   ACIM, W-pI.135.14, p. 254.
[133]   ACIM, W-pI.24, pp. 36-37.
[134]   ACIM, W-pI.135.11:1-4; 12:1, pp. 253-254.
[135]   ACIM, W-pI.135.23:2-4, pp. 255-256.
[136]   ACIM, T-8.IX.2:1-2; 2:5; 3:1-3; 5:1-2, p. 158.
[137]   ACIM, T-9.I.14:1-5, p. 163.

Chapter 8
[138]   ACIM, W-pI.24, pp. 36-37.
[139]   ACIM, W-pI.31, p. 48.
[140]   ACIM, T-10.I.4, p. 182.

BOOKS

O is a symbol of the world, of oneness and unity. In different cultures it also means the "eye," symbolizing knowledge and insight. We aim to publish books that are accessible, constructive and that challenge accepted opinion, both that of academia and the "moral majority."

Our books are available in all good English language bookstores worldwide. If you don't see the book on the shelves ask the bookstore to order it for you, quoting the ISBN number and title. Alternatively you can order online (all major online retail sites carry our titles) or contact the distributor in the relevant country, listed on the copyright page.

See our website **www.o-books.net** for a full list of over 500 titles, growing by 100 a year.

And tune in to myspiritradio.com for our book review radio show, hosted by June-Elleni Laine, where you can listen to the authors discussing their books.

mySpiritRadio